ROUTLEDGE LIBRARY EDITIONS:
INDUSTRIAL ECONOMICS

Volume 9

FURTHER STUDIES IN
INDUSTRIAL ORGANIZATION

FURTHER STUDIES IN INDUSTRIAL ORGANIZATION

Edited by
M. P. FOGARTY

With a Preface by
G. D. H. COLE

Routledge
Taylor & Francis Group

LONDON AND NEW YORK

First published in 1948 by Methuen & Co. Ltd.

This edition first published in 2018
by Routledge
2 Park Square, Milton Park, Abingdon, Oxon OX14 4RN

and by Routledge
711 Third Avenue, New York, NY 10017

Routledge is an imprint of the Taylor & Francis Group, an informa business

British Library Cataloguing in Publication Data
A catalogue record for this book is available from the British Library

ISBN: 978-1-138-30830-5 (Set)
ISBN: 978-1-351-21102-4 (Set) (ebk)
ISBN: 978-1-138-57256-0 (Volume 9) (hbk)
ISBN: 978-0-8153-6954-7 (Volume 9) (pbk)
ISBN: 978-1-351-25257-7 (Volume 9) (ebk)

Publisher's Note
The publisher has gone to great lengths to ensure the quality of this reprint but points out that some imperfections in the original copies may be apparent.

Disclaimer
The publisher has made every effort to trace copyright holders and would welcome correspondence from those they have been unable to trace.

FURTHER STUDIES IN INDUSTRIAL ORGANIZATION

Edited by
M. P. FOGARTY

With a Preface
by
G. D. H. COLE

METHUEN & CO. LTD. LONDON
36 Essex Street, Strand, W.C.2

First published in 1948

CATALOGUE NO. 4442/U

THIS BOOK IS PRODUCED IN
COMPLETE CONFORMITY WITH THE
AUTHORIZED ECONOMY STANDARDS

PRINTED IN GREAT BRITAIN

PREFACE

THE present volume is a sequel to the series of *Studies in Industrial Organization*, edited by Mr. H. A. Silverman and published in 1946, to which I contributed a preface explaining the genesis of both. Mr. Fogarty, the editor of this second volume, has given a further account of the circumstances under which these four further studies came to be chosen for publication together out of a much larger number made under the auspices of the Nuffield College Social Reconstruction Survey; and there is little for me to add to what he has said. I have only once more to thank cordially the Survey's unpaid staff of Local Investigators, and especially those of them who collaborated in the making of this volume, and the advisers and staff, paid and unpaid, who helped in getting these studies into a publishable shape and in the tasks of seeing them through their various incarnations in type-script and in print. The full list of Local Investigators, having been given in a previous volume, need not be reproduced here: nor do I presume to thank Mr. Fogarty, in comparison with whose editorial labours mine have been merely nominal.

It is left only to add that Nuffield College takes no responsibility for the opinions here expressed. As a research institution it has no collective opinions, and limits its responsibility to satisfying itself upon the high quality of the material issued under its auspices.

G. D. H. COLE
Professorial Fellow of Nuffield College; formerly Director of the Social Reconstruction Survey.

October, 1946

CONTENTS

		Page
PREFACE		vii
INTRODUCTION		1

Chapter

I. FLOUR-MILLING — 21
Mrs. H. V. Edwards

II. THE WHITE FISH INDUSTRY — 101
R. K. Kelsall, in collaboration with Professor H. Hamilton, Dr.
F. A. Wells, and K. C. Edwards.

III. THE GRANITE INDUSTRY — 181
Professor H. Hamilton

IV. THE BREWING INDUSTRY OF EDINBURGH — 209
Dr. Mary Rankin

INDEX — 224

CONTENTS

INTRODUCTION

THE four studies included in this volume arose, like the group previously published in *Studies in Industrial Organization*,[1] out of the general work of the Nuffield College Social Reconstruction Survey. The Survey organization was set up in 1941 with wide terms of reference covering a large part of the reconstruction field. In practice, the chief part of its work was concerned with problems of the distribution of industry and population likely to arise after the war. A series of regional surveys, covering most of the industrial areas of Great Britain, was made to discover—so far as it could be discovered at the time—where and in what form problems were likely to appear. The Survey reports themselves were confidential, as they incorporated material supplied by Government departments, and were intended for these departments' use; but some of their results were summarized and published after the Social Reconstruction Survey finished its work in 1944.[2]

In the course of these surveys it quickly became obvious that a great deal of the essential background was missing. The question to be answered by the regional inquiries was whether, given the prospects of the individual industries important to each area, any problems were likely to arise of a kind requiring public intervention—especially, of course, problems such as those of the former depressed areas, or of congested districts such as Greater London where extensive changes in the siting of industry are required in the interests of good physical planning. But what were the prospects of these individual industries? For some much-surveyed industries such as coal, cotton, or iron and steel it was possible to make at least an intelligent guess, though a great deal of the most recent and valuable material even on these trades only became available at or after the end of the Social Reconstruction Survey's work. In other cases, including most of the less important or more prosperous trades, there was little or nothing to go on, and the Survey was forced to produce its own studies and forecasts.

Several of these studies were carried only as far as the Survey's main purpose required. They gave a broad impression of what future trends were likely to be. But there was often no question of studying industries for their own sake, or from the wider standpoint of industrial organization in general; and, in one or two even of those cases where this wider approach was adopted, the material collected was

---

[1] *Studies in Industrial Organization*, edited by H. A. Silverman, Methuen, 1946.
[2] *Prospects of the Industrial Areas of Great Britain*, by M. P. Fogarty, Methuen, 1945.

never worked up into finished form, or for one reason or another was not available for publication.

There remained at the end of the Survey's work rather more than a dozen studies which had been brought into finished or almost finished shape, were available for publication, and had some general interest over and above their function as a background for the regional inquiries. Most of the industries covered by this group are highly localized and were of secondary importance to the war effort; it was for this reason that it was possible to investigate them with reasonable thoroughness even under war conditions of shortage of staff, transport difficulties, and official secrecy. The results of one or two of the investigations have been published individually. Of the remainder, eight, dealing with various textile and clothing trades, were published in *Studies in Industrial Organization*. The four included in the present volume are more miscellaneous.

In spite of their apparent diversity, they have a number of features in common. One is geography. Three of the studies—fishing, granite, and brewing—happen to refer in part or whole to a single region, Scotland, and so help to clear up a general issue raised by several pre-war inquiries. The Barlow Commission pointed out that in all large regions of Great Britain the rate of growth of those industries which were expanding in the 'twenties and 'thirties tended to be about the national average. There were naturally variations in the case of individual industries; but, taking all these industries as a group, the rate of growth everywhere tended to be about the same. There were, however, divergences. Some regions did better and some worse than this tendency would lead one to expect; and it is important for future policy to know how far this was due to the peculiarities of individual industries and how far to special regional characteristics affecting all industries in a given area. Did Scotland and South Wales suffer from a general lack of local enterprise as well as from the fact that the industries which have grown fastest in recent years were always poorly represented in them?

In attempting to answer this question Scotland is a particularly good example to choose, since it happens to show the widest divergence of any major industrial region from the Barlow Commission's general rule. Seven 'local' industries, selling goods and services chiefly in their own neighbourhoods, increased their employment of insured workers in Great Britain as a whole between 1923 and 1937 by 57 per cent. The corresponding figure for the main industrial district of central Scotland was 43 per cent. The discrepancy was even greater in the case of the sixteen rapidly expanding 'basic' industries, selling chiefly outside their own areas, for which the Ministry of Labour supplied figures; over the same period, the increase in employment in these industries was 46 per cent for Scotland against no less than 66 per cent for Great Britain.

The report on *Light Industries in Scotland*, published shortly before the war by the Economic Committee of the Scottish Development Council, suggested that in at any rate some cases, including furniture and boots and shoes, this tendency for Scotland to lag behind was due not so much to difficult natural conditions, labour troubles, or distance from markets—factors largely outside the control of industrialists—as to sheer lack of enterprise on the part of the Scottish manufacturers. In the case of furniture, for example, it was pointed out that high transport costs were apparently no obstacle to the English firms which occupied by far the greater part of the Scottish market; if employment in furniture manufacturing in central Scotland increased between 1923 and 1937 less than half as fast as in Great Britain as a whole, it was alleged that the reason was the failure of Scottish firms to pay sufficient attention to modern methods of mass-production. How far can this case be supported from the experience of other trades, and how far was the lag of development in Scotland due to conditions which Scotland should have been able to remedy for itself?

A good deal of light was cast on this question by the Survey's reports on industries partly or wholly localized in Scotland, including jute, tweed, carpets, hosiery, and boots and shoes from the volume previously published, as well as the studies in the present volume on fish, granite, and brewing. It appeares that in industries such as brewing or tweed, where technique changes comparatively slowly and the craft element is still strong, Scottish firms have been able to hold their own. In other cases the light thrown on the minor Scottish trades is scarcely flattering. Where adaptability to new markets or techniques is required, or readiness to shift from declining trades into more profitable lines of activity, there seems to have been a real tendency for Scottish light industries and other minor trades to fall behind. There are honourable exceptions, including notably some firms in carpet manufacturing; but the general impression is the same as was given by the Scottish Economic Committee's report. In view of the small initial representation of many growing industries in Scotland it would have been unreasonable to expect the same absolute rate of growth there as in the South. But, over and above this handicap, there has also been a definite regional tendency to lack of enterprise in the expanding trades. Apart from its direct effects, this tendency limited the growth of local purchasing power, and so indirectly impaired the attractiveness of Scotland to enterprise originating elsewhere.

Apart from geography, the industries covered in this volume have in common that they all raise in one form or another the question of the relations of industry to the Government and the public. The issue of public relations emerges most clearly in the case of flour-milling. The flour-milling industry has been organized since 1929 in a powerful and highly efficient trade association, the Millers' Mutual Association, which by 1939 controlled approximately 80 per cent of the total output. Practically the whole of the remainder was produced by the Co-operative Wholesale Society, the only large concern outside the association; and it appears that even the C.W.S. adheres broadly to association prices. Thanks to combination, effective price-fixing, and drastic rationalization, involving considerable reduction of capacity and employment, the millers' margin[1] per sack of flour rose nearly 75 per cent between 1928 and 1936. The price of imported wheat fell by $31\frac{1}{2}$ per cent, while the price of flour fell by no more than $18\frac{1}{2}$ per cent. Dividends rose sharply. Other manifestations of monopoly also increased and multiplied; in London, for example, the milling trade organized a deliberate boycott of flour factors who, in the true style of Adam Smith, justified their existence and disconcerted the millers by buying when flour was cheap and unloading their stocks when prices began to rise. In the circumstances, it is not surprising that there has at times been strong public criticism of the flour-milling industry as a peculiarly pernicious monopoly astride the supply of one of the necessaries of life. Criticism was reinforced early in the war by the suspicion that milling interests were blocking an increase in the rate of extraction—the substitution of wholemeal for white flour—required both to save shipping space and for the sake of national health.

Yet it stands out clearly from the study by Mrs. Edwards that the milling interests have in many respects deserved well of their country. Combination has not meant techincal inefficiency. The demand for flour is highly inelastic, and displacement of labour was inevitable in the early 'thirties if efficiency was to increase, whether through better productive technique or—even more important—through elimination of the excess capacity due to the First World War. It is to the credit of the Millers' Mutual Association that the labour displaced was generously provided for, and that conditions for workers remaining in the trade have been excellent. If millers' margins increased after rationalization, it could be argued that the previous margins represented a return too low to allow efficiency to be fully maintained in the long run; an argument fully borne out by the recent history of the coal and cotton trades or (to take a smaller example from the present volume) by the history of the white fishing industry at Fleetwood or Aberdeen. It could also be argued, as Mrs.

[1] Including the value of milling offals as well as the margin between wheat and flour prices. Chapter I, p. 55. The margin referred to is the official margin: if allowance were made for unofficial discounts, which greatly diminished after reorganization, the proportionate increase would be still greater.

Edwards points out, that extensive exploitation of consumers by the milling interests was impossible while Dominion flour was allowed free entry and foreign flour was subject, even after 1932, to a duty of no more than 10 per cent. The milling interests have been valuable allies of those who look with suspicion on schemes for subsidizing British wheat, object to being ordered by authority to eat the bread which is good for them instead of the bread which they like, or fear that agreements for the bulk purchase of food imports, involving as they must a loss of the freedom to pick and choose in world markets which many British industries besides flour-milling have recognized as a main asset, will prove both expensive and inconvenient to British consumers.

There is room for legitimate differences of opinion in weighing up these factors. It is possible to hold that too high a price has been paid for the benefits of rationalization, and that equally good results could have been attained by other means. In general terms, the case for the defence on the issue of price is that, in what Professor Schumpeter has called the 'storm of creative destruction' by which capitalism progresses, the accumulation of a mass of profits in the hands of genuinely enterprising economic strategists such as the leaders of the flour-milling industry is likely to help economic advance more than it hinders it. There are some who would reply that competition would bring about the same results at considerably less cost to the consumer. Others might suggest that the introduction of a greater element of socialist planning, in the form either of nationalization or of control of profit margins, would eliminate a great deal both of the storm and destruction, and of the need for the mass accumulation of monopoly profits, without in any way impairing economic creativeness.

It is possible to feel a certain scepticism about these counter-arguments as applied to actual conditions between the two wars. Competition proved an uncommonly slow rationalizer in the conditions of the 'twenties and 'thirties, in flour-milling as well as in other industries; and, whatever may be thought of the relative merits of public and private ownership, the fact remains that most of the industries where problems similar to those of flour-milling arose before 1939 were and are likely to remain in private hands for as far ahead as can be foreseen. Political facts are as hard as any others, and in the atmosphere of the pre-war years those who called for the nationalization even of flour-milling were crying for the moon. Even the combination of public control, professional self-government, and freedom for individual firms which is being hammered out at the time of writing by the Board of Trade's working parties demands a technique on the side of the Government and an attitude on the part of industry which fifteen or twenty years ago did not exist.

It is not unreasonable to argue that in such circumstances as these reorganization on the lines of the Millers' Mutual Association must often have been the quickest way to economic progress. There is no question that rationalization under strong leadership and with the prospect of a period of generous profits would have been the salvation of many British industries between the two wars. Admittedly, the necessary leadership was, and is, often absent. Where it was present, it is for those who object to this form of reorganization to prove that there was a better alternative, in the sense of an alternative which, besides being technically sound, fair to employers and labour, and cheaper to the consumer, had a reasonable chance of being carried into effect in existing economic and political conditions. If some strong personality had done for coal or cotton what was done between the wars for flour-milling or shipbuilding, he would no doubt have incurred the same bitter unpopularity as the Chairman of National Shipbuilders' Security Ltd., or the same charges of profiteering as some of the leaders of the flour-milling trade. But it is also possible that coal and cotton, like milling and shipbuilding, would not to-day have been a national problem on account of technical backwardness, bad labour relations, and chaotic organization; and it is quite certain that vigorous leadership could have achieved more for these industries than was or could have been brought about in any other way.

Flour-milling is admittedly an extreme case, since there is no denying that the profits made by millers in the 'thirties were more than generous; it is not suggested that this particular method of reorganization would be ideal in the very different conditions of the 'forties. Policy to-day would at least demand control of millers' margins. But would it really have been worth while in the public interest to prevent these profits being earned, if the only practical alternative was to leave the trade to flounder in the same slough of stagnation as so many other industries struck by depression after 1918? It is easy enough to condemn the Ranks and Lithgows of this world by reference to an ideal which in fact was unattainable. But it is not good history; and it is not always easy to see what purpose it serves beyond stoking the fires of political controversy.

Whatever view may be taken on these questions, or on the wider social issues bound up with them, it is at least clear that judgment in this matter can properly be passed only after careful and detailed examination of the balance of evidence in each particular case. Any sweeping approval or condemnation of the past policies of the flour-milling industry—or any other—is likely to neglect factors of considerable economic and social importance. If unnecessary public suspicion is to be avoided, and a correct line of economic policy is to be worked out, it is important that for the future the essential facts about this and other industries should be made known regularly and through some agency generally accepted as reliable. A group of economists, business men, and trade unionists who discussed problems of post-war industrial organization at a series of conferences organized by Nuffield College stressed as a main conclusion that:

'Industry after the war must be so conducted . . . as to command the confidence of the people, as workers, as consumers, and as investors. . . . Fuller publicity is an indispensable instrument for the creation of this new spirit of confidence—candour towards employees in laying bare the financial aspects of the affairs of firms and business associations, candour towards investors in the presentation of accounts, and candour towards the consuming public in matters of price-fixing and the regulation of economic relations.' (Statement on *Employment Policy and Organization of Industry After the War*, Oxford University Press, 1943, p. 13.)

The flour-milling industry is an ideal case in point.

While flour-milling raises the problems of an almost too luxuriant prosperity, the granite trade and certain sections of the fishing industry present the picture of sleepy mediocrity more familiar to students of British economics. The granite industry might almost have been excluded on the principle that *de minimis non curat lex*, since even in its main centre at Aberdeen it employed in 1939 a mere $2\frac{1}{2}$ per cent of the insured population. The principle *de minimis* was in fact invoked on one occasion, as Professor Hamilton mentions in his study, to justify a refusal of protection to this trade.

But, small as it is, the granite trade is an illuminating example of a tendency widespread in British industry. Plenty of attention has been given in recent years to the rehabilitation of decaying basic industries. Not nearly enough has been given to speeding up the rate of development in industries which, like granite, fail to take advantage of their opportunities to expand. Economic progress demands a continual shift in the relative importance of different trades, and unemployment may appear and opportunities of raising the standard of living be lost—as no region has more reason to appreciate than Scotland—through missing chances of growth as well as through permitting unnecessary decay. Important as it is to overhaul cotton or steel manufacturing, it is not less important, though easier to forget, to prod the leaders of more comfortably situated industries who have fallen asleep by the wayside.

The British granite industry has not been depressed; nor has it been conspicuously inefficient. If it has failed to retain its proportionate share of an expanding market, plausible reasons can be alleged in its defence. There appears to have been a genuine measure of undercutting by low-wage industries abroad, and certain foreign countries, particularly in Scandinavia, have been able to offer products of a quality and variety which for geological reasons are not to be had in this country. Yet it is difficult not to feel, with Professor Hamilton, that more might have been done. Better technical methods; more co-operative action on the marketing side to match the co-operative methods already used to some extent in purchasing raw material; perhaps greater facilities for new entrants into the industry, with concentration, at the other end of the scale, into a smaller number of relatively large units—by action on any or all of these lines output might well have been increased, and employment, which in practice remained stable, have been allowed to rise.

The recent history of the white fish industry is an even more forcible illustration of the same point. Landings of white fish in Great Britain increased between 1913 and 1935 by 2,700,000 hundredweight, or almost a quarter. Over the same period landings at the four main fishing ports other than Hull remained practically stationary, a noticeable fall at Aberdeen being balanced by an increase at Fleetwood. At the minor ports there was an actual decline in landings, amounting to nearly 40 per cent. It was at Hull alone that there was a really striking increase, amounting over the twenty-two years to no less than 3,900,000 hundredweight; landings at Hull were multiplied practically by four.

The reasons for this remarkable contrast stand out most clearly from a comparison of the position at Hull and at Aberdeen. The national increase in landings arose chiefly from the equivalent, in the conditions of the fishing industry, of cheap mass-production. The more distant fishing-grounds were exploited by a section of the industry with a high degree of organization and relatively modern equipment, catching principally the rougher and commoner varieties of fish and disposing of them largely through the expanding market offered by fish and chip shops. In this movement Hull took the lead. Hull trawlers are relatively modern and organized in comparatively large fleets. Nearly half of them in 1934 were less than ten years old; more than half were already owned by firms with fleets of twenty or more, and three-quarters by those with fleets of not less than ten. Hull owners have shown considerable readiness to co-operate among themselves for such purposes as the supply of ship's stores or the processing of fish by-products, and to co-operate with owners in other ports for such purposes as the prevention of over-fishing. They have also maintained relatively good working conditions. They have taken the lead in exploring new sources of supply; when the nearer grounds showed signs of exhaustion, it was Hull trawlers which led the way to such areas as Bear Island or the Barents Sea. The part which Hull has played in developing the market for cheap fish is sufficiently illustrated by the value figures for 1934. White fish landed at Hull in that year was worth around 13*s.* 6*d.* a hundredweight; the corresponding figure for Aberdeen was just over a pound, and for Fleetwood and Grimsby around 24*s.*

In every one of these respects there is a clear contrast between owners at Hull and Aberdeen. Aberdeen has clung to its reputation for relatively high-grade fish, and has played little part in opening up the newer and more distant grounds. Its organization has remained old-fashioned as well as its ideas. More than two-thirds of all Aberdeen trawlers in 1934 were owned by firms with less than ten vessels apiece, and this dispersal of ownership was not made good by co-operation. A certain amount of interlocking between the directorates of fishing concerns and of the firms supplying stores and equipment appears to have added little to efficiency and a great deal to ill-feeling between owners and men. Most Aberdeen trawlers are old; in 1934 no more than 11 per cent of them had been built since 1919, and the position had not changed greatly by 1939. Working conditions are correspondingly bad.

Aberdeen owners have admittedly a case for not slavishly following the path marked out by Hull. They are in particular justified in laying more stress than owners at Hull on high-grade fish; for Aberdeen is subject to the double condition that its vessels can land their catch two days sooner and fresher than trawlers from the Humber, and that Aberdeen fish, when once landed, has to bear a relatively high transport charge. But it is impossible for anyone who reads Professor Hamilton's account of the Aberdeen fishing industry to doubt that it was seriously backward in the years between the wars. Serving a high-grade market is no excuse for refusing to co-operate to serve it more efficiently, for persisting with out-of-date equipment, for offering inferior working conditions, or for antiquated and uneconomic methods of marketing.

Whom did this backwardness benefit? Certainly not the consumer; it was the Hull section of the industry which sold fish to households which could never have afforded it before. Certainly not the men in the industry; and, equally certainly, not the owners. It was the Hull firms which made the profits; Aberdeen owners were averaging a steady loss through the early 'thirties. Some ancillary firms at Aberdeen may have done fairly well even at that time; but it is permissible to suspect that they would have done even better if, instead of attracting an unreasonable share of the proceeds of a static industry, they had taken a smaller slice out of a trade expanding at the rate achieved at Hull. It is literally true to say that the inertia of the Aberdeen fishing industry has involved loss for every interest connected with it.

Aberdeen fishing is, in fact, one more illustration of the truth that the danger to employment and standards of living in Great Britain does not lie with the conspicuous and forward-looking monopolist.

A dose of the medicine administered to flour-milling would have done the fishing industry a world of good, and, if profits had been made in the process, it is highly probable that consumers and workers would still have been better off than they actually were; for those concerns which do least for the public benefit tend to be in every sense of the word unprofitable servants. Even the text-book monopolist, pressing continually for maximum profits, has as great an interest in minimizing costs as in forcing up the price-level; and it would be rash to assume without further inquiry that text-book monopolists make up the leadership of a really successful trade association such as that in flour-milling. It is doubtful whether even flour-milling profits were ever maximized in the text-book sense. In other industries leadership is at least as likely to come from hard-driving entrepreneurs interested as much in power and prestige as in profits, or from professionally minded managements which, while aiming at a profit margin substantial enough to maintain a steady inward glow among shareholders, are interested less in expanding profits beyond that level than in a reputation for efficiency and public service. The great danger to national economic efficiency—efficiency it is understood, first and foremost in terms of service to the consumer—does not lie with these classes. It lies with the lazy-minded, the unco-operative, and the missers of chances; to convert a phrase from another context, with *Lumpenkapitalismus*.

To put the same point in terms of theory, the price policy of a typical British firm is determined not by the conditions of monopoly or monopolistic competition, in which a producer is faced with a determinate and smoothly sloping demand curve, but by a condition of oligopoly in which the demand curve is either uncertain or kinked. The effects of departing from standard prices are unknown, but more likely than not to be unpleasant. There is frequently, in addition, an almost complete and inevitable ignorance of the marginal costs which the theory of monopoly assumes should be equated to marginal revenue. As a further factor operating in the same direction, it is common to find firms aiming at a 'fair', 'just', or 'equitable' price; a price determined as much by moral considerations of what is due in justice to the producer as by a desire to maximize his returns. As a combined result of these factors firms tend to fix prices on the basis of 'full cost' or cost plus, with a view not so much to maximum as to standard profits. While this deliberate adjustment of prices to secure a standardized margin may not allow profits to fall to the level attainable in more competitive conditions, it does tend to prevent them from rising to the extent likely under conditions of monopoly or monopolistic competition. It therefore diminishes very considerably the chance that consumers may be exploited by forcing prices to the level likely to yield the maximum return, in either the long or the short run, on the lines suggested by the traditional theory of monopoly.[1] But, at the same time, standard margins and "ethical" prices put a definite premium on the conformist firm, content to live and let live, and place a real obstacle in the way of the path-breaker and pioneer; for the pioneer is inevitably also to some extent the price-cutter and the disturber of established harmonies.

However, to go back to the actual case under discussion, the fact remains that no leader or group has arisen in the fishing industry to drive it along the path taken by flour-milling; inefficiency, low wages, and lack of profits were allowed to drag on in several sections of the trade until the war drastically reduced the number of trawlers and sent prices rocketing. Even the war cured merely the trade's lack of earning power. It scarcely touched its inefficiency. Indeed, in some respects inefficiency was even for the time being increased, since it was naturally the newest and most efficient fleets, particularly those sailing from Hull, on which Admiralty requisitioning fell most heavily. In cases of this kind, what is to be done?

The policy actually applied to the white fish industry under the Sea Fish Industry Act of 1938 consisted of a combination of self-government with State supervision. There was to be a White Fish Industry Joint Council, bringing together all sections of both the producing and the distributive ends of the trade, and a White Fish Commission was to be appointed by the Government to supervise the industry and to initiate, approve, and if necessary assist schemes of development. Reorganization on these lines is tending since the end of the war to become common form for all industries requiring reform, though not on the schedule for complete nationalization, and it would have been of great interest to quote the lessons of pre-war experience in the white fish industry. But in this case war and rumours of war prevented the scheme from going fully into operation; and there is no other case among the industries studied in this volume in which comprehensive reform under Government control was attempted at all.

What can be gleaned from these studies—taken all together, not merely the study of white fishing—in the absence of experience of comprehensive official schemes of reorganization, is a certain amount of information about the weapons of which such schemes might make use. The weapon to which classical economic theory attached most importance, competition, emerges from the comparison with more credit than might be expected in days when the emphasis is more on working parties and industrial boards; if not, perhaps,

[1] See, on all this, Harrod, *Price and Cost in Entrepreneurs' Policy*, and Hall and Hitch, *Price Theory and Business Behaviour* in *Oxford Economic Papers* No. 2; Fogarty, *The Incidence of Rates on Houses, Review of Economic Studies*, 1942, particularly pp. 9–10 and Appendix; and, on the same theory as seen from the business angle, Johnson-Davies, *Control in Retail Industry*, 1945.

with the full glory which might have been attributed to it forty years ago. The free entry of Empire flour and the existence, alongside the main flour-milling association, of independent Co-operative mills has undoubtedly been a safeguard both to consumers and to the industry itself; if the State has kept its hands off flour-milling, and public discontent with high milling profits has been kept within bounds, by no means the least important reason has been the existence of important competitive sources of supply. It must be admitted that one of the two checks has worked with only limited efficiency. The Co-operative Wholesale Society sells only to co-operative retail societies, and has been content to participate in the high profits made by efficient British millers. Grain-milling is one of the most profitable lines of co-operative production, and it appears that before the war the 'surplus' on co-operative milling was considerably higher than the average rate of profit of mills owned by ordinary capitalist firms.[1] But, though following association prices, the C.W.S. has normally kept a little below them; and, from some knowledge of the machinery of the co-operative movement, it is permissible to doubt whether public opinion inside the movement would have allowed the C.W.S. to associate itself for long with any outrageous exploitation of consumers.

In the case of the fishing industry the effects of competition have taken a considerable time to work themselves out; but they have not for that reason been less important. It is the pressure of competition from Hull which has brought matters in the industry to a head, and at the same time has indicated lines which reorganization might follow. On the assumption that full employment is maintained, the competition of other industries with white fishing is likely to show itself a good deal more strongly in future than in the past; for, as Mr. Kelsall points out, if alternative work is easily available, and if existing conditions in fishing continue, fishermen may prove as hard to come by as coal-miners or cotton operatives. The evaporation of the labour force under conditions of full employment has been a powerful influence behind the progress made since 1941 towards the reorganization of coal and cotton; its effect in the fishing industry should prove to be at least as great.

Industrial self-government, like competition, emerges from these studies considerably less tarnished than acquaintance with some of the better-known basic industries might lead one to expect. Self-government may take a great many forms, according to the precise weighting of the different sections of an industry within its governing body, to the inclusion or exclusion of labour interests, and to the degree of supervision exercised by the State. Whatever the precise

[1] Carr-Saunders and others, *Consumers' Co-operation in Great Britain*, 1938, p. 441.

balance of interests, the essential fact is that industrial self-government means government primarily by and for producers. There is an inevitable suspicion that organization on these lines will tend to assist exploitation of consumers, and that the exploitation of consumers will tend to increase in proportion to the freedom of each section of producers to monopolize its own line of trade.

In the light of the studies in the present volume any such generalization must appear highly misleading. Definite and considerable gains to the public, as well as to shareholders, have been realized through co-operative action in flour-milling, granite, and fish; and, once again, it is not always the most obviously self-centred forms of organization which do least for the public welfare. It is sometimes suggested—the report in 1945 of the Eire Government's Commission on Vocational Organization is one case in point—that the disadvantages of producers' self-government can be overcome by off-setting the different interests within each trade against one another; a balance of interests should make it impossible both for one section of the trade to exploit the rest and for the trade as a whole to exploit consumers. The White Fish Industry Joint Council is an illuminating example of what this means in practice. It appears that the balancing of different interests within the Council has in fact prevented it from doing much harm. But, as Mr. Kelsall points out, there is no great gain in preventing a self-governing industry from doing harm by preventing it from doing anything at all; and that appears to have been the chief effect of the checks and balances in the Council's constitution. The genuinely valuable results produced by joint action in the white fish industry have arisen, as in the case of the co-operatives for fish processing and ship's stores set up by the Hull owners, from the purely self-centred action of relatively homogeneous sections of the trade.

It would be contrary to human nature to expect self-government by the owners of industry to bring down profits. But there is all the difference in the world between high profits combined with the offer of new scope to vigorous and progressive leadership, and high profits combined with a constitution of checks and balances which, with the best possible intentions, amounts in practice to a charter for stagnation. And, as the case of the white fish industry shows, in conditions of constitutional paralysis even the high profits may not be forthcoming.

The studies of brewing, and of course flour-milling, throw more light on the same point. The study of brewing suggests a case where checks and balances within an industry may fail even in their primary purpose of preventing positive harm—actual exploitation of consumers. Barley prices in the course of the war reached fantastic levels, and, if the industry had been subject to an elastic demand, some drop in barley sales might reasonably have been expected. In actual fact the demand for beer proved in war-time to be remarkably inelastic even in the face of heavy increases in taxation and prices; the high price of barley could therefore be recouped, to the mutual satisfaction of farmers and brewers, at the expense of the consumer. An incidental and possibly not unintentional effect was to provide farmers with an additional subsidy which, from the political point of view, had the merit of concealment.

The demand for flour is also inelastic; but in this case the producers have put up a stronger fight against attempts to increase the price or restrict the choice of raw materials by bulk buying of imports or the substitution of home-grown for imported wheat. The clash of interests within the grain-producing and processing trades has served a genuinely useful purpose; at the same time, the system of checks and balances has never been carried so far as to prevent vigorous action by the more progressive sections of these trades. Self-government in flour-milling has admittedly not been hard for the idealist to criticize. It has been frankly and openly government by and for the industry's owners, with no question of participation by labour interests or Government representatives. Politicians, economists, and both sides in industry itself have been feeling their way since the war towards a form of association modelled more on the organized professions, with their limited profits, high sense of public responsibility, and measure of public control, and less on the traditional British type of trade association; the aim has been to find the best compromise in the consumer's interest between the claims of owners, managements, and organized workers seeking a responsible partnership in the control of their trades. By contrast with this aim, self-government in flour-milling in the 'thirties represented merely the first crude stage of organization in the manufacturers' own interests. But at least it was effective, within its limits, and much of what it effected was good. And, once again, it is an open question whether any great further advance towards the ideal would have been possible at that time.

On the question of direct Government or local authority intervention in industry the studies in this volume provide a number of useful pointers, though hardly enough to justify any far-reaching conclusions. One minor point, which is of some interest at a time when more and more local authorities and local or regional development councils are looking round for ways of assisting industry, is the contrast between the relatively rapid progress of the Grimsby and Aberdeen fishing industries in their early days, thanks to the active building of docks, fish markets, and other facilities by the local authorities, and the relatively slow progress at Hull where similar assistance was delayed.

A more important point is suggested by the different attitude of governments to the more and less progressive industries covered. It is obvious from several references in Mrs. Edwards's study that the leaders of the flour-milling industry have been continually looking back over their shoulders at the pursuing forces of bureaucracy, and that the threat of Government intervention, though never explicitly formulated, has been a continual stimulus to progress and a restraint on the undue exploitation of markets. Once again, there is a marked contrast between the experience of an explosively progressive industry such as flour-milling and the industries which, like granite, have preferred to take life easily, or, like sections of the white fish industry, have sunk peacefully into permanent depression for lack of the intellectual vigour to think themselves out of it. A trade which is controlled by a notoriously successful and wealthy monopolist is a natural target both for semi-political competition such as that of the Co-operative Wholesale Society and for the interest of political parties. The leading flour-milling firms have accordingly figured in recent years in a good many left-wing schedules of industries for public control or early nationalization, in company both with other concerns of the same stamp, such as Imperial Chemical Industries, and with important trades subject to creeping paralysis such as coal and steel.

Coal and steel happen to be too important for their faults to be ignored; but the left-wing tendency to measure the degree of a firm's menace to society by the size of its dividends has allowed a great many equally worthy candidates for drastic reorganization to slumber undisturbed. The firm which does well for itself and the public is subject to continual outside stimulus and criticism. The firm which misuses labour and capital to no particular profit, even to itself, is allowed to go its way in peace, unless it happens to belong to one of three or four basic industries of the highest and most obvious national importance. It is only since the end of the war that there has been a serious threat even of investigation of such cases as these; and it is difficult not to feel that even now the official attitude towards them includes a great deal too much sympathy and far too little contempt. There is a natural reluctance to think of the bloated capitalist as a living embodiment of the Invisible Hand, harmonizing his own and the public interest, or of the marginal firm or industry struggling on the verge of extinction as the real menace to economic progress. A great deal more of that attitude will be needed if official intervention is for the future to be directed to the right address.

There are other minor cautions on public intervention in industry to be gathered from various parts of these studies. The flour-millers' case against national purchasing of imported wheat deserves careful consideration; so also does their case against anything more than a moderate permanent increase in the proportion of home-grown wheat to total consumption. If these claims cannot be entirely met, it is at least desirable that the fullest possible allowance should be made for them in working out the details of future policy.

Taking a rather different point, the study on brewing suggests forcibly that the existing basis of taxation on alcoholic liquor is in urgent need of revision. Although the consumption of beer per head of the population in the United Kingdom was halved between the two wars, liquor taxes—in the lower income groups, overwhelmingly on beer—were estimated in 1937–8 to take about a shilling in the pound of the income of an average family with 40s. a week, about 9½d. in the pound at the level of £4 a week, and no more than 5d. in the pound in the case of higher salaried workers in the range from £500 to £1,000 a year.[1] By the middle of the war the tax on the lowest incomes had risen to 1s. 7d. in the pound, while the charge on the middle-class incomes approaching £1,000 a year was still only around 6d. British taxation before, during, and since the war has been seriously regressive on the lowest incomes, and to this state of affairs the tax on beer has been one of the main contributors. The beer tax has a high yield and great administrative advantages; but is there not a case for shifting the emphasis away from a tax which falls so heavily on those least able to afford it, and which is 'avoidable' (in the terms of the text-books on public finance) chiefly at the cost of avoiding the society of fellow human beings? High war-time income-tax has made indirect taxation more fashionable than it was; is there not perhaps a risk that the pendulum may swing too far?

The general lesson of the four studies can be summed up in three propositions. First, it is essential that in future more attention should be given to the less obvious sources of inefficiency, slow progress, and unemployment; to the minor trades which rub along after a fashion at the bottom of a slough of depression; to the more prosperous trades which are content to wait for opportunity to knock twice; and to the causes underlying the lack of enterprise in particular regions. The appointment in 1945 by the Board of Trade of Working Parties of employers, trade unionists, and independent members to investigate some fourteen major and minor trades has been a valuable step in the right direction. Its value will be even greater if it is followed, as the working parties themselves almost unanimously recommend, by the establishment of permanent investigating bodies of the same kind.

In the second place, no easy generalization is possible about the most effective methods to adopt where inefficiency or unduly slow progress is revealed. Competition, industrial self-government, and

---

[1] Shirras and Rostas, *British Taxation*, pp. 52–3. The figures are for a family of man, wife, and two children, with tastes about the average for their class.

State or local authority intervention all have both their advantages and their disadvantages; which method, or combination of methods, is most appropriate to each industry depends on the widely varying circumstances of particular times and cases. It may very often depend on purely personal factors such as the presence or absence of strong leadership within a trade.

Thirdly, to go back to the point just raised in connexion with flour-milling, it is essential that for the future a regular stream of information should be available on the organization, efficiency, and progress of every sector of the national economy. Problems of industrial organization have had to force themselves on the public attention in the past either through some national disaster, such as the collapse of employment in the staple trades of South Wales or Central Lancashire, or through the notorious and obtrusive prosperity of a trade such as flour-milling. It will be necessary in future to throw more light on problems which fall into neither of these categories, with a view both to promoting efficiency and, as with flour-milling, to preventing wholly or partly unfounded public suspicion of an industry's activities.

Preventing public suspicion might almost be classed as a special case of the problem of promoting efficiency, since psychological tensions inside industry are at least as likely to reduce efficiency as defects of equipment or organization. Psychological causes of friction and inefficiency have been important enough in the past, coal-mining being only the most glaring example of tendencies which could be paralleled in many other trades. They are likely to be even more important in future if full employment is maintained. As in the case of the white fish industry, there is every reason to expect that, once alternative work is easily and permanently available, public suspicion of an industry will be reflected in growing labour difficulties and a tendency for the labour force to migrate elsewhere. Coal-mining in the 'twenties and 'thirties was the storm-centre of British industry; yet, though not as efficient as it might have been, British coal-mining remained a going concern right down to the outbreak of war. It was war-time full employment which strengthened the mineworkers' hands and enabled them, in effect, to threaten the public with an acute shortage of miners and coal and with sharply and persistently declining efficiency if their demands did not receive attention.

Ways and means of securing the necessary publicity will no doubt be many and various. The reform of company law on the lines proposed by the Cohen Committee will help to a certain extent. So also will a further development of the movement towards greater voluntary disclosure of companies' affairs, which has made noticeable progress in recent years. The new reformed and annual Census of Production will be of the greatest value; though it will not, of course, cover the qualitative aspects of industrial organization, which also need to be kept under continuous review. The deficiency might be met either by attaching to the Census a series of official monographs on the organization, development, and potentialities of particular industries or industrial groups, or, if it were thought that official monographs might not be sufficiently outspoken, by securing regular published reports from such bodies as the Cotton Board or the permanent Councils proposed for other industries in the Reports of Working Parties. The first batch of Working Party Reports all include detailed recommendations to this end. It may be hoped that sources of this kind will be supplemented by a reversion on the part of economists to an interest in realistic studies of economic organization. Whatever the method, the essential point is that an adequate volume of information from reliable sources should for the future be regularly available to the public.

There is, of course, no inconsistency between an approach to problems of industrial organization along the lines followed here, with the emphasis on increasing efficiency and on promoting expansion at industry's potential growing-points, and what might be called the full employment approach adopted by Lord Beveridge and others. Rising efficiency will be as desirable under full employment as in the depression of the 'twenties and 'thirties, and a policy of stimulating laggards and giving the more enterprising and active concerns their head will incidentally make full employment considerably easier to attain. A policy which exclusively emphasizes efficiency cannot guarantee the high level of monetary demand needed to ensure full employment, and for that reason may even incidentally defeat its own ends; for full employment should prove (and is already proving) an effective ally against concerns which rely for survival more on cheap labour than on efficiency of technique and organization. But that is not to deny that in a world of efficiency and abounding enterprise the political and economic steps to full employment will be far shorter than at present and much less likely to meet with obstruction.

The fact that the two approaches are not inconsistent needs to be stressed only because in recent controversy they have tended to appear not as complementary but as alternatives.[1] It would almost be true to say that they have become characteristic of the outlook of different nations; the British approach has tended to put first the question of full employment, while the American approach has been to concentrate, at any rate in practical policy, on increasing efficiency and production through allowing the freest possible play to enterprise. At the time of writing, the Washington agreements for an American

---

[1] See, for instance, the contrast of approach between Lord Beveridge's *Full Employment in a Free Society* (1944) and Professor A. G. B. Fisher's *Economic Progress and Social Security,* published in 1945.

loan to Great Britain, along with the Bretton Woods Agreement for an International Monetary Fund, are being challenged in Britain on the ground that the United States is not yet prepared to guarantee a high enough permanent level of internal spending to ensure full employment. Americans may not unreasonably object in return to being asked to underpin the economy of a country which in so many respects has failed to take to heart the other half of the lesson.

Both approaches of course need to be supplemented with studies of the personal problems of industry—that is, of its political problems in the widest sense of the term. Lord Beveridge's masterly analysis of the economic problems of planning for full employment stopped short at the point where the State launches out on a voyage among the shifting and dangerous currents (his own phrase) of personal and group relationships. Similarly, the four studies in this book are concerned primarily with commercial and technical management, and only secondarily with the attitude of the man on the job. Perhaps they might have gone further in this direction; but it is not easy to shake off the habit of mind acquired by most of those who learnt or practised economics in the 'twenties and 'thirties. The Civil Servant or politician with a new plan, in those days of one to three millions of unemployed, was a subject for the economist's great if sceptical interest. The enterprising business man with a factory to found was a public benefactor to be greeted with open arms, while established firms with an undue tendency to price or output control were cast for the prominent if unflattering role of the villain. The manager, the scientist, and the engineer were obviously vital contributors to the national standard of living and the struggle for existence in world markets. Of all the human factors in industry, it was only the ordinary worker whose point of view was usually and understandably treated as unimportant.

That did not happen to the same extent in politics; for the politician had to bear in mind that the man in the street kept his vote even when he lost his job. But the economic investigator, concerned with the internal power politics of industry, could quite reasonably treat him as a mainly passive factor. The economist might study the minor subject of Industrial Relations, a little off the beaten track of economic theory and organization, and concerned at that time chiefly with institutional factors such as collective contracts or trade union histories. He might plan better conditions for the ordinary worker, or join a political party to fight for his rights. But always at the back of his mind was the feeling that the rank-and-file worker stood on a different footing from the manager, the technician, or the Civil Servant, inasmuch as his primary business was to take orders and not to give them. He was a man to whom things happened, for better or for worse, not one who made them happen; and the queues outside the Employment Exchanges were there as a guarantee against any undue display of initiative on the part of either the individual worker or his trade union.

> 'Smile at us, pay us, pass us: but do not quite forget,
> For we are the people of England; and we have not spoken yet.'

Chesterton died a few years too soon to see the transformation in the relative power of labour and management—particularly the financial and economic side of management—brought about by full employment. The people of England, if they speak at all, still speak with a multitude of confusing voices; but it can at least be said that full employment has given them, individually and collectively, a direct influence in industry which at times has proved as startling and embarrassing to the professional friends of labour as to their official opponents. The studies included in this volume, like the reports of the Working Parties, serve first and foremost to indicate the need for further continuous research in all the industries covered; and there is no direction in which this need is greater, in view both of past neglect and of present problems, than in the field of relations in and between working groups. The classic American inquiries which laid the foundation for so much of modern management theory still await a parallel here.

The chapters which follow were drafted during the war; printing and other difficulties have held back their publication for upwards of two years. Inevitably, they refer largely to pre-war material, and it has not in all cases been possible to bring them fully up to date. They will serve nevertheless as part of the historical background of reconstruction, and they carry many general lessons in economic organization whose value will not grow less with time.

December 1946

CHAPTER I

FLOUR-MILLING

By Mrs. H. V. EDWARDS

FLOUR-MILLING represents one of the most highly mechanized and organized industries of modern times. The basic principles on which the processes of milling are founded are, of course, far from new. Corn was being ground on handstones or querns as far back as six thousand years ago. Mechanization of the milling operation developed gradually throughout the centuries. At first millstones were driven by hand or by cattle; the next stage was the development of the water-wheel about 400 or 500 B.C., and this method was common until windmills began to come into prominence some thousand years later. The windmill-watermill era continued up to the time of the invention of the steam engine, the first steam-driven mills being operated in 1784. All these methods were similar in principle as far as the actual milling of the grain was concerned, and it was only the driving mechanism which underwent any real changes. In the latter half of the eighteenth century, however, experiments were made abroad on a new type of milling process, which reduced the grain not by simple crushing or grinding, but by a more gradual and gentle method. The new type of mill was called the roller mill, and it consisted in essence of two metal rollers, each with a finely toothed surface, which in turning against each other broke open the grain without crushing it. The new method remained in the experimental stage for many years, and it was not until the 1820's that serious attention was paid to it on any commercial scale. From this time onward improvements and further developments in technique proceeded apace, and by the 1870's the roller system had obviously come to stay. German millers in particular were using rollers to a considerable extent. The British milling industry had not yet taken up the new process, but were now definitely showing signs of interest, and in 1877 a deputation of millers went to Hungary to see the roller mill for themselves, and were favourably impressed. Four years later a demonstration was held in the Agricultural Hall, London, at which a number of complete milling plants were erected and operated. In the next decade the new system was quickly adopted by a number of the more progressive millers in this country, most of whose names are famous in the industry to-day.

At the same time the structure of the industry was undergoing a radical alteration. This came about through the large-scale development of wheat-farming in the prairie countries at a cost considerably lower than was possible at home. Home wheat production in consequence entered a period of rapid decline, and failed to keep pace with the consumption needs of a rapidly growing population. Imported wheat supplies advanced in importance, until in 1939 they accounted for about nine-tenths of the flour-milling industry's requirements.

Thus the development of the industry and changes in its structure came about in two main ways: the development of mechanization led to the concentration of production in larger units; and the growing dependence on wheat imports led to the location of mills at the ports, country mills declining in importance as home-grown crops contributed a decreasing proportion of the industry's supplies, and as the large units at the ports invaded their markets.

Between the beginning of the century and the outbreak of the Great War development along both these lines was taking place at a fairly rapid rate. The War of 1914–18 arrested this development, and to a certain extent reversed the trends of the preceding years. The need to economize in shipping made for a considerable increase in the use of home-grown grain, and this brought with it a resuscitation of the country mills, many of which expanded their output considerably beyond pre-war production. Consequently, at the end of control in 1921 there was an excess of productive capacity, and a period of intense competition followed, during which the industry experienced very lean times. Only the strong were able to survive. At the end of the 'twenties the industry, through the leadership of the largest concerns, got together and reorganized. The total capacity of the industry was reduced to proportions commensurate with the country's current consumption, and output was fixed between mill and mill so as to prevent over-production. This was, in fact, a classic example of rationalization. The organization remained solid during the ensuing ten years up to the outbreak of war in 1939—though it was showing some signs of wavering towards the end—and during this period the industry enjoyed considerable prosperity.

The industry itself is singularly clear-cut, representing as it does a processing rather than a manufacturing industry. There is no great diversity of either raw materials or of products, though both are of many different grades and prices. Mechanization, in virtue of the extreme regularity and standardized nature of production, has been able to advance to very great lengths; and this industry, which produces sufficient flour for the needs of over forty million people, employs the services of only about 15,000 operatives.

The milling industry of Great Britian to-day claims to be the foremost in the world, and there are no serious contestants to this claim. On the technical side, British milling engineers have for years been the forerunners in many fields of development; and the British milling industry has achieved a standard of organization not surpassed in any other country in the world.

Modern milling, as has been said, is very highly mechanized. In the most modern mills the whole system, from the arrival of the grain at the mill to the delivery of the flour and meal in bags, is completely mechanized, and it is said that the only scope for further mechanization (apart from minor improvements of design of existing machinery) lies in more complete automatic control, though this is already far advanced. There are one or two mills specializing in stone-ground flour which operate on the old principles of grinding, but apart from these one or two exceptions the methods and machinery used are the same throughout the industry, in both large and small mills. The latter lack the elaborate systems and specialized machinery of the larger units, but in the main part of the milling process the machinery is essentially similar, and the larger units merely comprise greater numbers of the respective machines.

The passage of the material through a mill from the grain to the flour stages usually takes place in a downward direction from the top floor of the mill to ground-level, in order to make full use of gravity in the transfer of the grain from one stage to the next. A mill may comprise anything from four to seven floors, though many of the smaller mills may have fewer than four. Intake of the grain at all but the smallest mills is by elevator or suction. Bucket elevators are employed at some of the medium-size mills, but where the volume of grain used is large enough to justify them pneumatic suction plants are generally employed. The grain is received in a storage silo, sometimes receives a preliminary cleaning, and is transferred as required to a small service silo feeding the wheat-cleaning plant or screen-room. In the case of the large modern mills the silos are of reinforced concrete; in many small- to medium-size mills they are of laminated wood. Silos normally hold at least one month's wheat requirements, which in the case of the larger mills amounts to some 5,000 tons. In the screen-room all impurities are removed from the grain by special sorting machines which throw off the various types of foreign matter (or 'screenings') into their respective groups, such as maize, oats, barley, or melilot. The wheat is now washed and, in all but the smaller mills, is conditioned by heating and by augmenting or diminishing the moisture content in order to bring the grains to the most suitable texture for the milling process which follows.

The actual milling process is extremely elaborate in practice, but the principles involved are clear. It is a very gradual process, and its aim is to separate the outer parts of the grain from the starchy interior. A normal wheat grain consists of about 83 per cent of endosperm, which is the inner portion of the grain and forms the food reserve on which the wheat embryo or 'germ' draws for its early growth. This portion consists mainly of starchy material and provides the basic raw material of white flour. The outer layers of the grain form about 15 per cent of its weight and are commonly known as bran. The germ, which is easily detected in the grain on account of its oily appearance, makes up about 2 per cent of the wheat. This, being the live part of the grain, is rich in both fats and vitamins, and provides one of the main sources of natural vitamin B.

The mechanical operations involved are carried out on series of rollers, and the stages in the passage of the wheat through the mill are broadly as follows:

1. Breaking open of the wheat grain and scraping the interior endosperm (which yields the flour proper) from the outer skins (which make up the bran) in successive stages. This is carried out on the 'Break' Rolls, of which there are normally four sets. They consist of a pair of finely fluted cylindrical rollers, usually about three feet long, revolving at different speeds. After the grain has passed through the first 'break' the resultant stock is sifted and graded by being passed over sieves of progressively finer mesh (now commonly carried out by means of the agitating Plansifter, which has an action similar to ordinary hand-sieving); and the fine flour and bran made during the roller process are also drawn off by purifiers, which carry out the division by a combination of sieving and separation by means of air currents (or 'aspiration'). The numerous grades of stock separated off by this sorting process are passed through to the appropriate processing rollers—either the next Break Roll or the Reduction Rolls. A similar process of sifting, grading, and sending the stocks forward to different parts of the mill follows the passage through each of the four Break Rolls.

2. The reduction rolls grind the stock down into flour, each different type of stock going to a different roll.

3. The flours and meals ground on the reduction rolls are now 'dressed', i.e. sifted through silk bolting cloths of varying mesh. The number of grades of flour produced in the mill varies: in the larger mills the number of grades usually falls between twenty and thirty; the smaller country mills usually limit themselves to about five.

4. The different varieties of flour are made by running together proportions of selected grades.

5. The coarser parts of the wheat grain, representing about 30 per cent of its weight (in normal times), are also divided off into various grades of wheat feed (or offals as they were formerly called);

these are used for cattle feed. The germ, which may or may not be drawn off from the stock, is generally separated off about half-way through the milling process. Some of the germ is unavoidably mixed in with the flour, and if it is not sifted off the rest of the germ finds its way into the feed.

All the different grades of stock and flour which are separated out during the milling process are examined from time to time during the day. The different stocks are laid out in piles and are tested, usually by the foreman, for texture and colour. In this way faults which may have occurred in the machinery, or adjustments which might with advantage be made in their setting, are determined. The finished flour stocks graduate in colour from the creamy white types to the light brown tones of those which are nearest to the feed stocks.

The reason for the success of the roller milling process was that it enabled the endosperm of the wheat grain to be more completely freed from the outer skins of the grain and from the germ. Under the older method of milling by grindstones much of the outer husk was reduced to powder and could not be separated off from the flour. This, by present milling standards, is an unforgivable sin. The texture, colour, and, most important, the baking quality of flour suffer if the bran is included in any quantity, and its keeping quality is impaired if the germ is included. The roller mill process produces a flour of excellent colour and baking quality. But the germ and bran, which are excluded from the flour, contain the mineral and vitamin (principally B and E) elements of the wheat grain. The germ and its surrounding tissue, in particular, contains about 70 per cent of the total B_1 content of the grain. White flour, therefore, while it provides very valuable food in the form of carbohydrate, is deficient in certain quantities of vitamin and mineral food which the whole wheat grain could provide. This fact has given rise to an enormous amount of controversy. In earlier days nearly all the germ was allowed to go into the cattle feed, but in more recent years increasing quantities have been extracted and used, usually after some form of cooking to enable it to be kept for fairly long periods, in the manufacture of patent foods and in proprietary flours, and also for medicinal purposes.

The main case against wholemeal flours has been that the public have clearly shown a very decided preference for white bread and flour; and this is an unanswerable argument while the public are allowed to exercise a free choice. White bread is said to be assimilated more easily than brown—the 'roughage' in wholemeal bread is one of its characteristics—but the difference is not outstanding or highly significant. One of the points against wholemeal flour is its relatively poor keeping quality, precisely on account of the inclusion of the germ, which contains about 10 per cent of fat.

The subject of white versus wholemeal bread has undoubtedly proved a happy hunting-ground for dieticians of all kinds. The milling trade's research body carried out a number of experiments during the middle and late 'thirties which showed that whereas wholemeal flour had a vitamin B content of 600 to 800 I.U. white flours contained only 80 to 150 I.U. The industry frankly acknowledged the claim of wholemeal flour to a higher vitamin content, but pointed to the obvious public preference and to the fact that bread formed only part of the nation's diet and that in a normal mixed diet sufficient vitamin B was absorbed without making it necessary to retain all the vitamin of the wheat grain in the finished flour. But nutritional surveys carried out in 1938 under Government auspices demonstrated that about half the country's population were not, in fact, taking sufficient B_1. In 1938 the milling industry started negotiations for the supply of synthetic B_1, to add to white flour.

Another charge levelled against modern milling methods has been the use of chemical agents. This again applies particularly to white flours, and more especially those used for the manufacture of bread. It is said in milling circles that about 95 per cent of the flour used in England is treated by chemical means, the cost varying between $1\frac{1}{2}d.$ and $2d.$ a sack (280 lb.). The chemical agents are usually termed 'improvers', since they have the effect of 'strengthening' the flour and increasing its adaptability to varying methods of fermentation.[1] Three types of treatment have been employed: by the use of powders, e.g. acid calcium phosphate, ammonia persulphate, and various branded chemicals; by gases, e.g. chlorine, Beta gas, nitrogen trichloride (Agene); and physical treatment, usually by heat. Treatment by gases is probably the method most widely employed. A great deal of research has been carried out by the millers on this aspect of milling. It is clearly an important side of the milling process. The whiteness of a flour is a weighty factor in its saleability. Improvers, moreover, remedy some of the defects of a weak flour and enhance its baking quality; their use has therefore had the effect of up-grading different types of flour. There is no doubt that the advances made in flour treatment have made a number of users doubtful of the intrinsic value of the flour which is offered for sale, and hesitant of using their judgment of a flour by its outward appearance. A number of users, including some of the big bakeries, biscuit manufacturers, and the Army, stipulate that their flour shall have been subjected to no artificial treatment whatsoever. In general, however, bakers prefer to buy treated rather than untreated flours, although the latter are available.

[1] See p. 80.

During the 'twenties continued public agitation on the whole question of food purity and of treated flour in particular caused an official inquiry to be made into the use of chemical agents in flour. The Departmental Committee on the Treatment of Flour with Chemical Substances issued its report in 1927. Its findings, however, were far from conclusive. While it considered certain chemical agents —including chlorine gas—to be more obnoxious than others and recommended that their use should be forbidden, it failed to produce any substantial proof that the use of any one of the chemical substances used in flour treatment was actually deleterious to health when taken in the quantities in which it appeared in flour. It looked as though the Committee had started out with certain preconceived ideas which proved extremely difficult to substantiate scientifically. Naturally enough, no legislation bearing on the treatment of flour was put into effect as a result of the Committee's report, though the Minister of Health, under the Food and Drugs Act, is empowered to 'prohibit or restrict the addition of any substance, or the application of any treatment, to flour intended for sale or for use in the making of bread for sale'.

PRODUCTION

It has been seen that the manufacture of flour involves the simultaneous manufacture of other wheat products. Apart from brown or wholemeal flours, which form only about 3 per cent of the total flour output, flour is of about 70 per cent extraction.[1] The other 30 per cent of the original wheat grain is used for the most part in cattle foods, and is now generally termed wheat feed, the older designation of 'offals' being discarded by the trade as unpleasant and possibly prejudicial to sales. It may be divided into two broad groups —bran and weatings—weatings being the more finely ground product. There are various grades of feed, in the same way as there are numerous grades of flour (though they are not so numerous), which are run together to form the various types of wheat feed marketed by the miller. Small quantities of other wheat products are also manufactured by some flour-mills, including rolled and flaked wheat, which is used for patent cereal foodstuffs, and cut and kibbled wheat, which is generally used for poultry. Germ is extracted in very small quantities—probably at most $\frac{1}{2}$ per cent of the total weight of flour —but it is a highly profitable by-product.

The total output of the industry varied little in the last pre-war years. The Wheat Commission's figures give the following annual net quantities of home-milled flour manufactured by United Kingdom millers during the seven years ended 31 July 1939:

---

[1] Statements of this kind in the present chapter relate to milling practice before the outbreak of war in 1939.

QUANTITIES OF FLOUR DELIVERED BY U.K. MILLERS

Year to 31st July				Thousand tons
1932–3	.	.	.	. 3,978
1933–4	.	.	.	. 3,864
1934–5	.	.	.	. 3,899
1935–6	.	.	.	. 3,941
1936–7	.	.	.	. 3,829
1937–8	.	.	.	. 3,835
1938–9	.	.	.	. 3,939

The failure of production to expand with rising population over the thirty years to 1939 is seen by comparing the figures of output for the period before 1914 and those for the 'thirties. The available statistics are those of the Census of Production, which do not offer exact comparisons for all the years. For 1907 and 1924 the output of all firms, however small, was included; in the later years only that of firms with more than ten employees was taken account of. However, the contribution of the small firms was not very significant —not more than 1 per cent—and a correction has been made in the figures for the later years to take this into account.

U.K. OUTPUT OF FLOUR AND MEAL

				Thousand tons
1907	.	.	.	. 3,904
1924	.	.	.	. 4,174
1930	.	.	.	. 3,889
1935	.	.	.	. 4,078

The figures for the middle 'thirties do not exactly square with those of the Wheat Commission. Part of the discrepancy is accounted for by the fact that the Census figures include a certain amount of meal as well as flour, and there may also be a certain amount of duplication through the purchase by millers of imported or home-milled flours for blending purposes. In some years the latter item may have accounted for as much as 4 per cent over-statement.

In 1935, 71·5 per cent of total output consisted of meal and flour, 27·8 per cent of bran and weatings, 0·3 per cent of rolled and flaked wheat and cut and kibbled wheat, and the remaining 0·4 per cent of other products, including germ. For 1939 roughly 30 per cent of the total output, or broadly the same proportion as in 1935, was officially classified as offals: by 1944, as the war made it necessary to raise the rate of extraction, this figure had fallen to 15½ per cent.

The value of the output of flour is subject to considerable variation. This is because a very high proportion—about 75 per cent—of the cost of the flour is made up of the cost of raw materials. Between 1924 and 1938 the price of wheat ranged from over 50s. per 400 lb., in the middle 'twenties, to below 20s. in the period 1931–3, and flour prices have naturally fluctuated widely according to ruling prices for wheat. Flour prices are also partially dependent on the price which the by-product, wheat feed, fetches on the market, this price being offset against costs in arriving at the price of flour. Wheat feed prices do not necessarily move with the price of wheat, but follow the general course of the prices of animal feeding-stuffs. Thus, for instance, during the depression, when wheat prices fell more heavily than those of other cereals, the cost of wheat feed to the farmer was actually higher than the price received by him for his wheat.

In 1924 the average price of flour ex-mill London was 44s. 3d. a sack; after 1926 prices began to fall, until in 1931 they were below 20s. a sack. After 1934 they again began to rise, and by 1937 had reached 37s. 6d., but fell again during the following year. The changes were due almost entirely to the fluctuations in wheat prices during these years; the course of the two sets of prices between the two wars is examined in more detail later (p. 54). Other costs contributing to the final cost of flour may be roughly estimated as follows:

Wages	10d. to 1s. 6d. a sack
Power	6d. a sack
Selling costs	6d. to 9d. a sack
Fair average costs of delivery .	1s. 6d. a sack

Total expenses amount to round about 5s. a sack, and of these between 50 and 60 per cent may be taken to be manufacturing expenses (including depreciation), about 15 per cent selling expenses, and about 30 per cent overheads. It is generally assumed that the average net profit on a sack of flour is round about 2s. 6d. to 3s. Such figures are clearly extremely rough, and are to be taken only as indicating the general level of costs and profits.

For what such figures of value are worth, it may be stated that in 1935 the value of all wheat products, all but a minute proportion of which was accounted for by the flour-milling industry, totalled some £46 to £47 million. In 1930 the corresponding figure was £58 to £59 million, and in 1924 £82 to £83 million. Of these totals, the value of flour output amounted to about £38 million in 1935, compared with about £48 million in 1930.

Normally the price of wheat feed is about two-thirds that of flour, rolled and flaked and cut and kibbled wheat falling somewhere about midway between the two, but, as has been said above, the sets of prices do not necessarily move entirely in sympathy with one another.

The industry is not troubled with the difficulties of seasonal production, though at times the influx of quantities of cheap foreign flour may temporarily reduce the output of certain mills. Even in the comparatively slack season, when consumption tends to fall during the warmer months of the year, the mills are able to continue production with but little interruption. The uniformity of the product, the absence of any sudden change in demand from the point of view of fashion or preference for different types of flour, and the fact that flour may be stored without deterioration—and in fact with some advantage—for many months, make it possible for production to be maintained at a fairly constant momentum.

Different types of wheat produce correspondingly different types of flour, ranging in 'strength' from the relatively weak flours made from English and other Western European wheats to the very 'strong' flours from high-grade Canadian wheat.[1] 'Strength' cannot be defined in any precise scientific terms, but its meaning is clearly understood. It is the capacity of a flour to make a large, well-risen, shapely loaf of bread, of fine even texture. Relatively strong flours are essential for commercial bread-making, while weaker flours are suitable for cakes, biscuits, household use, and for animal foods. Even when the purpose for which the flour is being used is known, different methods of manufacture (particularly, in the case of bread, as to the type and time of fermentation) influence the selection of the grade of flour, and a good all-round bread flour is so blended as to stand up to varied treatment. For biscuit manufacture flours are made in great variety and to a high degree of specialization.

Perhaps the most important factor in turning out a particular brand of flour is that it should be of standard quality through the year, and it is the aim of every miller to maintain consistent standards in his flours. This calls for expert knowledge of the various wheats which are available at different seasons in order to arrive at the correct blends.

The following are the broad classes of flour manufactured:

Bread-making Flours. These flours, as has been mentioned before, require a good proportion of strong wheats. Usually the strong wheats, such as Manitoba, account for between 30 and 50 per cent of the mixture, the rest being composed of medium-strength wheats (or 'filler' wheats), wheats which give a good white colour ('coloury' wheats), and weak wheats. Practice, of course, varies considerably between mill and mill, and particularly between port mills and inland mills. The latter use a relatively high proportion of weak local wheat —usually between 40 and 50 per cent—and the rest of the grist has to be made up of wheat yielding a very strong flour. Port millers, however, use less of the very weakest wheats and thus require proportionately less of the strongest types. Flours have to be varied to suit local tastes—thus, London prefers strong flours, the North adopts a shorter baking process and requires a slightly weaker flour, while the long Scottish baking process demands very strong flours. A typical London flour might be blended as follows:

[1] See also p. 65 et seq.

40% high- and medium-grade Canadian (Manitoba) (strong wheat)
45% fillers
10% Australian (coloury wheat)
 5% English or other weak wheat

while a typical North Country flour might be made up of:

35% Manitoba
35% fillers
10% Australian
20% weak wheat

The great majority of bread flours are white, only about 5 per cent of the nation's bread being made from brown, wholemeal, or other non-white flours. In normal times white flours are of about 70 per cent extraction, i.e. they contain about 70 per cent of the total wheat grain. Bran and germ, as has been seen, are separated off as far as possible during the milling process. A fair-size mill normally separates out between twenty and thirty different grades of flour, which are blended to form the various commercial grades put on to the market. Years ago the blending of flours used to be carried out in large part by the baker himself, often with extremely inadequate knowledge, but now blending is undertaken almost exclusively at the mill. No standards of flour quality are laid down and no exact qualities are associated with any particular types of flour; there is, moreover, no uniformity between mill and mill. This is, of course, in the nature of the industry: wheats vary so much, from season to season, that any absolute uniformity is out of the question, though, as has been said before, millers seek as far as possible to keep uniform standards even with the varying mixtures which pass through the mill. Four broad types of flour are sold to the baker—Patents, Super, Bakers, and Households—though these terms are by no means universal. The first-named consists of the highest quality flours and represents varying proportions of the total flour output of the milling operation; clearly its quality varies inversely with the proportion taken off: a normal quality patent flour represents about 50 per cent of the total flour passing out, but the figure may sometimes be as high as 70 per cent (though rarely higher) according to current demand. Supers form from 20 to 30 per cent of the total flour output. Households represent the poorest grade flours and contain a greater proportion of the outer layers of the wheat grain. A straight-run flour is by definition the flour produced by running all the flour streams together; a commercially termed 'straight-run' does not, however, conform to this description, but represents the flour left after the Patents have been drawn off. The chief flours sold by a mill are usually sold under brand names.

The finer brown flours contain in general all but the outer coarse brown layers, and comprise varying quantities of the germ, which, as we have seen, is rich in fats and represents about 2 to $2\frac{1}{2}$ per cent of the total wheat grain. The inclusion of some of the outer skins of the grain in these flours lowers their strength, and they produce a much less bold dough than do white flours taken from a similar mixture of wheats. For this reason they are made with a far higher proportion of strong wheats than are white flours. The inclusion of the germ gives a sweet taste to the loaf; and some proprietary flours have added malt or other substances to give a loaf of a sweet sticky texture. One of the disadvantages of brown flour is its poor keeping qualities compared with white. This is due to the fatty nature of the germ, which tends to become rancid after too long storage. Some proprietary brands of brown flour contain more than the natural quantity of germ which is present in the wheat; added amounts of 'free' germ, which is subjected to some form of partial cooking, are put into the flour during the last stages of manufacture.

Wheatmeal and wholemeal flours contain from 90 to 100 per cent of the whole grain, but there are no fixed standards. Wholemeal, properly so-called, should, of course, contain the whole wheat. Some proprietary brands of wholemeal flour are made by the old methods of stone-grinding and not on the modern roller-mill system. Here again, the use of the stronger wheats is necessary to produce a bread flour strong enough to suit the baker. Some of the meal which is made does not go for human consumption at all, but is used for cattle food.

Self-raising Flours and other Flours for Household Use. These are usually made from weak and filler wheats. A considerable proportion of the household flours are imported. The ingredients added to render the flour 'self-raising', i.e. capable of aeration without the aid of yeast, are bicarbonate of soda, together with cream of tartar or acid calcium phosphate (A.C.P.). The latter is more commonly used, mainly on account of its cheapness. The addition of these chemical ingredients is made either by millers specializing in such flour or by bakers and retailers themselves.

Biscuit and Cake Flours. The characteristics of biscuit flours are their lack of 'spring' and their poor gluten content. The most suitable wheats for such flours are home-grown or other weak varieties, and their manufacture is the preserve of the country millers, many of whom mill biscuit flours almost exclusively, using the local wheat. Imported flours from the Continent are also on the market. Some port mills or mills in large centres which make a certain quantity of biscuit flours may use imported wheats, but English wheat is superior in flavour. The wide range of biscuits made, varying from dry crackers to special fancy mixtures, requires a correspondingly large range of flours, and biscuit flours are therefore made in great variety.

Cake flours are for the most part somewhat stronger than biscuit flours in order to give sufficient boldness and a good texture, and contain small proportions of strong wheats.

LOCATION OF FLOUR-MILLS

The location of the industry is governed primarily by transport costs, first in respect of supplies, and, secondly, of markets. Flour-milling is a processing industry rather than a manufacturing industry, and the cost of the raw material contributes about three-quarters of the value of the finished product. The weight and bulk of both wheat and wheat products are great in proportion to their value, and their final cost to the consumer is clearly governed in no small measure by handling and transport costs. The importance of the handling side of conveying material and products should perhaps be emphasized. Flour and feed have in any case to be handled for distribution however close the market, and cannot be treated in bulk in the same way as wheat. For this reason—and the development of road transport and the consequent cheapening of distribution in recent years has increased the weight of the argument—the main economies to be made lie in lowering the cost of handling and transport of the grain; and to-day the prime factor in the economic operation of a mill is the ease and cheapness with which it obtains its wheat supplies, a factor involving both location on the water-front, and a unit of sufficient size to effect direct intake of the wheat.

As has been said, the growing importance of overseas wheat (in the years before 1939 foreign grain made up on the average about 90 per cent of the wheat converted into flour in the United Kingdom) made the ports the natural centres for the establishment of flour-mills. The largest port mills are situated on deep-water sites which are capable of taking ocean-going vessels. The economic advantage of receiving the grain direct into the mill from the steamer is great; extra charges are incurred in transferring wheat from the ship to a lighter or barge, and still more in unloading grain at the dock and subsequently transferring it, either immediately or from the grain merchants' stores, to road or rail containers for delivery inland. Where the mill is of smaller size and docking facilities are inadequate to accommodate large ocean-going vessels, the grain may be transferred to lighters which are loaded overside from the large ships. The time taken in transferring the wheat from the ship's hold to the mill's silo is an important factor in the total cost of the grain, and the capacities of the intake plants of the largest mills go up to 300 and 400 tons an hour. The medium-size port mills are, for the most part, situated on the river or canal front and take their wheat from barges which are loaded overside from vessels lying in the dock or river. This is the cheapest method of transport failing direct intake.

2

The port mills, it will be clear, rarely take in either appreciable or regular supplies of home-grown wheat; to do so would be to ignore their special locational advantages, since home-grown wheat is carried in comparatively small lots and could not be handled with the ease and speed as in the case of the large loads arriving by sea. It is said that on the average only about 2 to 3 per cent of the port mills' grists is made up of home-grown wheats.

The growing importance of provender-milling and the association of flour-milling firms with this closely allied and technically similar industry emphasize the advantages of a port location, since practically the whole of the seed and grain requirements of the animal feed industry have to be imported.

Other considerations which govern the siting of a mill are adequate supplies of pure water—which is used in very large quantities for washing and conditioning the wheat—and power supplies. But these last two properties may be found in most large centres of population and are not peculiar to the ports, though they are always to be found there. The singular advantage of the port location, it must be stressed, lies in its favourable situation as regards wheat supplies. Auxiliary advantages, of lesser importance, which nevertheless contribute to the efficiency of a mill—such as local transport facilities, public utilities, a large local market, an adequate labour pool—and which are found at the ports, are also available at all large consuming centres.

The port mills have the added advantage of being in a favourable position for exporting their products, but this is not of very outstanding importance; in 1935 only 3·2 per cent of the total flour output of the country, representing about 5 per cent of the port mills' output, was exported, and the general trend has been one of continuous decline.

The strategic disadvantages of a concentration of large mills at the ports is obvious. In London in 1939 there were four large mills with a combined capacity representing about 10 per cent of the total capacity of the United Kingdom, all concentrated within a very small dock area. Two of these mills were, in fact, destroyed by air attack during the war.

Country mills may be divided into two broad classes: those producing all-English flours for biscuit manufacture and retail sale, and flours with a high proportion of home-grown wheat for cake-making and retail sale; and those producing ordinary bread flours, which require higher proportions of strong imported wheats.

'All-English' country flour-mills are in a special position, and the port mills in general do not attempt to compete with them in their specialist products. They are naturally situated in wheat-growing districts, and though the grain may have to be brought in from some distance around if the mill is of considerable size, transport costs are relatively low, and certainly lower than if the wheat were taken to a port mill for processing. About 70 per cent of the flour produced goes to biscuit manufacturers, the remainder being taken up by factors or other millers for blending purposes, or used for self-raising or household flours.

The position of country mills producing bread flours is different, and for the most part they represent survivals from earlier times. They do use a certain amount of local wheat, the delivered-in costs of which are reasonable, but a considerable proportion of their grist must be imported in order to give the necessary strength to the flour. This proportion varies according to the quality of the English harvest, but in general forms at least 60 per cent of the country mill's grist, and considerably more in the case of a mill situated near a port. As far as possible inland mills are situated on a waterway, and where the mill is of sufficient size the grain is brought in bulk or sacks by barge, but for many of the small mills the canal service is inadequate, and transport costs may be considerable. It was suggested by the trade in connexion with the Barlow Commission[1] that the difference in grain transport costs alone between receiving wheat at a port mill and at an inland mill might be of the order of 4s. a ton on the average, i.e. an average increase in the cost of flour of between 8d. and 9d. a sack. The main advantage of the country mill lies in its local distribution of both flour and feed and its close relations with local farmers, with whom it often trades on a reciprocal basis. The loyalty of country bakers to their local mills must also be taken into account, and is not to be regarded as of small moment; the feeling of loyalty is strong, and although port mills send their representatives into these districts, local bakers generally prefer to continue to trade with the local miller.

It is clear that country mills in general are of comparatively small size; the advantage which they derive from having supplies of wheat and a small market available in the neighbourhood would be lost if the wheat had to be brought in from and the flour distributed over too wide an area. It does in fact sometimes happen that a country mill has to take a considerable quantity of its home-grown wheat from districts well outside its normal supply radius on account of the inadequate supply or quality of the local harvest. This uncertainty is often an important adverse factor. And the supply of home-grown wheat, it should be remembered, is seasonal and farmers are usually anxious to get their wheat threshed and off their hands as quickly as possible. This entails relatively large storage facilities and heavy pressure of work in the last quarter of the year—it has been estimated

[1] Report of the Royal Commission on the Distribution of the Industrial Population, 1940. Cmd. 6153.

that 45 to 50 per cent of the sales of home-grown wheat take place between September and December. The limitation imposed on the size of the country mill by the restricted market which is available within an economic radius makes it more economic not to run on a three-shift system, which is the common practice in the large mills, and nearly all country mills achieve the output determined by local demand by running in the daytime only. Many of the disadvantages of the country mill as compared with the port mill therefore arise from the smaller scale on which they operate, though this factor, in turn, derives from the situation of the mill.

It is clear that the locational advantage lies very definitely with the port mills, particularly in so far as normal bread-baking flours, which account for the major proportion of their output, are concerned. The country mill comes into its own when transport and handling charges for the particular types of wheat and flour with which it is concerned can compare with those applicable in similar circumstances to the larger port mills. The importance of the country mill is obviously very closely linked with the contribution which home-grown wheat makes towards the total wheat requirements of the trade. Before the war, about 10 or 15 per cent of the total quantity used in the trade was home-grown. The ability and willingness of the country mills to absorb the greater part of the home crop has left the port mills free to obtain their supplies in the most advantageous market. It was this factor which made it possible for the trade to hedge the Government off from its proposed scheme for making all mills use a minimum proportion of home-grown wheat in their grists when the Wheat Bill came before Parliament in the early 'thirties. If the small country mills were scrapped and production concentrated in the larger units, home-grown grain would have to be taken up in greater measure by the port mills. The supply of flour to the small inland centres of population would then entail double transport charges, of wheat one way and flour and feed the other, between these centres and the ports, in place of the single transport of wheat to the inland mill which takes place at present. That the larger units are able to operate more efficiently cannot be denied, but they would not be able to produce flour as cheaply as they do now if they were restricted in any way in their freedom of choice in the wheat market. If the country mills were to fall further into disuse through intense competition on the part of the port mills—as happened before and during the process of rationalization of the industry —Government policy aimed at maintaining home wheat production would force on the trade some form of compulsory quota arrangement. The danger of such a situation, which would entail, for the port mills in particular, not only restriction and less economic operation, but inevitably a considerable amount of Government control in effect if not in name, is being recognized by the trade, though this was not always so. Mr. Dence, the Chairman of Hovis, said in a letter to the trade press in 1941:

> 'Millers have been short-sighted indeed in permitting so many country mills to fall into disrepair and disuse, and they are still far too apathetic to this vitally important link in their trade organization. . . . The position should be studied by the N.A.,[1] our Advisory Committees, and by millers individually, and a serious effort should be made to build up a chain of useful depots and mills through all our agricultural areas.'

If this injunction is acted upon it looks as though the port milling interests may seek to take some direct interest in maintaining the country mills in being.

The shift of the milling industry to the ports was already well advanced by the end of the nineteenth century, and continued to progress throughout the period up to 1935, though in the latter part of the 1930's the transference of output appeared to have slowed down almost to a standstill. The Census of Production gives the following figures for comparison:

	Percentage of total flour output			
	1912	1924	1930	1935
Port mills	62%	70%	72%	75%
Mills at large inland centres	} 38%	12% }	} 28%	} 25%
Country mills . .		18% }		

It should be noted that the Census classification includes as 'port' mills all mills which have direct access to the sea, whether they are actually on the coast or not. For example, the mill at Sowerby Bridge, near Leeds, is classed as a port mill in virtue of its situation on the Rochdale Canal. This is probably the most logical way of defining a 'port' mill, since the advantages of a mill's location on a canal front are similar, though they differ in degree, to those of a mill situated on the docks. In the trade a 'port mill' is understood to mean one capable of direct intake of wheat from the ship. In either case the term implies that the mill receives all but a very small proportion of its wheat from overseas sources.

Apart from the division between port and inland location, the industry is distributed fairly evenly throughout the country. All the large ports contain a number of flour-mills, and these supply to a large extent the needs of the population not only of the ports themselves but of the surrounding areas within a considerable radius. The port mills, in fact, send their flour to all parts of the country, and it will be seen by a study of the map of Great Britain that all but a

[1] I.e. the National Association of British and Irish Flour Millers.

few districts—excluding the remoter areas of Scotland—are within a fifty-mile radius of one or other of the large ports, and that all except the Scottish areas lie within a radius of seventy-five miles.

The relative importance of the various ports as regards flour-milling capacity can be judged to a certain extent from the figures of wheat imports through each. It must, however, be remembered that wheat for the inland mills also enters these ports; not all the quantity imported is for processing at the port. All the ports are concerned in a certain amount of this transit trade in grain: probably Hull is more outstanding in this respect than any other port, supplying large quantities of wheat to inland mills in Yorkshire and the East Midlands. The following figures must therefore be taken with reserve, but they do indicate where the main centres of the industry, as far as the ports are concerned, lie.

AVERAGE ANNUAL IMPORTS OF WHEAT OVER
THE PERIOD 1934–8

	Percentage of total U.K. wheat imports
London	26%
Liverpool	19%
Hull	15%
Manchester . . .	10%
Bristol and Gloucester .	9%
Cardiff and Swansea . .	5%
Glasgow	4%
Edinburgh . . .	3%
Newcastle . . .	3%
Southampton . . .	1%

Derived from Annual Statement of Trade

There are a number of fairly large and medium-size mills situated in the large inland towns, particularly in the industrial centres of Lancashire, Yorkshire, and the Midlands. These mills are not so closely linked with wheat-growing districts as are the smaller country mills, though in many cases they are very old-established and date back from the times when the city or town was of comparatively small size and surrounded by an agricultural fringe. These mills may, in fact, take considerable quantities of home-grown wheat, but they also receive large quantities of imported wheat. The fact that transport costs of flour and wheat are on the average about equal enables them to compete with the port mills' flour in the town in which they are situated and its immediate neighbourhood. The majority of them are situated towards the outskirts of the towns on the side of a river or canal to ensure as economical transport as possible.

The small country mills not situated in large towns are, naturally, most heavily concentrated in the wheat-growing areas in the East of England, but they are in evidence in the whole of the South of England. North of a line from the Severn to the Humber they are singularly absent. The fact that a great part of this latter area includes the hilly regions of the west coast and the Pennines makes the absence of inland mills readily understandable.

There is, of course, no hard and fast dividing-line between the mills manufacturing bread flours located in country districts and those attached to large centres of population inland. For the most part all inland mills producing bread flours are situated in or near population masses, whether small or large, and most towns of any size possess one or a number of mills, even though these may not— and this is generally so in the case of inland towns—be sufficient to cater for all the needs of the town.

SIZE AND STRUCTURE OF THE INDUSTRY

The size of the industry has already been partially indicated in the figures of production of flour, for home consumption and for export, and the output of the industry as measured in terms of flour has been seen to amount to between 3·9 and 4 million tons a year.

The size of a flour-mill is normally reckoned in terms of output of sacks of flour (of 280 lb.) per hour: thus a thirty-sack mill is one which is capable of turning out thirty sacks of flour every hour. It has been seen that the flour output of a mill represents about 70 per cent of the total weight of wheat which is milled—i.e. that the flour is of 70 per cent extraction—and the size of a mill is reckoned on the basis of a 70 per cent extraction rate. It is obvious that if, as in war-time, the extraction of flour is raised and the flour represents a higher proportion of the total weight of wheat milled, the actual productive capacity of the mills as measured by the number of sacks of flour delivered every hour is increased in proportion.

If every mill worked full-time—that is on a three-shift system— an output of 4 million tons of flour a year would, at 70 per cent extraction, be produced by mills with a total capacity of about 5,300 sacks. The actual productive capacity of the industry is rather higher than this: first, to allow a certain margin—which has been estimated in trade circles at about 5 per cent—and, secondly, because the smallest country mills do not work on a three-shift system, but operate in the daytime only. The present output capacity of the industry, taking into account the fact that the smallest mills work during the daytime only, may be taken as about 5,500 to 5,600 sacks.

The number of manufacturing units is comparatively small; in the 'thirties there were some 550 mills in the United Kingdom, and this number included some 250 very small units, some of which operated only intermittently as far as flour production is concerned. These very small units accounted for less than 1 per cent of total flour output. The number of mills in the United Kingdom employing more than ten workers—a complement which is very much below the minimum required to run a mill on an adequate scale for full-time three-shift production—was, according to the 1935 Census of Production, about 280.

The number of establishments in existence in the 'thirties represented a very much reduced total compared with those functioning at the beginning of the century. In 1907, according to the Census of Production of that year, there were altogether some 1,250 mills in the United Kingdom, half of these being very small units. In 1917 there were 600 mills with a capacity of five sacks or over. Immediately after the Great War, however, there was a sharp fall in the number of mills; this came about mainly through financial failures and through the activities of the larger firms in buying up smaller concerns. This process of gradual rationalization culminated in the reorganization of the industry in 1929.

The sizes of individual units vary from the small one- to two-sack plants of the country millers to the large port mills which have capacities up to 180 sacks. The Census of Production, unfortunately, gives particulars of size of unit for all grain-milling establishments together, including provender-mills as well as flour-mills. The provender-milling industry comprises a far larger number of small units than does the flour-milling industry, and the Census figures cannot therefore be taken as indicating the size ranges of flour-mills and the relative importance of each. The Census does, however, give particulars for port and inland flour-mills, and these give some impression of sizes:

OUTPUT OF PORT AND INLAND FLOUR-MILLS EMPLOYING
OVER 10 PERSONS, 1935. UNITED KINGDOM

	No. of Establishments	Output of Wheat Products '000 tons
Port mills .	108	4,251
Inland mills .	169	1,252
Total .	277	5,503

(Census of Production)

These figures show that the average size of the port mills in 1935 was about thirty-six sacks, and that of the inland mills about seven sacks. The latter estimate leaves out of account, of course, the fact that there are about 200 establishments with small outputs which do not figure in the Census figures; it also refers to the practical capacity of the small mills which are working by day only.

Further information on the size of mills is included in the *Report on the Marketing of Wheat*, published in 1928. This shows the location and size of mills in England and Wales at that date. Considerable changes have taken place since then, but changes in respect of the larger mills by way of new building have been recorded. Taking these changes into account and adding estimates for the mills in Scotland and Northern Ireland, it may be said that there are about thirty-five mills in the United Kingdom with capacities of fifty sacks or over. These are all either actually at the ports or have direct access to the sea by navigable river or canal. Most of the plants owned by the leading milling firms, in fact, have capacities well above fifty sacks, the most common range being from eighty to a hundred sacks. These large mills therefore account for between 50 and 60 per cent of the total output of the country.

In 1928 the number of mills between ten and fifty sacks in capacity in England and Wales was about 120. A number of the smaller mills in this class have been closed down under the reorganization scheme, and it is probable that, even adding estimates for Scotland and Northern Ireland, the present number of mills within this size group is no higher than 120, and may, indeed, be somewhat lower. They probably account for about one-third of total capacity. The rest of the country's output is produced by the small mills of less than ten sacks.

A flour-mill is one of the most highly mechanized units in modern industry. The extremely small numbers of operatives who are to be seen in a modern mill strikes a casual visitor most forcibly. Whole floors of machines can be seen with only an occasional worker inspecting them or examining the stocks as they pass from one set of machines to another. The capital cost involved in equipping a mill is naturally high. A large mill takes from eighteen months to two years to build and equip, and the pre-war costs were estimated[1] to amount to between £4,000 and £5,000 for every sack capacity— £1,000 per sack for machinery,[2] £2,500 to £3,000 for buildings and equipment, and further sums for offices, railway sidings, and the like.

The high degree of mechanization is well illustrated by the figures of power consumption. According to the 1935 Census of Production, the annual consumption of electricity per operative in the grain-milling trade was 10·9 B.T.U., compared with a corresponding figure of 2·7 B.T.U. in respect of all factory trades taken as a whole. The high capital cost—a large-size mill might have cost over £500,000 even before 1939—necessitates continuous operation, and all but the smallest mills aim at continuous day and night operation, working

[1] E. Leigh Pearson (article in *Milling, 1937*).
[2] As a minimum. Two country mills, each of eight sacks capacity, cost £10,000 each in respect of latest machinery.

on a three-shift system, resulting in a 120-hour working week or a 6,000-hour working year for the mill.[1] All the larger mills work to this number of hours, but as the capacity of the mill decreases, so also does the tendency to work to less than full capacity increase. There are no official figures in the latest Census of Production statistics to give any indication as to how far this occurs in practice. The 1907 Census, however, gave the combined capacities of the mills in the various size groups as well as their output, and these two sets of figures together showed the relationship between the average size of mill and the degree of full-time working very clearly.

OUTPUT OF FLOUR MILLS IN THE U.K. FOR WHICH DETAILED PARTICULARS WERE RECEIVED. 1907

Size of Unit Flour milled in the year '000 cwts.	No. of Returns	Total Flour milled '000 cwts.	Capacity		Percentage of Full-time Working (6,000 hours = full-time)
			Total Sacks	Average Sacks	
Under 10 . .	176	584	252	1·4	16%
10–50 . .	172	4,507	574	3·3	52%
50–150 . .	132	11,645	941	7·1	83%
150–500 . .	74	21,211	1,489	20·0	91%
500 and over .	23	22,204	1,478	64·3	100%

Full economies can only be obtained when the mill is able to run at full capacity; otherwise overhead costs are liable to be disproportionately high. Even when full-time operation is achieved, the larger unit tends to be more economical than the smaller unit, other things being equal. This arises from the fact that the labour complement tends to diminish in proportion to capacity as the latter increases, and the contribution of wages to the cost of flour to be correspondingly lowered. Mr. Leigh Pearson[2] in 1929 gave the number of operatives in a flour-mill of 20 to 25 sacks as 61, and in a mill of twice that size as 80 (see Appendix I). Comparative figures have also been supplied by the C.W.S., who have suggested the following levels for different size units:

5-sack plant	.	.	.	24 operatives
50-sack plant	.	.	.	87 ,,
100-sack plant	.	.	.	133 ,,

These figures must clearly be taken merely as illustrative and not as indicating the actual number involved in any particular unit. The special domestic circumstances of a mill, such as its method of grain

[1] The actual number of hours worked in a mill when working full-time is usually 125 to 127—representing 5¼ days' labour. But some allowance must be made for stopping and re-starting the plant, so that the effective weekly operation may be taken as 120 hours.

[2] *Organization and Management in the Flour-Milling Industry.*

intake, the extent to which conditioning of the wheat is carried out, and other technical factors must obviously cause the figures to vary considerably. Nevertheless, the general rule holds good, and the saving in operative labour is definite, though it may be only slight in proportion to total costs. In 1935 the cost of wages in the seven largest mills owned by the C.W.S., with an average capacity of between 50 and 100 sacks, represented between 3 and 4 per cent of total costs (including the cost of raw material); in two smaller mills, each with a capacity of 20 to 30 sacks, the percentage was about 5 per cent, and in two small mills of about 6 sacks, the proportions were 7 and 8 per cent.[1] The cost of wages, it has been seen, amounts to between 10d. and 1s. 6d. a sack, while the price of flour has ranged over the past twenty years between 18s. and 50s. a sack. Any saving in wage costs may make an appreciable difference in the margin of profit, which has been estimated at round 3s. a sack.

The question of an optimum size unit is very inviting, but one that can clearly not be discussed lightly. It cannot be readily determined by a process of trial and error, in view of the varying individual characteristics, especially as regards location, which influence the size of each particular mill. What may be the best size in one locality may be completely out of place in another situation. The port mills, for example, which are situated on the dock side in order to take in their wheat direct from the hold of the ocean-going ship, have clearly to be of sufficient size—of at least 50-sacks capacity, and generally considerably larger than this—to take up the large quantities of grain which arrive at the mill. All that can be said is that, other things being equal, economy increases as the size of the unit increases, both through the saving in overheads per unit of output and through the proportionately smaller labour force required. But comparisons are invidious: the large mills have far more elaborate cleaning, conditioning, and grading machinery than have the small units, and are able to cope more efficiently with varying grades of wheat for this reason. But the small mill in its essential plant is an exact replica of its larger counterpart, the roller mills, reduction rolls, purifiers, and the like being exactly similar.

In considering the optimum size of the technical unit, entirely divorced from external circumstances, it is held in some sections of the trade that the most efficient size for the mill proper lies somewhere round about the 80-sack mark. The optimum size of unit here is governed largely by the number of machines which can be effectively superintended by a single complement of mill-workers—manager, rollerman, purifierman, silksman, all of whom are highly skilled, and their assistants. In 1929 Mr. Leigh Pearson[2] declared that the

[1] Carr-Saunders and others, *Consumers' Co-operation in Great Britain.*
[2] Op. cit.

optimum size of milling unit at that time was considered to be one of about 50 sacks. Technical improvements and the experience gained by millers and milling engineers during the period of rationalization in the building of new mills and the modernization of others have caused this earlier figure to be revised upwards. Nevertheless, there is an upper limit for the size of the actual milling unit, and this limit does not apply to other sections of the mill—intake, screen-room, and warehouse. Thus a 120-sack plant, for example, is likely to comprise two 60-sack milling departments, each working quite independently, while the other departments of the mill cater for the full output of the plant. It is interesting to note that a new mill built a year or so before the war was equipped with storage and warehouse space capable of dealing with a mill of about 160-sacks capacity. Only one milling department, of half that size, was constructed, and was built up above half the area occupied by the warehouse and dispatch department, the other half remaining free for the future erection of a second mill, the decision as to whether this should be devoted to flour- or provender-milling presumably being left open.

THE FIRMS IN THE INDUSTRY

It is estimated that the three largest milling concerns—Ranks, Spillers, and the C.W.S.—control between them between 65 and 70 per cent of the country's total flour output. The tendency towards large concerns began with the introduction of the roller-mill process, which was first taken up by the bigger and/or more enterprising manufacturers. The pre-eminent firms of the present day had already established strong positions by the outbreak of the 1914 war by building new mills or acquiring other businesses, and they further increased their strength during the war. The last full year of control (1920), and 1921, in which control came to an end in March, saw amalgamations of fairly considerable size, including the formation of the Associated London Flour Millers by the seven leading 'independent' London millers, the joining of Spillers (already the result of the amalgamation of Spillers and Bakers) by W. Vernon and Sons, and the purchase and absorption by J. Rank Ltd., of a number of firms. By 1924 Ranks controlled at least eight other sizeable concerns, and by 1927 the Spillers group controlled thirteen subsidiaries which were liquidated in that year. After rationalization in 1929 Spillers bought up five large concerns, and Ranks, besides a number of smaller though still considerable amalgamations, absorbed the A.L.F.M. in 1933, and at the end of this year controlled about fifteen to twenty major milling establishments, besides directly owning four large port mills. Extensive building of large port mills was also undertaken by the big concerns, the new mills in general superseding a number of smaller mills in the area which were then closed down.

Large mills were built in London, Southampton, Belfast, Cardiff, Avonmouth, and Newcastle between 1932 and 1938, the first three being owned by the Ranks group[1] and the other three by the Spillers group. The C.W.S. was also modernizing and enlarging its mills during this period. In addition to new building, existing medium- and large-size mills owned by prospering firms were being extended, remodelled, and equipped with the most up-to-date machinery. A few new public companies were launched during the early 'thirties, but were unable to pay the dividends offered by the large concerns.

The position of the large firms before the outbreak of war was roughly as follows:

J. Rank, Ltd. At the end of 1938 the U.K. Ranks group owned a capacity of about 1,550 sacks, i.e. about 28 per cent of total U.K. capacity, and with the acquisition of John Greenwood Millers in 1939 the group's share increased to about 30 per cent of the total. This figure had risen from about 1,200 sacks since the incorporation of Ranks Ltd. in 1933. During the five years (1933–8) over £4,000,000 was spent in acquiring additional interests and business and financing increased stocks. At the end of 1938 the group operated directly six of the largest up-to-date mills—at London, Hull, Southampton, Barry Dock, Birkenhead, and Belfast. Subsidiary or associated companies operated in London, Manchester, Liverpool, Swansea, Bootle, Blackburn, Barnstaple, Selby, Thornaby, Doncaster, Winchester, Edinburgh, Glasgow. The total issued capital of the company is about £8,300,000.

Spillers Ltd., as has been mentioned, controlled thirteen subsidiaries which were liquidated in 1927. The group owns all the shares of seven companies and all the ordinary shares of the large West of England firm of Hosegood Ltd., which Spillers bought up at the end of 1938. It also directly operates one Canadian milling firm and controls another, and is actively concerned in shipping. Its largest mills are situated in London, Cardiff, Bristol, Birkenhead, and Newcastle; and it operates on a smaller but still very considerable scale at Plymouth, Manchester, Bolton, Birmingham, Leeds, Sunderland, Hull, Grimsby, Glasgow, and Londonderry. The Spillers group has, of course, concentrated particularly on the manufacture of animal foods, and the amount of actual flour-milling capacity which it controls is considerably less than that controlled by Ranks. The flour output controlled by the group forms about one-fifth of total U.K. output. Total issued capital (1942) is about £4,100,000.

The C.W.S. and S.C.W.S. cater exclusively for Co-operative Society bakeries and stores, and it is estimated that the C.W.S. supplies 90 per cent of English Co-operative flour requirements. The two

---

[1] The London mill belonging to the Ranks group was actually built by the A.L.F.M. in 1932.

wholesale societies own thirteen mills, with a labour complement of about 2,250, including large port mills at Manchester, Dunston-on-Tyne, Avonmouth, Hull, Glasgow, Leith, Edinburgh, and London. Inland mills are situated at Sowerby Bridge, Oldham, St. Albans, Drybridge, and Fyvie. The total output of Co-operative mills before the war, excluding eight small and two medium-size mills run by retail societies, was about 17 per cent of total U.K. production. In the London area the increasing requirements of co-operative flour users outstripped supply, and building was begun in 1938 on a new mill at Silvertown, said to be the largest unit to date, and which, but for the war, would have been in production in 1940.

Besides these three very large groups, there are a number of smaller companies. Hovis Ltd., the largest firm outside the 'big three', own nine flour-mills, including four operated by subsidiaries; not all of these are engaged on the manufacture of Hovis flour. The firm probably accounted for about 7 or 8 per cent of total U.K. production. McDougalls, who cater largely for the retail trade, own, as far as can be ascertained, three mills, output probably being in the region of 2 per cent of total U.K. output. Chas. Brown, with mills in London, also accounted for about 2 per cent of total output.

The above groups, as can be seen, control between them about 80 per cent of total output. Ranks and Spillers between them account for nearly half of total U.K. output, and are in a very strong position both as flour manufacturers and as wheat buyers; and their lead in matters of price and general trade policy is clearly recognized by other firms in the trade, including the C.W.S. More will be said on this subject in the next section.

TRADE ASSOCIATIONS: PRICE POLICY

The employers' bodies, in order of chronological seniority, are: the Incorporated National Association of British and Irish Millers, the Flour Milling Employers' Federation, and the Millers' Mutual Association. While all these bodies include the major part of the country's industry, none of them has a complete membership, though the number and importance of the non-members are quite distinct in the case of each of the three bodies.

The *National Association* was formed in 1878. It represents the industry in all its dealings on trade questions with official bodies and Government Departments; questions relating to labour and kindred matters it leaves to the Employers' Federation. In 1937 the National Association included about 225 out of some 500 millers in the British Isles, representing about 95 per cent of total flour output. It is said that the Scottish trade is less fully organized than the English. The Presidency is successively held by millers representing all the various interests in the trade—small inland millers, independent port millers, as well as the large combines. There are a number of sub-committees, including the following: the Wheat and Grain Contracts Committee, which was appointed in 1922 to deal specifically with the terms on which U.S. wheat was offered for sale, and is now actively concerned with all questions affecting wheat and other grain contracts; the Flour and Wheatfeed Committee, whose chief concern is with legislation, and particularly definitions, affecting the two milling products; the All-English Flour Committee; and the Home-Grown Wheat Committee, whose activities in conjunction with the National Institute of Agricultural Botany are directed to the improvement of the strains of home wheat. An interesting offshoot of the National Association is the Young Millers' Section, which had a membership of 91 in 1937–8. This group is composed of the sons of millers or other young men of similar status who are destined for the management of flour-mills.

The National Association is organized regionally through local associations of millers; there are about twenty such associations in the British Isles. These local millers' associations came into existence shortly after the inception of the National Association. They meet regularly, usually at weekly or fortnightly intervals (though when the price of wheat is fluctuating widely they meet more often) and discuss matters of general trading policy within the area, including the range of flour prices to be charged.

Prices are quoted delivered-in to the baker or other user. For price-fixing purposes the local associations are grouped into four main areas in England and Wales—London and the South-east, Liverpool and the North-west, Hull and the North-east, Bristol and the South-west, and Scotland and Ireland. The main responsibility for the fixing of prices within these areas rests with the associations operating at the ports. Each area is marked out in zones according to their distances from the port; prices naturally rise as the distance from the port increases, but within each zone the price is uniform. It should be emphasized that the prices fixed at the different ports vary considerably from one another. Quotations at Liverpool, London, Bristol, and Hull are rarely the same. This sometimes causes difficulties, particularly on the boundaries between the areas. The inland portions of the South-east area are notably liable to difficulties of this kind as the margin between wheat and flour prices to which London millers work tends to be higher than elsewhere. This 'border' trouble sometimes leads to an arrangement for differential prices within a zone; for instance, prices may be fixed at a lower level in Oxfordshire and Berkshire than elsewhere in the same zone of the South-east area in order to make the price coincide with offers from mills in the Bristol area. The local associations inform millers who operate outside but trade inside their areas of the prices ruling within, but there are often cases in which these extra-district millers under-sell in the area. The question of imported flour, always a thorny one with the trade, is also dealt with as far as possible by the local associations. Meetings are held with factors who handle imported flour to discuss prices, but the problem of distribution by factors is often a very difficult one; more will be said on their activities later in dealing with the question of distribution.

These local associations operate fairly successfully now that the trade has reached the requisite degree of organization. But after the First World War, when capacity was far in excess of demand and competition was of the cut-throat variety, their discussions regarding price were often so much wasted time and effort. Millers sold at the price fixed if they could, but were ready to quote lower prices if necessary. Before the rationalization of the industry in 1929, these bodies could therefore hardly be called price-*fixing*—they agreed on prices, but had no power to enforce them. There are still no direct powers, but the prices are more or less adhered to because the intense sales pressure is no longer necessary, output quotas being laid down under the rationalization scheme; but even now flour is often sold at prices below those agreed upon by the associations. The Co-operative mills, it should be observed, are not represented on these local associations, and although they are members of the National Association there is little co-operation between them and private millers. Their flour is sold exclusively to Co-operative bakers and other Co-operative users, though the converse is not true; Co-operative bakers are free to buy their flour elsewhere, and indeed have to do so in the case of proprietary brands. Co-operative prices, however, conform closely with those ruling in the rest of the trade.

It was stated in 1937 that steps were being contemplated to ensure that the membership of the National Association should be absolutely complete. But what those measures were was not divulged, and up to the outbreak of war no move of this kind had been made.

A Research Association was formed in 1923 in co-operation with the D.S.I.R. Its annual income is now between £12,000 and £13,000, most of which is drawn from the industry. The Association's laboratories are at St. Albans, and have a staff of about twenty. Its work is divided into five departments—milling and bio-engineering, with a staff of seven; chemistry and physics, with a staff of five; and analytical micro-biological, and nutrition departments, with a total complement of six. A very wide range of problems affecting the industry is investigated, including research into wheat-growing and into baking methods.

The Flour-Milling Employers' Federation was established at the end of the First World War in November 1918. It functions largely through the National Joint Industrial Council which was set up in the following year. All matters relating to wages, hours, and conditions of labour in the flour-milling industry are dealt with by agreement between the Federation and the workers' organizations. The Federation comprises most members of the industry, accounting for at least 90 per cent of the country's total flour output, but its membership is not quite so complete as that of the National Association. The majority of the non-members are small country millers, but this is not to say that country millers as a whole remain outside; taken by and large, the Federation is fully representative of the industry, including both large and small concerns, all of whom have an equal voice. The Co-operative groups, though the terms of their membership are somewhat different from those relating to private millers, are also represented on the Federation and take an active part on the Joint Council. One of the reasons given by country millers for not joining the Federation has been the relatively high wages paid in the industry under agreements made on the Council; a number of them resigned during the depression years when the wage-scales were left unchanged. Some country millers are dissatisfied with the margin fixed between wages at the ports and those in rural districts, which amounts to only 12s., or about 16 per cent of the wage paid to a skilled man at a port mill. The most outstanding block of non-members is found among the East Anglian millers, the greater number of whom remain outside the Federation. But most of the firms in the industry accept the decisions made by the Joint Council whether they are members or not; many of the non-members indeed consult the Federation in matters of interpretation, and make use of the organization in other ways affecting questions connected with the employment side of the industry. The National Joint Industrial Council has an admirable record of achievements as regards the welfare of the workers, and the prosperity of the industry after it reorganized in 1929 has in part been shared by labour. Many of the labour agreements made by the flour-milling industry have in fact been the first of their kind in the industrial world, and wages have compared well with those in other industries. The activities of the Council will be discussed in more detail later in considering the labour side of the industry.

The Millers' Mutual Association. This body was set up in 1929. It represented the long-awaited reorganization of the industry which had been pressed for with such vigour throughout the 'twenties, and, in fact, before the First World War. The growth of the industry and the increase in the size of units throughout the thirty years after the introduction of the roller-mill process in the 1880's was already by 1914 resulting in short-time working, and shortly before the outbreak of war a financial expert who had already reorganized other trades, put forward a reorganization scheme; but when war broke out the scheme was dropped. During the war of 1914–18 millers did very well indeed, profits being fixed according to capacity. In spite of E.P.T., all of them, and particularly the larger millers, enjoyed very prosperous conditions, and milling capacity was considerably increased. The excess capacity of the industry at the end of control was estimated at 1,500 sacks at least,[1] representing over a quarter of the capacity needed to satisfy current demand. The result was inevitable. Throughout the 'twenties cut-throat competition was the order of the day. The vital need for some sort of co-operation within the industry was keenly appreciated by the leaders of the trade, who recognized as soon as control came to an end that there would be trouble without some agreement as to prices, output, and grades of flour. But the rank and file of the trade would not give any support to a scheme. The result was a price war which assumed very serious proportions as the task of pushing sales of large quantities of flour on an unwilling market became more Herculean year by year. Intense pressure, in which the leaders of the trade came to the forefront, was now put upon the market—by price-cutting, the offer of forward contracts, multiplication of travelling salesmen and extended distribution—and this continued right up to the time of reorganization in 1929, and to a certain extent even beyond it. The policy of the leaders of the industry has been called one of 'aggressive expansion';[2] their object was to capture a sufficient proportion of the trade to make rationalization a practical objective.

Published official prices of flour fixed by the local associations were normally about 2s. to 3s. a sack above those which firms were prepared to accept, and towards the end of the decade the difference was often in the region of 5s. to 6s. In 1929 the position became so fantastic that the London Association refused to publish official prices. Forward selling of flour was usual, six months contracts being quite common and twelve months contracts not unknown. This was, in actual fact, justified between 1925 and 1930, as wheat prices throughout this period fell fairly steadily, but this did not excuse the frankly speculative nature of the deals, and official trade opinion was obviously very much against the practice. In 1929 it had probably reached its height, and trade journals were talking about the 'perilous' proportions it had assumed—one firm in this year was offering to supply unlimited quantities of flour at reigning prices for an unlimited period—and this at a time when wheat prices were lower than they had yet been since the end of the war, and it seemed impossible that they could fall much further: though, in fact, they were to drop heavily during the next two years.

Trade circles assessed the losses of the industry as a whole during

---

[1] E. Leigh Pearson, op. cit.
[2] A. F. Lucas, *Industrial Reconstruction and the Control of Competition.*

the middle and later 'twenties at about £5,000,000 annually. The Royal Commission on Food Prices obtained figures from a large number of millers for the years 1922–3 and 1923–4; according to these figures, the average profit per sack of flour for the year 1922–3 was under 4*d.*, and for the following year 1*s.*, compared with a pre-war rate of profit estimated by the Flour Mills Control at 1*s.* 4*d.* a sack. The different classes of millers fared differently: mills owned by the large companies and by the Co-operative Societies showed higher rates of profit, those mills at the ports outside the large groups showed a net loss of 3*d.* a sack in 1922–3 and only 7*d.* a sack profit in the following year, while the town and country mills registered profits slightly below the average. The large concerns were able to show small profits largely by astute wheat-buying, but large numbers of the smaller old-fashioned mills closed down. The Co-operative mills were shown to be in a far better position than the other large concerns, mainly because they had not expanded their capacity unduly during the war, so that output was still commensurate with the demand from Co-operative consumers; in addition to which, of course, having an assured market, they were spared the cost of travelling salesmen, estimated by the Royal Commission on Food Prices to amount to up to 9*d.* a sack. Towards the middle of 1924 conditions began to improve slightly, as the price of wheat moved upwards, but after 1925, when wheat prices started on their steady downward movement, the position greatly worsened.

In 1924 the National Association formed a Trade Organization Committee to issue a report on the state of the industry. The outcome of the report was a proposal to form a Cartel. The Committee suggested a subscription from each mill, on a sliding scale according to its capacity, to form a fund to be used to buy up and close down inefficient firms. It also proposed the formation of a limited company to control output and to purchase, close, and sell redundant mills. Each policy-holder in the company would provide information on output over a specified period which would be used as a basis for his fixed quota, to be increased *pro rata* as mills were closed or demand increased. If his deliveries of flour exceeded the quota allotted to him, an additional premium was to be paid into the company, and if they fell below the prescribed amount he would be entitled to compensation. Under certain conditions the company should be empowered to buy and sell the right to the registered output of any policy-holder.[1]

The Council of the N.A. passed a resolution asking Spillers and Ranks to get together with a view to agreement on the principles of trade reorganization. Capacity was bought up by the two firms, often acting in co-operation, which, both were anxious to point out,

[1] E. Leigh Pearson, op. cit.

was limited to these special operations, during the 'twenties, and it became evident in 1929 that the leaders in the industry had reached a point at which they were in a position to dictate terms to the rest of the trade. *Milling*, in its issue of 6 July 1929, said:

'Obviously we have not exaggerated the situation when we have said that the industry was in a bankrupt condition, and it has been accomplished in a few years, during which tremendous losses have been incurred . . . reserves have been depleted or exhausted, heavy overdrafts have been taken up, and it has been accompanied by an inevitable and general depression of values. All this is quite apart from the annual loss of profits. Numerous firms, some of them old-fashioned, have had to close their doors and realize miserable assets.'

Later that month an anonymous manifesto was sent round to milling firms which asked why the 'insane price-cutting' should continue, and quoted part of a speech by Mr. Rank:

'If, owing to the fact that we have far more milling capacity in the country than can be fully occupied, we find it impossible to secure a reasonable return for our energies except by reasonable co-operation, we have every right to get together and secure that return, the same as so many other trades have done.'

Meetings were held with millers all over the country, and Mr. Rank expounded the proposed scheme for reorganization. The formation of the Millers' Mutual Association was announced in the Press in August 1929. At that time it represented about 90 per cent of the flour trade outside the Co-operative groups, which remained apart from the scheme; members of the M.M.A. therefore accounted for over three-quarters of the total flour output of the United Kingdom. By 1939, the proportion of the non-Co-operative trade included in the M.M.A. was assessed variously as between 95 and 97 per cent, i.e. about 80 per cent of total flour production. No details of the workings of the M.M.A. were made public, but it was announced that output would be regulated by means of quotas based on a datum period production, that members would pay into the organization according to their capacity, the money being used to buy up redundant mills, that levies or compensation payments were to be made in cases of production over or under the allotted quotas, and that no new mills were to be built except by purchasing the quota rights from existing establishments. It was clear that the M.M.A. was being run very much on the lines suggested by the N.A. Trade Organization Committee. The limited company suggested in this body's report came to birth in the Purchase Finance Co. Ltd., directed exclusively by the seven foremost firms in the industry, each of whom held one of the seven sole issued shares. Some hundreds of thousands of pounds were spent in buying and closing down redundant capacity. No figures are available of the numbers of firms closed down as an immediate result of M.M.A. policy: *The Miller* stated that 177 firms were closed down between 1921 and 1931, but, of course, many of these had been closed before 1929. Compensation was paid on a generous scale to both dispossessed owners and workers, as high profits in ensuing years were anticipated, and were, in fact, to follow in full measure. A number of the millers who were bought out took up provender-milling, which was still in a relatively unorganized state. Other avowed objects of the M.M.A., beside the regulation of output and the closing down of redundant mills, were to reduce costs of manufacture and of distribution. Costs were reduced through the elimination of the less efficient units and increased centralized buying, and distribution costs, through the elimination of competition, were also lowered; but it is doubtful whether any of these reductions was reflected in lower costs to the consumer.

The M.M.A. itself made no provision for price-fixing. The price-fixing bodies were already in existence in the form of the local associations of millers operating under the National Association, and their ineffectiveness in the past had been due merely to over-production. Now that output was regulated, and 90 per cent (gradually increased to 95–97 per cent) of the non-Co-operative trade was controlled by members of the M.M.A., there was no reason for members to under-sell, though, as has been said, competition of this kind has not been completely eliminated. All the port area associations have strong representation of the large millers, and the prices fixed in the port areas more or less determine the prices which rule all over the country. It is very rare that inland mills can work to as high a margin of profit as the port mills, for reasons which have already been discussed; the competition of lower prices, in fact, more often acts the other way, port millers' flour being available in the inland districts at prices below the local rates, or, as has been seen, differential rates at different ports may operate unequally in certain border districts. When such anomalies occur, adjustments are made to cope with the situation.

The success of the British milling industry in its reorganization was regarded with a certain amount of envy in other countries where flour-milling capacity was greatly in excess of requirements and millers were experiencing lean times. The Irish trade made contact with British millers in 1932, and a scheme of reorganization was carried out in Ireland with the help of English capital; Ranks Ltd. are strongly represented in Eire at the present time. The Dominions were still in the unhappy position of being grossly over-milled—it was estimated that only about 40 per cent of Canada's capacity was being fully used, and hardly any of the companies were paying dividends—and when the Ottawa proposals were being discussed, and on subsequent occasions, representatives of the British milling industry strongly recommended their Canadian and Australian counterparts to undertake some form of rationalization to bring down their capacity, and suggested that the three countries should then come together and agree on the regulation of export markets. But there is traditionally little love lost between British millers and their colleagues overseas, mainly on the grounds of the power which the former wield in the international grain market, and not a little on the grounds of their obvious prosperity. Whatever the reason the proposal seems to have been regarded with suspicion by the Dominions' millers, and nothing came of it.

It was well for the industry that it reorganized when it did. Shortly after the formation of the M.M.A. the economic depression set in, and during 1930 wheat prices fell by about half. Without organization, price-cutting would have reached new record levels. As it was, the trade entered into an extremely prosperous period. New plants were built, and extensions and modernizations effected in others. As an editorial in one of the trade journals said at the beginning of 1933: 'There are few industries in the world which have been more richly blessed than the flour-milling industry of this country during the last four years.'

The M.M.A. was scheduled to run for ten years: at the end of this term there was a certain amount of doubt as to its continuance, and the fear of unleashed competitive conditions in the future was, as far as can be judged by trade press comments, a very real one. However, the M.M.A. was continued, and if anything placed on a firmer foundation.

The prosperity of the milling industry has inevitably led to accusations by antipathetic spokesmen that the trade, through the M.M.A., has held up prices unduly, and that whatever benefits were obtained through rationalization have passed into the pockets of the millers and not to the public. It is difficult to make any very close estimate of the way in which prices moved as a result of M.M.A. policy, because any estimate of the average price of flour over a given year, in the absence of data giving the quantities sold at each price throughout the year, must be based on a simple average of periodic quotations. The same difficulty applies to wheat quotations, but in this case a better idea of the actual position, particularly as it affects the port mills, can be obtained from the import figures which give both the price and quantity of imported wheats.

The following table shows the average c.i.f. cost of all imported wheats, including duty, the average price of flour ex-mill London, excluding quota payment, and the average price of British bran. The figures are worked out to show the position in regard to the price of flour per sack. Wheat prices are therefore indicated in terms of 400 lb., which, at 70 per cent extraction, produces one sack of flour. It must, of course, be understood that the figures in the final column do not purport to represent actual profits or loss; no account has been taken of operating costs. But, as showing the margin between the bare ex-ship cost of wheat and the price of the products of that wheat, within the limits of the price data, they do indicate the trend of the margin out of which costs and profits could be taken.

	Average cost of Imported Wheat	Average price of Flour ex-mill London	Average price of Milling Offals	Margin per sack of Flour
	(1) Shillings per 400 lb.	(2) Shillings per 280 lb.	(3) Shillings per 120 lb.	Shillings per sack
1925	50·1	48·6	8·9	7·4
1926	46·6	45·4	7·6	6·4
1927	44·0	40·3	9·2	5·5
1928	39·7	35·3	9·4	5·0
1929	36·9	34·9	8·1	6·1
1930	29·4	29·9	5·9	6·4
1931	18·2	19·6	6·1	7·5
1932	22·0	21·4	7·0	6·4
1933	20·3	21·9	6·0	7·6
1934	19·9	20·6	6·5	7·2
1935	22·2	23·2	6·6	7·6
1936	27·2	28·8	7·1	8·7
1937	37·3	37·6	8·7	9·0
1938	27·1	27·6	8·0	8·5

(1) Annual Statement of Trade.
(2) *Board of Trade Journal.* From 1935 onwards prices of flour are quoted 'delivered-in' and not 'ex-mill'. The difference between the two is taken by the Board of Trade to be about 1s. 6d. a sack, and this amount has been deducted from the published figures for 1935 onwards to give an estimated 'ex-mill' price.
(3) Ministry of Agriculture. Averages of the prices quoted for bran and middlings.

It will be seen that from 1924 onwards the general trend followed by the 'margin' was downwards, and that after 1929, the year in which the M.M.A. was formed, the 'margin' recovered and rose fairly steadily throughout the 'thirties, tending throughout, except for the all-important 1929–33 period, to move in sympathy with wheat prices. During the four years 1929–33, when the industry was 'richly blessed' the opposite occurred. The fall in the 'margin' in 1932, when average wheat prices were higher than in the preceding year, should be considered in the light of the fact that record imports, amounting to nearly six million tons, and 13 per cent greater than those for 1932, took place in 1931 at extremely low prices. It should be observed that throughout the period 1925 to 1939 no changes in wage rates took place. Part of the advance which took place in the margin from 1934 onwards can be attributed to the rise in wheat prices, involving increased capital costs in the form of stocks. This being so, the increase in the margin by 50 per cent between 1928 and 1933 is the more remarkable in that wheat prices fell by half during that period. In order to take into account the effect of changing wheat prices on the tying up of working capital—though for the most part other overhead charges remain constant irrespective of wheat prices—the margin may be expressed as a percentage of the cost of wheat:

	Average cost of Imported Wheat Shillings per 400 lb.	'Margin' expressed as a percentage of cost of Wheat
1925	50·1	15%
1926	46·6	14%
1927	44·0	13%
1928	39·7	13%
1929	36·9	16%
1930	29·4	22%
1931	18·2	41%
1932	22·0	29%
1933	20·3	37%
1934	19·9	36%
1935	22·2	35%
1936	27·2	32%
1937	37·3	24%
1938	27·1	32%

This table tells very much the same story in regard to increased margins as the earlier one. It is evident that rationalization brought beneficial results to the industry, but not to the public as a whole. Trade profits increased, not only through reduced costs of production and distribution resulting from rationalization, but also through the swollen margins between wheat and flour prices with which the consolidated trade was now able to tax the consumer. It must at the same time be acknowledged that the profits of the trade had been extremely poor, and indeed often non-existent, during the latter 'twenties, but this was due, not to the officially quoted prices of flour (which figure in the preceding table) being too low to allow of a reasonable profit, but to the fact that these were not adhered to by millers: it has been mentioned that taking prices were 2s. and 3s. and often as much as 5s. below the official figures.

Prices have undoubtedly been maintained at a level sufficient to allow of considerable prosperity on the part of holders of capital. The industry, and particularly the highly efficient large firms, made very substantial profits indeed after rationalization. Spillers ordinary shares, for instance, advanced from about 15s. before rationalization to over 60s. in 1934: profits in fact were so handsome that in this year the Board recommended that the Chairman and Deputy Chairman should receive salaries of £8,500 and £6,500 respectively in addition to their fees; and after a three-year period up to 1929 when dividends on ordinary shares were nil, the increase in profits made possible the payment of a constant dividend of 15 per cent from 1931–2 onwards. Hovis, which had maintained dividends throughout the difficult 'twenties, paying 10 per cent in 1924–5 and 12½ per cent in the two succeeding years, increased payment to 15 per cent up to 1930–1 and from 1931–2 onwards dividends were paid at the rate of 20 per cent, two capital bonuses of 10 per cent being issued in addition. In 1934 Joseph Rank was described as the wealthiest man in the country. The M.M.A. has a sufficient monopoly of output to ensure that its decisions are adhered to by the trade as a whole. The C.W.S. and the S.C.W.S. are not, of course, members of the M.M.A., and they claim to stand in the way of a complete monopoly; but even discounting Co-operative output, the M.M.A. controls at least 75 per cent of the country's flour production, and the C.W.S. could not, at its present level of output, provide a really effective bulwark—and it has been seen that the C.W.S. organization adheres to the price-levels formulated by the bulk of the trade. It is true that many of the small independent millers have no particular affection for the large trusts. But the amount of trade which the latter hold is ample to prevent this independent section from engaging them in a trial of strength. Nearly all the independent firms bowed to the inevitable in 1929 and joined the M.M.A.—and it certainly paid them to do so. They are clearly not in a position to break away from the monopoly organization, and the majority recognize that it would be against their interests to do so: that without the M.M.A. at the back of them they would be the first to go to the wall. The relative inelasticity of demand for flour forms an ideal setting for the maintenance of price-levels, for there is little reason to suppose that there exists a latent demand which a reduction in price would satisfy.

But when all this is recognized there is little justification for some of the violent attacks which were made during the 'thirties on the milling industry in regard to its price policy. The price and quality of British flour compare favourably with those ruling abroad. Were this not so, there is little doubt that the market would be flooded by imported flour. There is no protection against Empire-milled flour, and all flours enter this country free of quota restriction.

Dominion millers complain that the extremely powerful position of the British miller in the world wheat markets and his ability to buy wheat often at very favourable prices, while the Canadian or Australian miller is confined to the use of the home crop, gives British firms an advantage with which it is difficult to compete. Nevertheless, Empire flour during the 'thirties made up about 8 per cent of total flour supplies in the United Kingdom, and the pressure behind the sales was considerable. As long as the present comparative absence of protection and the present competitive spirit between the home miller and the overseas miller, and between the home miller and the flour importer, persist, there would seem to be little ground for fearing that any anti-social price policy on the part of the millers would have any chance of success. In viewing profits, too, it is as well to assess them in terms of prices paid to the consumer in the form of bread and flour purchases. It has been said[1] that the effect of M.M.A. policy was to maintain a net profit of 2s. 6d. to 3s. a sack. In evidence before the Royal Commission on Food Prices in 1924 Sir Albert Humphries, the President of the N.A., gave the normal rate of profit at between 1s. 6d. and 2s. a sack, and the Report of the Royal Commission stated that the pre-1914 rate of profit, as estimated for the purposes of E.P.D., was about 1s. 4d. a sack. A sack of flour produces about 180 2-lb. loaves. A profit of 3s. a sack, therefore, is translated into a charge of $\frac{1}{4}d.$ on each 2-lb. loaf, and $\frac{1}{8}d.$ per lb. of flour. This puts milling profits into their proper perspective. By way of comparison, it may be mentioned that the subsidy granted to British agriculture in respect of wheat-growing in 1938-9 entailed a payment of twice this amount.

RELATIONS WITH THE BAKING TRADE

In contrast to the highly integrated milling industry, the baking trade is still a fruitful field for the small entrepreneur, though during the past ten or twenty years the growth of larger units has been steadily squeezing out or absorbing a number of small producers. It was estimated in 1942 that there were some 27,000 baking concerns; of these only about 10,000 were members of the trade organization. But the trade has been regulated in so far as conditions of work are concerned since 1938, when a Trade Board was established.

The interests of millers and bakers are to a very large extent mutual. This is particularly the case in regard to stable agreed prices. Widespread under-selling in the bakery trade means the purchase of cheap flours and under-cutting among flour-sellers, more especially on the part of factors. Throughout the early 'thirties there was very strong competition in the bakery trade and a great deal of cut-throat under-selling. The quantities of cheap imported flours which were

[1] T. C. Smith, *Britain's Food Supplies.*

entering the British market at this time were both cause and effect of cut prices: they were in large part to blame for the under-selling, which led to demands for cheap quality flours on the part of bakers forced to meet this competition. And the whole process was felt to militate against the interests of millers and bakers not only by reason of reduced profit margins, but through the inevitable lowering of the quality of the bread and the effect of this on consumption.

The baking trade has local associations similar to the millers' local associations which meet to discuss matters of general concern, including the prices ruling for bread in their areas, but, as has been seen, a large proportion of the baking trade remains outside the official body. Bakers, particularly those in the North-west and North-east of England which were most severely affected by competition, appealed to the local millers' associations to assist in the maintenance of bread prices by employing Flour Contracts embodying Sale Note clauses in their dealings with bakers. The relevant section of a current Flour Contract reads as follows:

'Buyer agrees that during the currency of this Contract Buyer will not sell any flour sold in packages of less than 140 lb. weight or bread at a price below the specified price nor enter any Contract for the purchase of flour (over whatever period deliverable) except subject to provisions similar to those contained in this section. No restriction as to price attaches to bona fide sales to any Government Department or Public Body.'

These Sale Note clauses were first drawn up in 1921, and were haphazardly employed for some years—the principle was discussed by the Royal Commission on Food Prices in 1924—but their use became more general during the 'thirties, when the bread 'price-war' threatened to get out of hand. Their increased use led to the issue of a report on the practice by the Food Council to the Board of Trade in June 1936. The Food Council approached the N.A.B.I.M. and asked them to 'use their influence with their local associations to prevent their well-organized industry from being used as a tool to enforce excessive prices for bread and thus to hamper progress in the baking industry'. The Council suggested that the Sale Note clause should apply only where under-selling below the Council's maximum prices amounted to more than $\frac{1}{2}d$. a 4-lb. loaf, and that the baker should have the right of appeal to an independent tribunal for an investigation of his costs to decide whether his low price was justified; if this were found to be the case the Sale Note clause should not operate. These provisions were agreed to by the milling trade; the 'specified prices' for bread laid down under the Flour Contract are now $\frac{1}{2}d$. a quartern below the maximum rates specified by the Food Council.

The relative change in the fortunes of baking and milling is interesting. In the seventeenth century the baker was the dominating party, and, particularly in London, did a considerable amount of business in merchanting both corn and meal; as a body the bakers had the whip hand of the millers, who were prevented from forming any association. But the millers gradually rose from their subsidiary position and early in the nineteenth century there are records of bakers being financed by millers and 'mealmen' or factors, largely through the formers' inability to meet their flour debts. The baker in this case became a virtual employee of the miller or factor. The latter particularly made a practice of setting up bakers in business, and organized bakery chains. A witness before the Parliamentary Committee of 1815 said, 'Two Millers have forty shops in London and they put bakers into them and send them flour and pay them wages, I believe, or settle with them in some way or other'. A number of these miller-baker enterprises went out of existence after the 1880's when the increasing size of the milling units made the going too difficult for the smaller millers, and a number of them gave up the milling side of their business and concentrated on baking. The case of a Liverpool concern may be cited; the firm was established as a milling concern in 1849, and afterwards acquired a string of bakers' shops as a market for its flour on the tied-house principle, though these tied shops did not absorb all the flour of the mill. Eventually the firm decided that its position would be more satisfactory if it devoted its energies to either milling or baking; and as a small concern it decided on the latter.

In noticing that the tendency was for the integrated units to disintegrate as the milling trade became more and more concentrated in the large productive units, it is important to compare the sizes of the two concerns. The bread-baking trade, as has been mentioned, is still largely in the hands of the small producer-retailer, but though the number of large 'automatic' baking concerns with a trade of over 400 sacks a week, corresponding to a staff of over 20 employees, is comparatively small, their importance is growing, and in 1935 they accounted for about 40 per cent of bread consumption. This, of course, includes Co-operative bakeries. A bakery firm using 1,000 sacks a week, of which there were about 450 in 1935, would keep a mill of 8 to 10 sacks employed full-time, while a string of a dozen bakeries of this size would be able to take up the output of a large-size mill of about 100 sacks capacity.

The dissimilarity in size between the producer units in milling and baking, and more particularly the wide difference in the sizes of controlling units in the two trades, have been the main reasons for the absence of vertical integration on any appreciable scale at the present time. The Report on the Marketing of Wheat, etc. (1928) said:

'Some hold the view that it may eventually prove to be good policy for millers to follow the brewers' example and link up with retail establishments so as to provide a regular outlet for the products of their mills. Among the larger provincial millers, there are instances of steps being taken in this direction and a few relatively small country millers dispose of all or nearly all their flour through directly owned or associated bakeries with very successful results.'

The stability created in the industry by its reorganization in 1929, however, seems to have lessened considerably the argument for linking up in this way. There is certainly little evidence of it at the present time. Where it does occur—often through the financial difficulties of the baker through which the miller comes to hold a mortgage on the business and stipulates that he shall be the sole supplier of flour—it is on a very small scale. There was a case where a producer of a special germ and malt flour was forced to manufacture the bread and distribute it to bakers because the wide variation in the quality of the loaf when bakers were left to undertake manufacture threatened the reputation of the flour; but this is an isolated case. It is said that the larger milling interests have in recent years begun to take a more vital interest in financial integration in an attempt to counteract the growth of powerful buying units in the baking trade, of which the huge Weston group, with its 51 bakeries and biscuit factories and 450 retail shops, is the most important. The miller's influence is said to be exerted largely by way of financial support for bakeries and bakery chains, but to what extent the practice exists is not known. Market rumour, according to the *Financial News* of July 1943, has it that millers may attempt to secure a foothold in the baking trade of the North, where there is scope for expansion owing to the decline in home baking as a result of the war. Progress along rationalized lines in the baking trade was temporarily held up during the Second World War owing to the need for decentralization, but it is expected to continue when controls end, and it is anticipated that the milling combines may play an important part in its development.

LABOUR FORCE

The number of operatives employed in the industry before the Second World War is usually taken in the trade to be about 15,000. This figure is in fairly close agreement with those suggested by the Census of Production statistics. The total number employed in the grain-milling industry in units with over ten employees was 22,855 in 1935, and of these approximately 75 per cent were stated to be operatives. A reduction of the resultant number of operatives in the ratio of the quantity of wheat flour and by-products to the total quantity of grain products milled by these firms brings the figure for the number engaged in flour-milling down to 14,900. To this must be added a further 1 per cent in respect of the smaller units with fewer than ten employees. The total number employed, on this reckoning, was just over 15,000 in 1935—a few hundred less than the corresponding number in 1930. At this figure it seems likely to remain. To quote a statement by an expert, Dr. A. E. Humphries, as early as 1933— 'I should be surprised if further mechanization, taken by itself, results in any further appreciable number being unemployed.' Rationalization has already proceeded to such lengths that any really significant reduction on this score is not likely. The reorganization of the industry at the end of the 'twenties reduced employment by a considerable extent. Between 1929 and 1935 it was estimated that between 3,500 and 4,000 workers—nearly 20 per cent of the total employed—were thrown out of the industry; but, failing quite unforeseen developments, this operation appears to have been completed once and for all.

Of the total of 15,000 workers engaged in the industry, roughly three-quarters can be classed as flour-milling workers proper. The remainder, comprising workers in the power-house, dispatch department, and on miscellaneous jobs, might be attached to any trade, and have no special qualifications in flour-milling as such.

For the most part, all the operatives employed in the mill proper, including the screen-room and mixing-room, with the exception of the labourers, may be said to be skilled. Their work involves setting the various machines and seeing that they continue to operate efficiently, and this requires years of experience, together with a sound technical background. In other parts of the unit it is less easy to determine how far the work is skilled or unskilled, but the major part of it should probably be classed as unskilled. Flour-packing, for example, while it demands experience, is a repetition job calling for no specialized knowledge, and the same is true of the intake and warehousing parts of the mill. On a rough basis of calculation it might be said that the skilled labour attached to all the departments concerned in the operational side of a mill, including dispatch and power-house, amounts to between 30 and 50 per cent of the total labour involved, according to the size of the mill. A small mill needs a higher proportion of skilled workers than does a large unit, where the skilled man can take charge of a greater number of machines. A mill of up to 20-sacks capacity may be taken roughly as requiring about 50 per cent of its operative labour to be skilled; for a mill of between 40 and 50 sacks capacity the corresponding proportion drops to about 40 per cent and for a 100-sack plant the figure falls to about 30 per cent.

The skilled jobs in a flour-mill are the exclusive prerogative of men. And there is little room for women in the unskilled jobs, because much of the work is heavy in itself or may involve heavy manual labour on occasion. The sweepers in the mill may, for example, have to assist in removing the rolls from the roller mills, or may be involved in the cleaning of machinery. The only parts of a milling unit where women are permitted are the sack-house, on sack mending and cleaning; the packing department, on packing small bags of under 60 lb.; on sweeping or cleaning—cleaning of machinery, however, being strictly barred; and, as a recognition of woman's proper place in industry, 'attendance in the mess-room'.

Flour-milling workers are organized in the Transport and General Workers' Union, and their main activities are conducted through the National Joint Industrial Council. The large majority, probably at least 95 per cent, of the 15,000 employees in the industry are organized in the union. The unorganized 5 per cent consist of groups of workers employed in small and often out-of-the-way country districts, with whom the contact necessary for trade union organization is difficult to maintain, largely for purely physical reasons of distance, but also to some extent through the quasi-feudal outlook of the small-town worker; and it is no coincidence that in the mills whose owners choose to remain outside the Employers' Federation, and therefore outside the N.J.I.C., the employees also are for the most part unorganized.

Wage-rates have been regulated by the N.J.I.C. since its inception. At the outset three classes of mill were recognized, according to location: class A—mills in the big centres, large towns, or principal ports; class B—mills in towns and industrial areas other than A; class C—small country towns or rural areas. Later the classification was further subdivided by adding classes AA and BB, between A and B, and B and C respectively.

Under an agreement made at the end of 1923 wage-rates are allowed to fluctuate with the standard of living as shown by the Ministry of Labour index, a 1s. rise being granted for every 5-point rise in the index. During the period of control in the 1914–18 war wages rose to 75s. for a labourer class A, and this rate obtained from May 1920 to July 1921, after which it fell continuously down to 51s. in August 1923, and then rose again up to 57s. in November 1924; after that date wages remained stable up to June 1939, when a further increase of 3s. was granted. It may be noted that no cut was made in wages in this industry during the depression years. The 1939 rates were as shown on page 64.

The rollerman is the highest paid operative. Wages for the intermediate rates between rollerman and labourer are fixed by Joint District Councils in each area. As an illustration of the order of seniority of the different occupations in a flour-mill, the following

Class	A	AA	B	BB	C
	s.	*s.*	*s.*	*s.*	*s.*
First Rollermen:[1]					
Grade 1 . .	73·0	70·6	68·0	64·6	61·0
Grade 2 . .	71·0	68·6	66·0	62·6	59·0
Grade 3 , .	—	—	—	60·6	57·0
General Labourers:					
All grades . .	57·0	54·6	52·0	48·6	45·0

rates of pay were operating in one mill during the inter-war period.[2]

	s.	d.		s.	d.
Rollerman . .	75	6	Flour topper . .	62	6
Assistant rollerman .	60	6	Sack cleaner . .	57	6
Silksman . . .	64	–	Warehouseman . .	59	6
Purifierman . .	67	–	Siloman . . .	60	6
Flour packer . .	60	6	Wheat receiver . .	66	6
Bran packer . .	59	–	Assistant receiver .	59	6
Screensman . .	70	6	Sack machinist .	31	6
Assistant screensman .	61	–	(woman)		

Foremen's rates vary, but they are generally about £1 higher than that of the highest paid worker in the department.

It has already been mentioned that the flour-milling industry has shown a most progressive attitude towards labour since the First World War, and relations between employers and employees in the Joint Industrial Council have been extremely good. Possibly the best illustration of the mutual confidence which exists between them is given by the treatment of the workers who were displaced through reorganization in 1929: funds running into many thousands of pounds were provided by millers, and these were administered by the Joint Council in resettlement schemes. Many other agreements with the workers were far ahead of similar arrangements in industry as a whole: holidays with pay were granted as far back as 1919; wages were maintained at their 1924 level even during the depression years; a guaranteed week was brought in in 1937; the working week was reduced in the same year—to 42 hours for shift-workers and 44 hours for day-workers; a pensions scheme was set up in 1930, which over half the workers in the industry in 1940 had joined.

The N.J.I.C. took over from the National Association the question of technical education, and for this purpose formed a Technical

[1] Grade 1 applies to mills which have a total roller contact of over 1,000 inches equivalent to about 10 sacks; Grade 2 with 1,000 inches or less; and Grade 3 with 250 inches or less.
[2] E. Leigh Pearson, op. cit.

Education Committee, on which representatives of the Board of Education, the City and Guilds of London Institute, and principals and teachers in technical colleges, sit in addition to representatives of employers and workers in the industry. The Committee greatly raised the scientific standards of the technical course which provides both for the needs of the skilled operative who is content to remain an operative and for the needs of those who aim at management. The present course of evening study is four years, the first two concerned mainly with flour-milling technology, and the last two dealing more fully with the scientific aspect of flour-milling, the course being arranged so that the first two years' study provides an adequate background for the less ambitious skilled worker. Before the Second World War there were about twenty centres in which classes were held, and the number of students was over 700, the numbers having shown a fairly steady rise from the 500-odd students in 1932–3. In addition to these centres, which are situated for the most part at the ports and chief inland milling towns, a correspondence course is conducted through one of the trade journals, the numbers of students varying between 100 and 200.

WHEAT SUPPLIES

Apart from a small quantity of chemicals used in the bleaching and 'improving' processes during flour manufacture, the only raw material employed is the grain itself.

Wheats differ considerably in size, shape, colour, and hardness of grain, and each type is suitable for a particular type of flour, either alone or in combination with other classes of wheat. Wheat is classified as hard or soft, yielding strong or weak flours. Hard wheat is rich in the protein gluten, and comes in general from areas with extreme continental climates. It naturally generally commands higher prices than a softer wheat, other things being equal. For the most part the strongest wheats are grown in Canada, the United States, and Russia. Canadian (Manitoba) wheat of high grade is considered to be the best in the world. Wheats which are medium in strength are generally known as 'fillers', though each of them has its own characteristics which must be taken into account in blending a flour to suit a particular purpose. South American and Indian wheat, for example, are used as fillers, though Argentina produces fairly wide ranges of varieties of different strengths. Certain other wheats are valued for their colour. Australian wheat in particular, though of only medium strength, is frequently expensive and is added to a wheat mixture for the express purpose of improving the colour of the flour. English and other West European wheats grown in damp and temperate climates are the weakest: their gluten is of poor quality, and they have, moreover, a high moisture content which

3

makes them compare unfavourably with wheats from sunnier and drier climates in regard both to storage and to milling, although they usually yield a flour of good flavour and colour. The high moisture content of these wheats is naturally reflected in their price, which is always well below that of stronger wheats—and in comparing the relative prices of wheats of different origins, the miller must take the valueless water content into account.

It has been seen that bread flours, which form the bulk of total flour output, require to be of good strength, and a percentage of hard imported wheats is therefore essential for their manufacture. Port mills, in fact, use imported wheats of both hard and soft types almost exclusively for the complete range of flours which they manufacture; while inland millers, with the exception of those using large proportions of home-grown wheat for the manufacture of biscuit, cake, and household flours, also have to purchase considerable quantities of imported strong wheats in order to produce a flour of sufficient strength for bread-baking.

The proportions of the various types of wheat milled in any one year vary considerably, depending on the size and quality of harvest in each supplying country both absolutely and relatively to one another, and on the prices ruling for each. There is no rigid formula for any particular type of flour, and the miller, while maintaining as far as possible a uniform standard in his branded flours, has usually a fairly wide choice of wheats from which to select the most suitable from the point of view both of quality and price. This ability to pick and choose in the world wheat market has been the British miller's chief advantage in competing with overseas manufacturers who have the benefit of excellent quality home-grown wheats. It is a factor of paramount importance to the prosperity of the British milling industry, and any arrangements which would weaken this power to purchase freely in a free market must react unfavourably to the trade. Millers have jealously guarded their right to buy in the markets of their choice, and have fought strongly against any rigid quota schemes such as were put forward in preliminary discussion in connexion with the Ottawa Agreement and the Wheat Act, and also against the monopolistic tendencies of wheat producers in seeking to restrict wheat production and maintain a high level of prices through the operation of world wheat agreements.

It is common knowledge that the United Kingdom is the foremost buyer of wheat in the world, and that as such it exercises a predominating influence on the world wheat market. During the 'thirties the quantities of wheat used annually by the British milling trade for manufacture into flour averaged some 5,600,000 tons, and of this total about 90 per cent was made up of overseas wheat.

The methods of wheat-buying in respect of both imported and

home-grown supplies, formed the subject of a lengthy report in 1928,[1] and although the position has changed somewhat in relation to the home-grown wheat trade since the operation of the Wheat Act in 1932, the general features of the selling and marketing of wheat are unchanged, and little need be said here on the subject. What must be stressed is the fact that the grain trade has in large part been put out of business by the milling industry, and by the three large firms in particular. Before the First World War most of the imported wheat was handled by the grain trade, and the miller's function was limited to processing the wheat and distributing the flour and wheat feed. But the milling combines as they increased in importance by-passed the grain merchants and operated on the wheat markets independently, taking their seats on the Corn Exchanges and conducting 'futures' operations. In this way they effected considerable economies. Already by 1926 60 per cent of the grain arriving at British ports was being taken up by millers direct, and the corresponding percentage before the outbreak of war in 1939 was nearer 70 per cent. The big milling companies do not operate entirely separately from the grain trade; they still buy a small proportion of their requirements through brokers and, very rarely, through importing merchants, but dealings of this kind are not very important, and the port distributing merchant in grain in particular has practically gone out of existence. The merchant trade now operates as an intermediary for the flour-milling industry for the most part only in relation to purchases of grain by the small and medium-size millers, who still buy nearly all their wheat in this way.

Many country millers have close business connexions with farmers; the reciprocal trading between the two, the miller buying wheat and selling wheat feed, is a feature of the country milling business; and many of these millers are provender millers also. Very often these millers act in the capacity of merchants, buying wheat in excess of their own requirements and re-selling it to other millers. Home-grown grain on the whole is handled to a greater extent proportionately by the merchant trade than is imported wheat.

The buying of wheat has formed a most important part of the miller's business, and was undoubtedly one of the factors hastening the development of the large-scale port mill and the decline of the smaller mills. The ability of large millers in the period of competition after decontrol in 1921 to offset bare margins of profit, or even losses, on the manufacture of flour by advantageous buying in the wheat markets when prices were fluctuating gave them an enormous advantage over smaller millers who were less able to recoup themselves in this way. The value of wheat-buying to the miller was acknowledged

---

[1] *Report on the Marketing of Wheat, Barley, and Oats in England and Wales.* Ministry of Agriculture and Fisheries.

by Dr. Humphries, the then President of the National Association, in evidence before the Royal Commission on Food Prices in 1925:

'Q. 1133. Is a material proportion of the miller's profits made out of milling operations from day to day, or from intelligent anticipation of future market movements?

'*A*. The latter, certainly.'

The predominance of the millers in the overseas wheat market was illustrated when the Government arranged for purchases of security wheat stocks from the United States in 1938. The fact that these purchases were on Government account was kept secret at the time, and the business was transacted by the three large milling companies. The grain trade was deeply hurt, to say the least, but there is no doubt that had the grain trade contracted for the large quantities of wheat which were involved, immediate suspicion would have been aroused that the State was behind the deal.

Violent price fluctuations characterized the world wheat market between the two wars, with particularly serious results for the overseas producer. Co-operative producer organizations were established in a number of overseas countries between the two wars—the most outstanding of these was the Canadian Wheat Pool—but the absence of really close co-operation in many of the countries and, more important, the lack of real co-operation between the individual producing countries, rendered their avowed object of stabilizing wheat prices ineffective when the pressure of supplies on the world market became at all abnormal. The successive lowering of wheat prices during the late 'twenties and the attempt of the Canadian farmers to stand out for what they considered a fair price for their crops, reduced the Canadian Wheat Pool to a state of bankruptcy, and the Pool was forced to apply to the Government for official backing. Most of the overseas schemes, in fact, are supported in some way by the respective Governments. The limited success of the London Wheat Agreement of 1933, which was the first attempt at international planning of the production and distribution of world wheat supplies, is a pointer to the difficulties in the way of stabilizing the market. Within a year of its birth, the Agreement was almost completely upset by a record harvest in Argentina, and although the international committee remained nominally in existence its influence on prices was insignificant.

The elimination of cut-throat competition in the home milling trade through reorganization in 1929 reduced the need for millers to take risks on the wheat exchanges. But buying is of necessity a risky undertaking; in 1929–30, for example, Spillers incurred a heavy trading loss through injudicious buying, which the directors frankly admitted.

The economies effected by large-scale centralized buying form one of the most important factors in the prosperity of the large firms. Little individual initiative is exercised by mill managers in the selection of wheats for their grists, though in other respects they are free to run their mills with the minimum of control from above. The major proportion of each mill's output consists of a limited range of flours; and, in fact, the large mills owned by the leading firms produce identical brands. The central wheat-buying department is informed of the mill's grain requirements and issues from the wheats which it has available, those which conform best to the mill's known needs. Mills bought up by the combines, which still trade under their old names, continue to market flours under their former brand names, but they too obtain their wheat in the same way through the central organization.

The trend of home wheat production since the end of the last century has been examined at length in numerous reports on the state of the country's agriculture, and it is unnecessary here to give more than the brief facts which most vitally affect the milling industry.

The average annual wheat production in the United Kingdom over five-year periods from 1910 up to 1930 was as follows:

UNITED KINGDOM AVERAGE ANNUAL PRODUCTION

	'000 tons
1910–14 . . .	1,609
1915–19 . . .	1,891
1920–4 . . .	1,661
1925–9 . . .	1,389

Ministry of Agriculture.

The unhappy condition of British wheat-growers after 1929 when world wheat prices underwent a drastic fall prompted the Government in 1931 to propose assistance for the wheat farmers in the form of the quota principle, already in operation in Germany, France, and other European countries for a number of years, whereby millers were required to use a definite proportion of home-grown wheat in their grists. The milling trade were strongly opposed to this proposal, constituting as it did both a check to their freedom of action in the wheat market and a possible beginning to Government supervision and control. An alternative scheme, which left the millers' freedom of choice unimpaired, was drawn up by the trade, and the Government agreed on all major issues. The resultant Wheat Act of 1932, administered by the Wheat Commission, composed of seventeen representatives of millers, farmers, bakers, and consumers, gave to growers of 'home-grown millable[1] wheat' a firm price and a secure

[1] I.e. 'capable of being manufactured into a sound and sweet flour fit for human consumption having regard to the customary methods employed in the milling industry for cleaning and conditioning wheat'.

market, but left the normal trade channels virtually undisturbed. The subsidy (or 'deficiency payment') which was given to registered growers for certified millable wheat, up to a maximum quantity of 27 million cwt.,[1] to make up the average price they received to 10s. a cwt. (45s. a quarter) was balanced by levies—which were called 'quota' payments although the scheme involved no individual quota arrangements—imposed on each sack of flour delivered for consumption in the United Kingdom, including both home-milled and imported flour. The flour bears the quota payment on passing from the miller, importer, or merchant, to the baker or other consumer, the former being responsible to the Commission for quarterly payment. The position of the miller in relation to the payment is therefore solely that of tax-gatherer. In effect, of course, the subsidy to the farmer is ultimately borne by the general public in the form of higher bread and flour prices. It may be noted that the movement of the quota payment inversely with world wheat prices has the effect of levelling out to a certain extent fluctuations in the price of flour to bakers.

As a result home wheat production advanced strongly up to the middle 'thirties, and the first years of the subsidy's operation were blessed with extremely good harvesting conditions.

ESTIMATED PRODUCTION OF HOME-GROWN WHEAT, 1930–9

Year (1st August to 31st July)	Estimated Production '000 tons	Sold and Certified as Millable '000 tons	Percentage Sold and Certified as Millable
1930–1	1,132	—	—
1931–2	1,013	—	—
1932–3	1,168	1,020	81%
1933–4	1,672	1,488	88%
1934–5	1,869	1,796	96%
1935–6	1,753	1,683	96%
1936–7	1,481	1,185	80%
1937–8	1,510	1,223	81%
1938–9	1,965	1,842	94%

Report of the Wheat Commission.

Of the millable wheat, by no means all was actually used for the manufacture of flour for human consumption. Nevertheless, the operation of the Wheat Act, together with the providentially good harvests immediately following its inception, resulted in an increase in the quantities of home-grown wheat used in millers' grists. The

[1] Originally fixed as 27 million cwt.; increased to 36 million in 1937.

estimated amounts used for flour manufacture rose from 537,000 to 876,000 tons during the first five years of the Act's operation, the greater part of the advance taking place up to 1934–5, after which the usage of home wheat by flour-millers expanded only slightly. On the average only about half of the millable crop was used in flour manufacture before the war, though the percentage varied from year to year. The greater part of the remainder was used for feeding poultry in the form of whole grain, the rest going to cattle, poultry, and other animal feeds.

ESTIMATED QUANTITIES OF HOME WHEAT TAKEN UP BY
FLOUR MILLS

	'000 tons	Quantity taken up as : Percentage of Total Home Crop	Percentage of Home Crop sold as Millable
1932–3 . .	537	46%	52%
1933–4 . .	503	30%	34%
1934–5 . .	837	44%	46%
1935–6 . .	847	48%	50%
1936–7 . .	876	58%	73%

(The Census of Production estimated the proportions of the total home crop used by flour-millers for the years 1933, 1934, and 1935 as 39·2%, 35·5%, and 41·7% respectively.)

Although the home wheat position was considerably improved by the operation of the subsidy, the importance of imported wheat remained very great. Over the five-year period 1932–7, imported wheat accounted for about 87 per cent of the total wheat converted into flour, home wheat contributing little more than one-eighth of the quantities milled, though the proportions were increasing throughout this period, and in the year 1936–7, 16 per cent of the wheat used for flour production was home-grown.

	Home Wheat used for Flour as a percentage of total Wheat used in Flour manufacture
1932–3	9·4%
1933–4	9·0%
1934–5	15·0%
1935–6	15·0%
1936–7	16·0%

It will be apparent that the price of home-grown wheat in the open market is lower than those of imported wheats, with the exception of West European grain. Comparative prices for different classes of wheat averaged over the monthly quotations during 1938 were as follows:

Price per cwt.

			s.	d.
British	.	.	6	9
Australian	.	.	7	7
Argentine .	.	.	7	8
Danubian .	.	.	7	5
Russian	.	.	7	7
Canadian.	No. 1 Manitoba		9	10
	No. 2 ,,		9	6
	No. 3 ,,		8	9
	No. 4 ,,		8	5

The quantity of wheat imported into the United Kingdom has averaged slightly over five million tons a year in the period between the two wars. Demand for wheat for flour manufacture has not increased in proportion with the increase in population on account of the declining consumption of flour per head (see later). The violent fall in wheat prices which occurred in 1929 and lasted throughout the depression years resulted in a distinct rise in the quantities of imported wheat retained for home consumption. After 1932, however, the operation of the Wheat Act at home, aided by the excellent quality of the home harvest for the first four years of its operation, and, more important, by relatively poor harvests in the main exporting countries and the recovery of world prices after 1933, caused a continuous decline in the volume of overseas wheat used throughout the years 1931-7. In 1938 imports rose again, partly because of the diminished quantities of home-grown wheat harvested in the two preceding years, but mainly owing to the recurrence of surplus world stocks and a consequent drop in world prices, together with the establishment of security stocks in this country to provide against the event of war.

Average Annual Net Imports, 1910–39			Net Imports, 1935–9			
'000 tons			'000 tons			
1910–14 .	.	.	5,227[1]	1935 .	.	.	5,032
1915–19 .	.	.	4,095[1]	1936 .	.	.	4,999
1920–4 .	.	.	5,019	1937 .	.	.	4,755
1925–9 .	.	.	5,149	1938 .	.	.	5,020
1930–4 .	.	.	5,407	1939 .	.	.	5,271
1935–9 .	.	.	5,015			

Statistical Abstract.

In contrast with the use made of home wheat, all but a very small proportion of imported wheat is used for flour manufacture. During the years 1933–5 about 5½ per cent of the available imported wheat

[1] Not excluding re-exports.

supplies were used, according to the Census of Production, for other purposes, mainly for cattle and poultry foods, either on account of their low price or because of deterioration.

The relative positions of the main wheat suppliers have undergone considerable change during the past thirty years. In the five years before the First World War and in the ten subsequent years Empire countries accounted for less than half of the total supplies. The Ottawa Agreement of 1932, which imposed (as from November 16th 1932) a tariff duty of 2s. a quarter (of 480 lb.) on foreign wheat, greatly improved the position of Empire suppliers. The original Ottawa proposals for assisting Empire wheat producers were based, in the same way as those originally put forward for assisting the home grower, on the principle of a definite import quota from each Dominion. Strong objections were raised by the millers on the grounds that Canada and Australia would have a virtual monopoly of a fixed percentage of Britain's wheat supplies, and, secure in this monopoly, would raise their prices; that marketing power would be transferred from the buyer to the seller, and the 'futures' market would to all intents and purposes be killed; that trade with Argentina would be severely damaged; and that the scheme—as with the original home wheat proposals—would mean some form of Government supervision of the industry. While the Ottawa Agreements Act was not as favourable to the home milling industry as might have been hoped, in that it allowed Empire flour to enter free of duty while foreign wheat was made liable to a duty of 2s. a quarter, it represented an enormous improvement over the original proposals, which would have reacted most unfavourably on the British milling trade, and, no doubt, on the price of bread to the consumer.

This encouragement to Empire wheat, together with the decrease in the acreage under wheat in the United States, in the early 'thirties, which changed the United States from a net exporter to a net importer of wheat in the three seasons 1934–7, resulted in a rise in the percentage of wheat supplied from Empire sources. In 1930–4 the proportion rose to 55 per cent,[1] and reached 62 per cent in 1935–9. The proportions varied considerably from year to year, the highest

[1] A ruling was given after the Ottawa provisions began to operate that freedom from duty in the case of Empire wheat should be given only in cases of direct shipment or shipment through foreign ports on a through bill of lading. It was said at the time that a considerable quantity of the wheat consigned prior to the Agreement from the U.S. had in fact been Canadian wheat. A considerable percentage of Canadian wheat (over 45 per cent) had been shipped via U.S. ports, but the Bill of Lading would have indicated the country of final destination. In the two years 1929 and 1930 the quantity of wheat consigned from Canada to the U.S. was only 17½ million bushels against 343 million bushels consigned to the U.K. It is clear, therefore, that the possible error due to imports of Canadian wheat being credited to the U.S. was very slight, if at all significant, and that general conclusions based on published import statistics are not likely to misinterpret the trends in this respect.

figure reached being 84 per cent in 1936. Both Canada and Australia approximately doubled their exports to this country, between 1909–13 and 1935–9, and became the only Empire suppliers of any importance. India, which supplied more wheat to us than did any other country in 1909–13, dropped right out of the market until the later 'thirties, owing to the extremely low world prices and her increased local consumption of wheat.

The relative importance of foreign suppliers also underwent a considerable change. Comparisons between one year's imports and another's cannot be taken as indicating necessarily any change in the import policy of this country. The size and quality of the wheat harvest in each surplus-producing country and the prices demanded are factors of prime importance. In 1909–13 the United States, Argentina, and Russia accounted for practically the whole of our foreign wheat, in fairly equal proportions. U.S. policy in reducing her wheat acreage in 1932–4 drastically lowered production, and this was further emphasized by poor harvests—production dropped from 25 million tons in 1931 to less than 15 million in 1933–4—and she became a net importer of wheat in 1935–6. Her prices, moreover, were relatively high. The U.S.S.R. dropped out of the market after the First World War and did not return to it until the 'thirties. The protectionist policies of the main European countries in the 'twenties and 'thirties and the increase in their home wheat production aided by tariff duties on imported wheats and the imposition of quota arrangements on their flour-millers brought quantities of European wheats on to the world markets in the middle 'thirties at extremely low prices. The quantities purchased from foreign sources during the inter-war years therefore varied enormously between one country and another. Russia's re-entry into the international wheat market further complicated the pattern, and no general trends can be followed during these years. In the later 'thirties the conservation of supplies on the Continent, and heavy purchases, notably from the United States in 1937 and 1938, for the establishment of security stocks also obscured any movements which might otherwise have been apparent. Argentina is normally this country's chief foreign supplier, though the disastrous failure of her crops in the year 1935–6 caused her share in British imports during the five pre-war years to fall very much below their previous level.

Mention should be made in passing of the suppliers of other requirements for the milling industry. Apart from the actual grain the requirements of the industry are few. Mill machinery, however, is a factor of very great importance. British milling engineers have achieved world-wide fame in this particular field, and to them must be given a great part of the credit for the good quality and cheapness of present-day flour. They are, for the most part, firms which were

CHIEF SUPPLIERS OF WHEAT TO THE UNITED KINGDOM
1909–39

Exporting Country	1909–13		1920–4		1925–9		1930–4		1935–9	
	Mill. cwts.	%	Mill. cwts.	%	Mill. cwts.	%	Mill. cwts.	%	Mill. cwts.	%
Canada	91	18	115	23	166	32	181	33	193	38
Australia	59	11	72	14	63	12	111	20	107	21
India	97	19	25	5	17	3	—	—	14	3
Argentina	84	16	99	20	113	22	116	21	69	14
U.S.A.	94	18	180	36	139	27	37	7	33	6
U.S.S.R.	79	15	—	—	—	—	59	13	25	5
France	—	—	—	—	—	—	—	—	23	5
Rumania	—	—	—	—	—	—	—	—	18	4
Germany	—	—	—	—	—	—	14	3	—	—
Empire	249	48	215	43	246	47	297	55	315	62
Foreign	268	52	289	57	272	53	247	45	191	38
Total	517	100	504	100	519	100	544	100	506	100

Derived from Annual Statement of Trade.

established before roller-milling came into existence and later specialized in milling plant. The chief suppliers are Henry Simon of Stockport, Thomas Robinson of Rochdale, and E. R. and F. Turner of Ipswich. Other firms specializing in particular types of machinery, such as scales, elevators, conveyors, and the like, include W. and T. Avery of Birmingham, Robert Boby of Bury St. Edmunds, and Spencer of Melksham. Chemical manufacturers which cater for the milling industry in supplying 'improvers' operate at most of the ports, but the main centres are London, Manchester, Glasgow, and Hull. Large supplies of sacks and bags are also required by the trade. They are made of either jute or cotton. Both have their respective advantages and disadvantages; cotton sacks are cleaner, take print more easily, their fibres do not shred, and they can be used afterwards for other purposes, where their print is held to have a considerable advertisement value; jute sacks, on the other hand, are cheaper, stronger, and can be used more often. Most home-milled flour is sold in returnable jute bags, while imported flour is generally packed in cotton bags. There are about twenty main sack manufacturers, just over half of whom produce both types of bag. Of the twenty firms, seven or eight are in Scotland (six in Dundee), four are in Ireland, and the rest are located in English ports—four in Liverpool, two in Manchester, one each in London and Ipswich. Numerous bag factors operate in each of the main milling ports.

CONSUMPTION

The consumption of wheat bread and flour goes through a type of cycle as the standard of living of a community rises. Wheat flour is not a staple article of diet in countries with a very low standard of living, the cereals making up the major portion of their diet consisting of rice, maize, millet, rye, and the like, according to the climate of the country. Higher in the scale, wheat tends to replace other cereals in the diet. As incomes rise still further, consumption of flour begins to fall; an increase in the proportion of prepared cereals, meat and fats, and of fruits, sugar, and prepared foods, in the diet produces a corresponding fall in the consumption of flour and bread. This fact is demonstrated by the different levels of consumption both in different countries and in families with different incomes in this country. Thus, in 1937, it was estimated that the *per capita* consumption of flour (not necessarily *wheat* flour) in the United States was about 25 per cent below that in this country, while in France it was about 11 per cent and in Germany about 12 per cent higher than ours. Estimates made by Sir John Boyd Orr of consumption of bread and flour by families with varying incomes showed that the highest income groups, with incomes between £400 and £800, took only three-quarters of the amount of bread and flour (in terms of flour) consumed per head by the lowest income group, with less than 10*s*. income per head per week.

Except during the two World Wars, flour consumption in this country has shown a progressive decline over the past century. Consumption per head of bread and flour in 1939 was at a level between 40 and 50 per cent below the corresponding figure a hundred years ago, and 30 per cent below what it was in the 1880's. The following table shows how the consumption of flour in the United Kingdom declined after 1918. The figures are not entirely reliable, since they are given from varying sources, but the Census of Production figures and those of the Wheat Commission are in fairly close agreement. The downward trend until 1938 is unmistakable. The main cause was the general improvement in standards of living; other factors have also contributed to the decline in consumption. Factories, offices, and schools have set up canteens to provide midday meals in place of the sandwiches which were formerly taken from home. The popularity of potato chips as a food for the lower income groups has grown enormously; and among families at all income-levels packaged cereals and breakfast foods have taken the place of a considerable part of the bread eaten at breakfast. The progress of the latter foods has been very striking: firms which set up after the First World War have been extraordinarily successful, and have pressed home their competitive attack by engaging in extensive advertising, often of somewhat dubious dietetic accuracy. The

Source	Year	United Kingdom Flour available for Consumption '000 tons	United Kingdom Consumption of Flour per head of Population	
			Per year lb.	Per week lb.
Beveridge: British Food Control	1910–14	4,520	223	4·28
	1914	4,535	220	4·23
	1915	4,430	216	4·15
	1916	4,560	226	4·33
	1917	4,930	244[1]	4·69
	1918	5,050	250[1]	4·80
Census of Production	1924	4,219[2]	210	4·05
	1930	4,103[2]	200	3·85
Wheat Commission[3]	1933	4,226	203	3·91
	1934	4,190	201	3·87
	1935	4,182	200	3·86
	1936	4,188	199	3·83
	1937	4,132	196	3·76
	1938	4,162	196	3·77
Central Statistical Office[4]	1934-8			3·75
	1940			4·01
	1941			4·56
	1942			4·37
	1943			4·43

slimming craze also played its part in the decline in the amount of bread eaten. Then, too, throughout the inter-war period, and particularly in the 'twenties, considerable publicity was given in the Press to articles, often extremely virulent, condemning the quality of the flour and bread being offered to the public, on the grounds both of the removal of the germ and bran from the wheat grain, and of the chemical treatment applied to the flour. White bread became

[1] For these two years the flour was composed of wheat mixed with varying proportions of other cereals.

[2] Assuming that 4 per cent of the given output of flour and meal in the Census was accounted for by duplication (imports or output of other millers) or by meal for purposes other than human consumption; this being the average percentage shown in the Wheat Commission's figures for 1932–7. Without this correction, consumption figures for 1924 and 1930 would be 218 and 208 lb. per year respectively. For 1930 a slight adjustment (less than 1 per cent) has been made for the small firms excluded from the Census.

[3] The Wheat Commission's figures refer to the year ended July 31st. Figures for the calendar years have been calculated as simple means of the two quantities for the years ended July 31st and beginning August 1st.

[4] Civilian consumption only.

the Aunt Sally of all types of people, from Harley Street doctors to food faddists of all kinds. Sir William Arbuthnot Lane at one time warned the public that white bread might be one of the causes of cancer, and in 1929 the popular Press was crying out against 'poison gas in our bread'.

All these contributory factors were clearly causing a very marked drop in consumption. Between 1924 and 1930 the (*per capita*) fall registered was about 5 per cent. Though the decline was to a certain extent counteracted by the depression years, which lessened the ability of many households to afford the more expensive foodstuffs and forced them back on to a diet containing a higher proportion of bread, the position was recognized by the millers as frankly serious. At the end of 1934 they launched a Bread Advertising campaign, which was planned to extend over a period of five years, at a total cost of half a million pounds. The trade was not greatly impressed with the results of this drive; but Census of Production estimates of the quantities of flour used for bread manufacture appear to indicate that it was not without effect.

	Estimated Quantity of Flour used for Bread Manufacture '000 tons	Weekly Consumption per Head lb.
1924 . . .	2,200	2·11
1930 . . .	2,250	2·11
1935 . . .	2,340	2·15

The improvement between 1930 and 1935 may, of course, have been due in part to the fact that, in the older industrial centres at least, the general level of prosperity was lower in the later year.

At this stage it may be useful to see the proportions of total flour output devoted to various uses. The following figures are based on Census of Production estimates of quantities used in each trade, given as percentages of the totals shown on page 28:

PROPORTIONS OF TOTAL AVAILABLE FLOUR USED IN VARIOUS TRADES

	1935	1930	1924
Bread	55·9%	54·8%	52·0%
Cakes, pastries	6·6%	6·5%	5·4%
Biscuits	3·5%	2·8%	2·1%
Flour for the retail trade, food preparations, cattle and poultry food manufacture and industrial uses	34·0%	35·9%	40·4%

It should be mentioned that a number of people in the trade consider that these figures do not represent the true state of affairs, and that the proportion of flour which is devoted to bread manufacture is considerably higher than that indicated above. The Census figures, of course, relate to consumption of flour and do not purport to give the relative quantities of different types of flour produced by British mills. It will be seen later in the section dealing with foreign trade that a great deal of the flour used for the retail trade, cattle and poultry foods, and other industrial uses is imported. The relative proportions of English-milled flour are more heavily weighted in favour of bread flours. Nevertheless, the Census figures should be treated with some caution.

The growing importance of biscuit manufacture is brought out clearly by the Census figures. During the depression years a great deal of very low-priced flour was exported to this country from European sources, particularly France, Germany, and Italy, and this flour was used to a very large extent in the manufacture of cheap biscuits by large baking firms who came on to the market and whose sales reached very high levels during the 'thirties. The success of these new cheap lines compelled the older biscuit firms also to produce ranges of lower-priced biscuits. It is not surprising, therefore, that the sale of biscuits registered a rise; the proportion which they took of the total flour consumed increased by two-thirds between 1924 and 1935. The quantities of flour devoted to the manufacture of cakes also increased, though not so significantly.

However unsatisfactory the figures relating to consumption of flour may appear, there is little doubt as to the general prospects for the future, and the flour-milling industry is fully aware that there is no reason why the downward trend of consumption should not continue, though more slowly than in the past. From the industry's point of view, output of flour is not likely to show a rise in the future unless there is a significant fall in living standards or a rise in the prices of non-flour foodstuffs in comparison with flour, or the population of the United Kingdom undergoes a considerable expansion. On present evidence it can look forward at the best to a stable demand for its products. The importance to the industry of maintaining or improving its present close organization in the face of its future prospects is evident. New entrants to the industry's ranks are not likely to be welcomed, nor, indeed, are they likely to be forthcoming, and the future is likely to see further consolidation rather than any extension.

DISTRIBUTION

All but a small percentage of home-milled flour is sold by direct dealings between miller and baker, grocer or other user, through travellers working for the various mills. Imported flour is distributed largely by factors. A certain amount of flour is bought directly from the mill or at the corn exchanges (this applies particularly to imported flour) by the larger bakers and grocers; and millers also buy flour at times for blending. Little home-milled flour is distributed by factors: in 1919 the Flour Mills Control stated that only $7\frac{1}{2}$ per cent of the flour manufactured in this country was so distributed, and the general impression is that the current figure is lower; this is probably correct, since the elimination of so many small millers in the 'twenties must have taken off the market much of the flour formerly handled by factors. The operation of factors in the market has inevitably caused difficulties in connexion with maintaining arranged prices. Factors do not operate only as importers or selling agents for country and other small-scale millers, they also purchase flour from the large millers and act as merchants, and millers (though not, perhaps, the consuming public) have often been embarrassed by factors who have bought quantities of flour on a rising market, and later, when prices have risen, have undersold the miller in his own product. In 1932–3 the practice caused such difficulties in the London area that the London millers came to an agreement to deal only with factors not concerned in the imported flour trade, and drew up contracts limiting the factor's function to that of a selling agent and precluding him from acting as a merchant for their particular flour. At that time they tried to persuade the country millers to do the same, but it appears that no definite arrangements were made.

As far as the employment of travelling salesmen attached to the mill's staff is concerned, it has already been mentioned that the intense competition in the trade after decontrol in 1921 led to the extended use of pressure salesmanship, and the port mills particularly employed large numbers of travellers, and sent their flour, which was offered at extremely competitive prices, to all parts of the country. Cross-transport was, in fact, one of the most prominent features of the trade before rationalization took place. London in particular received large quantities of flour from other ports, especially Hull, the flour being transported by sea. One of the arguments used for the rationalization of the industry was the saving in distribution costs which would result from planned production. It must be admitted that cross-transport was by no means always to the disadvantage of consumers. In 1924, for example, Liverpool millers were selling flour in Somerset at 3s. less than the local prices.[1]

Economies in distribution have not been achieved to any appreciable extent through a reduction in selling staff. The mills which were taken over continued for the most part to trade under their own names, and their managements and staffs remained unchanged. This is not an uncommon feature of large-scale amalgamations, for competition between the various branches of a group is an important factor in the promotion of efficiency. Moreover, goodwill is inevitably

[1] Liberal Industrial Inquiry, *Britain's Industrial Future*, 1928.

lost if old-established firms lose their trading identity or if the link between buyer and traveller, often very strongly forged, particularly in the case of the smaller buyers, is severed. So it happened, for example, that when the Associated London Flour Millers was formed in 1921 of seven old London firms, travellers from the seven individual firms continued to canvass as before, and in 1933 when Ranks Ltd. took over the A.L.F.M., representatives of both Ranks and of the various firms in the A.L.F.M. continued to cover their old ground. It was quite usual for small bakers taking only between twenty and thirty sacks a week to be called on by a dozen or more travellers regularly. Looked at from the standpoint of the industry as a whole, the multiplicity of salesmen appears highly wasteful in view of the fact that output quotas are laid down for each mill under the terms of the M.M.A. Their cost is said to amount to about 10 per cent of total manufacturing charges. But from the point of view of individual concerns a reduction in sales staff would lead to an inevitable loss of sales. Personal and psychological factors are not to be ignored. Despite the regulation of price and output, and the predominating position of the leading concerns, competition in the industry is by no means dead. Distribution costs are not likely to be reduced, moreover, while the present structure of the baking trade continues. Much of the high distributive cost is due to the small turnover of individual bakers and their inability to order more than small quantities at a time. It is with the smaller man, too, rather than with the sales departments of large bakeries, that the personal element of salesmanship is of such importance.

When flour delivery is considered, however, the economies brought about by rationalization were more significant. Eventually the two leading millers possessed substantial capacity at all the chief ports, so that all parts of the country lay within reasonable distance of their mills. Distribution was also arranged to make for maximum economy in respect of the trade of subsidiary firms; this was achieved largely by delivering flour to the buyer from the most convenient mill belonging to the group, preserving the subsidiary firm's identity by packing the flour into the latter's bags. Overlapping as far as distribution was concerned was therefore eliminated to a very great extent among the units now belonging to the large firms; but there was no demarcation of spheres of influence as far as the other elements of the trade were concerned. The Co-operative group, as has been seen, are in a special position: flour is ordered direct from the central distribution department, and no salesmen are employed. But Co-operative bakers and grocers are free to use other flour, and are therefore visited by travellers from other firms.

Flour is normally distributed by road, in charged sacks of 140 lb., the charge being refunded on their return. It is normally sold at a delivered-in cost; but some bakers, particularly those obtaining their flour from the big mills at the ports, often prefer to buy it ex-mill at a price equal to the price 'delivered-in', which is fixed according to the location of the mill, less an allowance for the actual cost of transport, and themselves arrange for its transport, but the practice tends to be discouraged by millers. A mill usually keeps its own fleet of vehicles, but the general practice is to maintain only so many as can be kept continuously employed, outside carriers being relied upon for any extra cartage that may be required at times of heavy pressure.

ADVERTISING

The products of the industry are peculiarly homogeneous; moreover, the major proportion of flour reaches the advertisement-imbibing public only indirectly, in the form of bread. Advertising can therefore only be of value to an individual firm in the case of a distinctive product which is either retailed direct or produces a distinctive loaf. All the patent brown and specialist breads fall into this category, and large sums are spent annually on keeping the names of the brands before the public. The leading makers of plain and self-raising flour also devote considerable sums to advertising. Press advertisement carries less weight than public posters and signs, particularly in the case of bread flours; the latter are also extensively advertised through the medium of the retailer or caterer by means of shop and restaurant signs and articles used in distribution. The firm of Hovis has developed this side of advertising very markedly, and a large part of its business is devoted to the manufacture of wrapping bags, books and stationery for bakery use, delivery vans, barrows, and carts; all of which provide admirable means of putting the name of Hovis before a very wide public, and, proving as they do a cheap form of advertisement, can be offered to the buyer at a price which represents good value for money. Other flours for bread, cakes, and biscuits, etc., are advertised in trade papers, but not to the ordinary public. Any public advertisement for these flours is of necessity communal and takes the form of 'Eat More Bread' or 'Bread for Energy'. Canadian millers inaugurated an advertising campaign in this country, and this, of course, pressed the claims of Canadian-milled flour, but apart from this one instance, the propaganda for stimulating flour consumption has been general in character and, as has been mentioned earlier, half a million pounds was spent by the trade out of M.M.A. funds during the years 1933–8 in an attempt to stimulate bread consumption.

FOREIGN TRADE

Imports of flour and meal into the United Kingdom showed a tendency to decline over the period after decontrol in 1921, though

they have fluctuated to a considerable extent with the general level
of world economic prosperity, naturally tending to rise during periods
of comparative slump and low prices and to slacken off at other
times. Total imports during the years 1935–9 were 20 per cent lower
than those during the corresponding period ten years earlier.

RETAINED IMPORTS OF FLOUR (Thousand tons)

1924	.	.	.	531	1932	.	.	422
1925	.	.	.	426	1933	.	.	487
1926	.	.	.	528	1934	.	.	469
1927	.	.	.	543	1935	.	.	399
1928	.	.	.	441	1936	.	.	418
1929	.	.	.	481	1937	.	.	426
1930	.	.	.	578	1938	.	.	383
1931	.	.	.	529	1939	.	.	316

U.K. Statistical Abstract.

Imports of flour accounted for about 12 per cent of the total
amount of flour consumed in this country during the middle
'twenties, for about 14 per cent in 1930 and 1931, and for about
10 per cent during the period 1932–7. Over the period 1932–9
imports were equivalent to the output of about four or five of our
big mills,[1] or about 10 per cent of the United Kingdom's flour-
milling capacity.

Imported flour is not uniformly distributed over the whole country.
Scotland is a far heavier importer in proportion to population than
is England and Wales. Scottish baking methods require comparatively strong flours, which are imported mainly from Canada. While
imports accounted during the five pre-war years for between 7 and
8 per cent of England's consumption requirements, about a third of
Scotland's flour came from overseas.

London is the most important port for the trade in imported flour,
with Glasgow taking second place. In 1937 the proportions of flour
received at the various British ports were as follows:

	%
London . .	42·1
Glasgow . .	23·2
Liverpool . .	11·3
Bristol . .	5·6
Leith . . .	4·6
Tyne ports . .	2·8
Hull . . .	1·1
Other . . .	9·3
Total . .	100·0

Broomhall Corn Trade Year Book.

[1] A total of about 550 sacks per hour.

By far the greatest quantity of flour is imported from the Dominions. During the five pre-war years Empire sources accounted for well over three-quarters of our imported supplies, Canada being the main supplier and Australia the second in importance. The position of Canada has remained fairly stable over the past fifteen years; she has supplied us on the average with just under half of our total imports. The decline in her importance seen in 1929 to 1931, which was due mainly to the high prices ruling for both wheat and flour of Canadian origin, under pressure from the Canadian Wheat Pool, compared with world wheat price-levels, was reversed by the operation of the Ottawa Agreement in 1932, and by the withdrawal of United States flour from the market. Australia advanced strongly in importance during the inter-war years: up to 1930 she supplied about one-seventh of British flour imports, and by 1936–8 her share had risen to over one-third.

SHARE OF SUPPLYING COUNTRIES IN TOTAL FLOUR IMPORTS

Exporting Country	Percentage of all Imports. By Volume										
	1925–8	1929	1930	1931	1932	1933	1934	1935	1936	1937	1938
Canada . .	49	38	39	36	47	44	45	53	49	47	48
Australia .	14	14	15	24	33	28	20	23	30	39	38
U.S.A. . .	26	26	28	19	5	1	1	1	1	1	5
Argentina .	7	8	5	7	6	4	3	3	3	5	5
Germany .	1	3	1	—	—	—	11	2	5	5	—
France . .	1	6	10	10	5	14	14	11	9	5	2
Italy . .	—	1	—	1	2	6	4	5	—	—	—

Annual Statement of Trade.

The main foreign sources of supply up to 1931 were the United States and Argentina. The decrease in the acreage under wheat in the United States at the end of the 'twenties made for a corresponding reduction in her flour exports to this country which was encouraged by the relatively high prices asked by U.S. millers. The imposition of the 10 per cent *ad valorem* duty on flour from non-Empire sources from March 1932 also contributed to the decline in importance of U.S. flour to this country, and between 1932 and 1937 it made up only 1 per cent of our imports, compared with over 25 per cent ten years earlier. Imports of Argentine flour also declined after 1931, and throughout the middle 'thirties they formed only about 3 per cent of our imports, compared with twice that proportion before 1932.

One of the most significant features of the flour-importing trade during the 'thirties, however, was the entry of large quantities of extremely low-priced flour from Europe, and particularly from France, Germany, and Italy. In 1934 imports from these three countries accounted for 29 per cent of total imports by volume, though only about 19 per cent by value. These cheap imports were a source of great concern to British millers, and the trade did all in its power to obtain some form of protection against them. The 10 per cent *ad valorem* duty imposed in March 1932 under the Import Duties Act on foreign flour hardly ameliorated the position, and in May of that year the millers appealed to the Import Duties Advisory Committee for the application of anti-dumping provisions to imports of flour. Dumping was clearly involved in the export of these continental flours: prices of both wheat and flour in these countries were completely controlled, and at a considerably higher level than world prices. Flour for export was being regularly offered at prices representing from a quarter to a third of those ruling in the countries of origin.[1] At times during the year the cost of flour from these countries, including freight and landing charges at a British port, was lower than the current cost of English *wheat*. Australia was also an offender, though on a smaller scale, in this respect: no doubt she was to a certain extent forced to adopt the practice in order to compete with the European countries which offered flour similar to and only slightly weaker than her own. Failing anti-dumping legislation, the millers suggested the imposition of a very much higher rate of duty on foreign flour—the rate proposed was as high as 50 per cent *ad valorem*. The Import Duties Advisory Committee, in weighing the evidence, consulted the National Association of Flour Importers, who took the opportunity of delivering an impassioned attack on the millers in which they stressed the inordinate prosperity of the trade over the past three years. The industry, they said, required no protective duties. They maintained at the same time that the greater proportion of the French flour was of very low grade, and was used, not for human consumption, but for cattle food, and did not therefore compete with the home flour trade except to a limited extent.

Importers also stated that the prices they quoted for continental flour delivered to bakers were on the same level as current prices for all-English flour. This being so, they must have secured very ample profit margins. It seems fairly clear that the importers, even though

---

[1] The accusation that French flour was actually 'dumped' abroad was refuted by the French authorities, who stated that the difference in the prices of flour sold in the home market and in the foreign market was due solely to the operation of a drawback which was allowed to millers in respect of the duty they had paid for imported wheat. However, most of the French flour which was shipped to this country was quite certainly manufactured principally of French wheat, and in any case the difference in price was too large to be explained by an adjustment of this kind.

they may have quoted prices equivalent to those for English flour, were in a position to offer favourable terms to buyers and still reap a substantial profit.

The Committee decided against any form of restriction. In 1932, however, when application was made to them, the situation with regard to continental flour had not yet assumed the serious proportions which it was to reach in the succeeding two or three years. Country millers of all-English flour were most vitally affected by the cheap imports since these were similar to flours made from home-grown wheat as regards strength, and were used, when destined for human consumption, for similar purposes—largely for biscuits, cakes, and retail flour. Nevertheless, all millers became alarmed at the situation: the port millers' particular concern was that the country mills might be squeezed out of existence by their inability to market sufficient quantities of English flour, and if this situation were to arise the port mills would be forced to take up increased amounts of English wheat in virtue of the obligations of the milling industry under the Wheat Act. During the period 1932–4, when the situation was worsening, the industry continued to press for some protective legislation, but to no effect. It even attempted to negotiate some kind of gentleman's agreement with the continental millers, but this too failed. However, after 1934–5 the fall in the quality of the continental harvests, together with the threat of a war in Europe, resulted in a decided fall in the quantities of flour which were shipped from abroad, though French flour continued to be imported at very low prices right up to 1939.

In 1938 there was a revival in the quantity of U.S. flour purchased in this country; in this year the U.S. provided 5 per cent of our total imports. Her stocks of both wheat and flour were particularly heavy, and she was prepared to subsidize her flour exports in order to get it off her hands. The British Government were at the same time negotiating with the U.S. Department of Agriculture for purchases of security wheat stocks, of which the United States was also anxious to rid herself. The negotiations on behalf of the British Government were undertaken by the three large milling concerns, and they effectively defeated the threat which this subsidy represented to the home industry by refusing to put through any deal for the wheat unless the U.S. agreed not to subsidize her flour exports.

It will be seen from the table that the highest-priced flour, even excluding the 10 per cent tariff on non-Empire imports, has normally come from the United States. As has been mentioned, imports from the U.S. were very small during the five or six pre-war years, and it is clear that the small quantity which was bought was of exclusively high-grade quality. The lower prices at which U.S. exporters offered shipments of flour in the last two pre-war years

C.I.F. PRICES OF IMPORTED FLOUR (EXCLUSIVE OF DUTY).
1934–8
Shillings per sack

Exporting Country	1934	1935	1936	1937	1938	Mean 1934–8
Australia . .	16·6	18·4	21·4	30·2	24·2	23·2
Canada . . .	21·4	23·8	26·0	35·4	28·6	27·0
Germany . .	10·3	15·2	16·1	—	—	12·8
France . . .	10·9	14·0	18·7	27·1	14·6	16·3
U.S.A. . . .	23·6	27·2	32·0	35·0	28·4	28·8
Argentina . .	10·5	12·6	15·9	19·8	18·3	15·9
All imported flour .	16·7	20·2	20·2	31·9	25·9	23·4

Annual Statement of Trade.

caused the average price paid for all imported Canadian flour in 1937 and 1938 to exceed that for U.S. flour. What has been said on the subject of cheap imports from France and Germany during the 'thirties is amply borne out by the figures. It should be noted at the same time that Argentina was also a supplier of extremely low-priced flours.

Flour imports play a very important part in providing a check on both the price and the quality of home-milled flour. The cheaper imports which are made up almost exclusively of soft flour and have therefore a limited market, are not of outstanding importance in this respect. But Canadian flour provides a measuring stick which must guide home-millers in fixing the prices for their different grades of flour. Canada is especially anxious to maintain or increase the level of her flour exports to this country, since by doing so she ensures that substantial amounts of Manitoba wheat will be bought by United Kingdom millers in order that English flour may compete in strength with the imported product. During the middle 'thirties, in fact, a vigorous advertising campaign was conducted on behalf of Canadian flour. Canadian opinion is that if her flour exports to Britain were hindered in any way British millers would no longer be compelled to purchase as high a proportion of strong wheat, but would be able to mill larger quantities of lower-priced wheats from non-Canadian sources.

The free importation of Empire flours, free of both duty and quantitative restriction, has been a fact which charges against British millers have often ignored. Those who from time to time during the past decade have condemned the industry as acting against the public interest have tended to look so long at the mounting profits of the industry that they have failed to acknowledge the fact that the price of flour in this country compares favourably with those ruling abroad.

British millers have always been able to retort, with perfect justification, that were they to attempt to maintain prices at an unduly high level they would very quickly be ousted from the home market by imported flours.

EXPORTS OF FLOUR

Flour exports have never been very large in proportion to total output. They were at their height during the first few years after decontrol in 1921, and steadily declined over the subsequent period. The percentage of production exported in 1924 was 7·6 per cent, in 1930 5·2 per cent, and in 1935 3·2 per cent; and during the five years 1935–9 the total volume of exports was less than half that of the years 1925–9. Even the drawback granted at the end of 1935 on the duty paid on foreign wheat which entered into the exported flour made no contribution towards arresting the decline.

The main cause of the decline in the quantities exported in the middle and later 'thirties was the loss of the Irish trade after September 1932 through the operation of quota restrictions and an almost impossibly high duty of 5s. a sack. Up to that year Eire had been far and away the best market, accounting for over 125,000 tons annually, or well over half of total exports. The loss of trade was equivalent to the output of about four large mills, with a total capacity of about 480 sacks. This loss was most keenly felt in the Liverpool area, where considerable short time was suffered in consequence, and one mill was finally (in 1937) forced to close down. It should at the same time be observed that the Irish market, while it was lost to Great Britain, continued to be substantially served by one of the British firms. Ranks Ltd. hold a very considerable interest in the Irish milling industry.

EXPORTS OF WHEATMEAL AND FLOUR
Thousand tons

Year				Tons	Year				Tons
1924	.	.	.	319	1932	.	.	.	239
1925	.	.	.	344	1933	.	.	.	155
1926	.	.	.	202	1934	.	.	.	145
1927	.	.	.	209	1935	.	.	.	130
1928	.	.	.	219	1936	.	.	.	118
1929	.	.	.	216	1937	.	.	.	78
1930	.	.	.	201	1938	.	.	.	106
1931	.	.	.	206	1939	.	.	.	81

U.K. Statistical Abstract,

In the middle 'twenties, when competition between British mills was at its height and the countries of Europe were still engaged in the process of restoring their war-damaged economies, substantial quantities of British flour were purchased, particularly by Germany, Poland, and Russia. As their home industries became rehabilitated these three countries dropped out of the market, but exports to Europe were maintained to a certain extent through the negotiation of trade agreements with the Scandinavian countries, which, though they took continuously diminishing quantities, accounted for about a third of our total exports during the five years preceding the outbreak of war.

But the main part of the United Kingdom's export trade in flour —and it should again be emphasized that this trade is small, representing in 1937 about one-fortieth of production—has gone in recent years to European communities in territories which are too small to carry out flour-milling for themselves on an economic basis. Thus, over a quarter of our exports during the year 1936 went to the British West Indies (including British Guiana and British Honduras), and nearly half the total exports were shipped to the British West Indies and to the Canaries, Madeira, the Channel Islands, and Gibraltar.

Liverpool is the major exporting centre. In 1937 half of the export trade was conducted through this port. The proportions of flour shipped from different British ports were as follows:

Liverpool	49·7%
London	17·3%
Hull	16·1%
Bristol	4·9%
Leith	4·4%
Glasgow	0·1%
Other ports	7·5%
Total	100·0%

Broomhall Corn Trade Year Book.

A note may be added on the foreign trade in the by-products of flour-milling—bran and wheatings. Since 1932 the United Kingdom has exported only very small quantities, nearly the whole of which go to Eire and the Channel Islands. Imports of wheat feed, on the other hand, have exceeded imports of flour in quantity, in the ratio of about 3 : 2 in the five years before the war, Argentina being the main supplier, contributing about half. The 1935–9 figures are as follows:

Thousand tons

	Imports	Exports
1935	596·9	3·7
1936	672·3	3·3
1937	614·0	3·4
1938	598·8	7·9
1939	555·6	16·5

Annual Statement of Trade.

The suggestion has sometimes been put forward by millers, particularly during the reign of cheap European flour imports, that if imports of flour were curtailed, greater quantities of home-produced wheat feed would become available and reduce our dependence on imported supplies. It is instructive to see the weight which should be attached to this argument. In the years 1935–9 average annual imports of flour totalled just under 400,000 tons. Had this quantity of flour been manufactured at home, about 170,000 tons of wheat feed would have been released, compared with average imports over the same period of some 600,000 tons. On the other hand, the argument used by representatives of the importers against this suggestion, namely, that British millers were exporting large quantities of wheat feed, is amply refuted by the official figures. The feed is exported for the most part only during the harvest months when there is an abundance of animal foodstuffs.

THE IMPACT OF THE WAR

The experience of the Government in flour and bread control during the First World War enabled early prearranged steps to be taken in respect of control in 1939. Whereas in the war of 1914–18 control of mills did not come into force until the third year of war, plans were prepared in detail well before September 1939, and stocks of wheat were laid by soon after the possibility of war became evident. Preliminary preparation was, in fact, begun already in 1935, when inquiries into production, storage, and distribution of food supplies were launched. At the end of 1936 the Board of Trade decided upon the establishment of a Food (Defence Plans) Department (Director, Sir H. L. French) which issued its report at the end of the following year on the most practical forms of control for the principal foodstuffs. The Department made plans for controlling and requisitioning stocks of cereals and flour, among other commodities, immediately war should break out. In 1938 heavy purchases of wheat were made on behalf of the Government to form a reserve of grain. At the beginning of 1939 the Board of Trade appointed a Cereals Advisory (Defence) Committee, composed of representatives of the Corn and Cattle Feed trades, Flour Importers, Millers, and Farmers, to advise on arrangements for the supply, control, and distribution of wheat, flour, and allied products in the event of war.

On the outbreak of war controlling agencies were set up by the Board of Trade to deal with the various stages of flour manufacture from the purchase of wheat to the distribution of flour to bakers. The Cereals Control Board became responsible for supplies of all imported cereals and cereal products, for the distribution of wheat, both home-grown and imported, to millers and of all cereals and cereal products for human consumption. It was organized in a number of Area Committees, composed of members of the grain trade, operating from each of the principal grain ports—London, Liverpool, Bristol, Hull, Glasgow, Leith, and Belfast—each of which served the surrounding counties. The Cereals Import Committee was set up to carry out the actual purchase of imported cereals and cereal products. Its direction came from, and it was responsible to, the Cereals Control Board. Its personnel was made up of grain traders, flour-millers, and importers. The Flour Mills Control Committee was an advisory committee in connexion with the administration of the various measures of control over mills. It was composed of millers representing all the interests in the industry, including the large millers, the C.W.S., and the smaller millers. In June 1940 these three bodies became divisions of the Ministry of Food.

Control Orders were issued on the first day of war whereby all the grain and milling trades virtually became State-controlled. Prices of grain and flour were fixed, and their distribution regulated. The first Order controlling mills, by which all millers were required to obtain a licence, made it quite clear that control was to be complete. It laid down that the licence could 'condition the activities of the mill as to kinds and quantities of cereals to be milled, the kinds and quantities of products, the management of the mill or its machinery, the regulation of work and employment, and deliveries into and out of the mill'. All millers were now required to do was to mill such grain as they received; they made application to the Port Area Grain Committees for the type of wheat they required—strong, 'filler', or weak—and were supplied according to the classes of wheat available. Competition in the industry was now completely ruled out. Although the Government's financial agreement with the milling industry was not announced until nearly two years of war had passed, it was clear from the start that the remuneration which individual mills received from public funds in lieu of their normal trading profits was not to be determined by war-time output. The agreement, which was announced in October 1941, provided that the industry as a whole should receive the average profits made during the three pre-war years, provided output did not fall below pre-war production—an unlikely contingency. The apportioning of the payment to individual millers the Government left to the industry itself, which formed for the purpose a body known as the British Millers' Mutual Pool. This body worked out, according to a secret and complicated formula, the amount payable to each mill on the basis of pre-war earnings. It should be mentioned that the agreement related only to bread flours, biscuit and other flours fell outside its scope.

But although the industry had to function entirely on an agency or contractor basis for the Ministry of Food, and individual mills were unable to exercise any of the independent judgment and initiative which were so important in peace-time, particularly as regards buying on the wheat market, it did not suffer any drastic reorganization such as was experienced by many other industries during the war. There was no concentration. Nevertheless, the war gave rise to problems of organization within the industry, similar in many ways to those brought about during the First World War and equally likely to test the industry's solidarity and the strength of its leadership once war conditions disappeared.

The changes in the structure of the industry were brought about mainly by air-raid damage. The high degree of concentration of flour-milling capacity at the ports, which formed natural targets for the enemy's bombing offensives, made it inevitable that a number of mills should be destroyed or damaged, and that for the most part these should be the large dock mills. Trade papers stated that the capacity destroyed in the bombing raids of 1940 and 1941 was estimated at between 10 and 20 per cent of pre-war capacity, with the probable figure rather nearer the lower than the higher estimate. Where possible, of course, production was continued after repairs had been carried out, but in several cases the damage was irreparable. Nevertheless, output in the industry as a whole was maintained at such a level that at no time, even when bombing was at its height, was there any interruption in the supply of flour to bakers. The substantial stocks of flour which had been built up at the beginning of the war were partly responsible for the absence of any break in flour supply; and the raising of the extraction rate from the 70 per cent which was prescribed at the beginning of the war to 75 per cent in September 1941 produced an automatic increase in the supply of flour from a given quantity of wheat of just over 7 per cent. Six months later the rate was raised further to 85 per cent. The rest of the deficiency resulting from the destruction of important mills was made up by extended output on the part of other units, and particularly of the inland mills; in addition, a certain number of mills which had been allowed to run into disuse before the war as a result of the industry's rationalization policy were brought into commission during the early war period. The contribution of the inland mills to the total output of the industry showed a definite expansion over the pre-war figure.

This readjustment of production within the industry not unnaturally caused some apprehension in the trade that all that happened after decontrol in 1921, with units which had been enabled to expand their trade during the war continuing to produce at their war-time levels, and units whose trade had fallen through no fault of their own attempting to regain what they had lost, might be repeated after the relaxation of control. But with this distinction: that whereas in the First World War the big firms advanced in strength and consolidated their position, this time the advantage was with the smaller units. The possibility that changes brought about by war-time contingencies might have a disruptive and disintegrating effect on the trade after the war was sufficiently real for the leaders of the trade to issue a warning to prospective disturbers of the pre-war balance of the industry.

The grain trade had perhaps even more cause for apprehension for the post-war period. Its function during the war was reduced to that of a distributing agency, the buying of wheat being carried out by the Cereals Import Division, which, though it comprised certain representatives of the grain trade, was directed by Mr. J. V. Rank. Spokesmen of the grain trade voiced the fear that the withdrawal during the war of its function as grain-buyer in overseas markets would result in some permanent loss to the trade, and that the damage to its merchanting function would not be reparable. The experience of the industry during the First World War was similar; during the 'twenties and 'thirties its activities underwent a continuous decline, and there was no reason for it to expect any reversal of the trend or even any stabilization at the pre-war position.

The industry linked with flour-milling at the other end of the process, the baking trade, suffered comparatively little from the effects of the war, and, in fact, remained more or less frozen at its pre-war position. The pre-war period, as has been mentioned, witnessed the gradual albeit slow decline of the small baker in the face of the growth of larger machine bakeries. In numbers the small baker was very greatly predominant, and it seemed that a very long time must elapse before he was crowded out altogether. Nevertheless, the trend was unmistakable. The importance of a dispersal policy in relation to supplies of such a vital commodity as bread during the war kept in being these smaller concerns, and many of them, under war-time regulation of prices and margins and the increased demand for their products, considerably improved their position. The trade as a whole strengthened its organization, and the membership of the National Association of Master Bakers, Confectioners, and Caterers rose appreciably. It established a research fund of £25,000. Before the war there was little or no co-operation between the milling and baking trades as regards research into the suitability of flour for baking or the improvement of baking methods. All the research that was carried out was conducted by the millers, and although much was achieved by them which was of direct benefit to the baking trade, the latter not unnaturally could not and certainly did not expect the millers' research body to direct its efforts to anything but the improvement of the milling trade, whether or not the baking trade benefited thereby. Large individual baking concerns carried out examinations of flour, but the bulk of the trade clearly was not in a position to do anything of the kind. The establishment of a research body devoted to the interests of bakers should do much to remove the inferiority complex which seems to have characterized the attitude of the baking trade as a whole in its relations with millers, and to further improvement in flour quality as well as in baking technique.

So much for the changes in the organization of the milling and allied industries during the war. Considerable changes, of course, took place as far as supplies and production were concerned.

Figures of wheat supplies were not available during the war, but it is possible to arrive at some idea of the course of events from unofficial and official statements.[1] Stocks of wheat at the beginning of the war were high, and consisted of high-quality grain, and throughout the first two years of war imports were maintained actually above the normal pre-war level. Meanwhile, home production expanded rapidly; the 1942 wheat acreage was about 35 per cent, and the 1943 acreage nearly 70 per cent, above the pre-war figure. The increased home wheat production in 1942 made it possible for wheat imports to slacken off as from the middle of that year, when shipping was diverted to military operations. Unofficial trade estimates of the amount of English wheat being issued to mills at the ports at the end of 1942 ranged from 35 to 40 per cent, and at the end of 1943 millers' grists in most parts of the country were composed of 60 per cent of home-produced grain. The employment of these large proportions of soft home-grown wheats—and with the added disadvantage of wet harvests—necessitated an increase in grain-drying plant at flour-mills, but even this was not sufficient to cope with the home-grown grain. The need for an increase in drying facilities for the home crop had been recognized as early as 1932, when the Wheat Act came into operation, and millers were urged to install drying plants. But the response was meagre, no doubt because those millers who had the necessary capital for installations of this kind were not themselves vitally concerned with the milling of English wheat. At the beginning of the war a scheme was drawn up for building fifteen silos and drying plants with a total capacity of 75,000 tons; by 1944 the majority were completed, and use was also made of the drying facilities provided by distilleries.

At the outbreak of war the futures markets in London and Liverpool were closed and the purchase of cereals was taken over entirely by the Government. Prices hardened immediately on the declaration

[1] This paragraph was written before the official war-time statistics were published. Actual war-time figures were:

	'000 tons			
	1939	1940	1943	1945
Home harvest	1,645	1,641	3,447	2,176
Imports of wheat and flour	5,671	6,331	3,975	4,092
Total Available Supplies	7,316	7,972	7,422	6,268

of war—quotations for U.S. wheat jumped from 56 to 79 cents a bushel in the first week, equivalent to a rise of 41 per cent—though prices had been falling steadily down to August; and, except for a sharp fall in the spring of 1940, prices maintained a steady rise throughout the course of the war. Already quite early in the war United States prices advanced well beyond the dollar-a-bushel level which in peace-time marked prosperity to growers, and by the summer of 1944 prices were about two and a half times those ruling at the corresponding period five years earlier. The Canadian Wheat Board guaranteed to growers a price of $1·25 compared with the previous guaranteed price of $0·90. Nevertheless, North American wheat prices at no time reached the levels attained during the war of 1914–18, when supplies were relatively scarcer. In Great Britain prices to growers also advanced considerably. Against the pre-war guaranteed price of 10s. a cwt., prices for the 1942 crop ranged between 16s. and 17s. 8d. a cwt.

The changes in the wheat situation as the war went on obviously had their effects on the quality of the flour. At the outbreak of war it was decided to make no change in the pre-war rate of extraction, which was fixed by order at a minimum of 70 per cent, and this rate remained unchanged throughout the first two years of war. The continued production of such flour was made possible by the huge stocks of wheat and flour which had been built up. The main change of practice in the manufacture of flour brought into force at the beginning of the war was the abolition of different grades of flour, only straight-run being permitted, except under special authority from the Board of Trade. Millers, in fact, encountered no special difficulties during the early part of the war. Though the wheats were not of their own choosing, the greater part of the grain issued was Manitoba wheat of good quality; and the flour was often superior in quality to the pre-war product. Temporary difficulties were met with in the shortage of the silk bolting cloth used for sieving the flour during the later stages of manufacture, which was normally imported from Switzerland. But in 1940 manufacture was undertaken in this country by milling engineers in conjunction with silk manufacturers.

During the early part of the war there was continual pressure from certain quarters of Parliament and the Press for the compulsory manufacture of flour of 100 per cent or near 100 per cent extraction. At the end of 1940 the Ministry of Food provided for the manufacture of a national wheat meal flour of 85 per cent extraction and launched an advertising campaign to encourage its consumption. Demand did not, however, at any time after the initial period reach proportions indicative of popularity; the highest percentage of total flour deliveries quoted was 7 per cent. But an increase in the supply of vitamin B to the public was recognized as of great value under the stress of war-time conditions and the loss of other articles of diet. Arrangements were made for the addition of synthetic vitamin B to the flour in 1940, but there was a good deal of criticism of such a policy, and the true facts were somewhat obscured. The extraction rate was raised compulsorily to 75 per cent in September 1941, and to 85 per cent in March 1942, and the question of synthetic additions was automatically dropped.

In contrast with the position during the early war period, millers were faced with distinctly difficult problems on the introduction of the 85 per cent extraction rate, since this change coincided with an increase in the quantities of soft home wheat issued. By the end of 1942 from 35 to 40 per cent of English wheat was being used, on the estimate quoted, and by 1943, some 60 per cent. Much was done by millers, milling engineers, and cereal chemists to improve the baking quality of the new flour; and an extension of the use of 'improving' agencies was necessary. By experiment and by modification of the existing milling process, and in some cases by the installation of additional conditioning plant its quality was gradually raised. Further problems faced the millers in 1943, when dilution of the flour by non-wheaten products was introduced. In view of all the circumstances, the quality of the flour manufactured during the war was excellent. The controlled price from October 1942 onwards was 38s. 3d. a sack—a stable price of bread being maintained by subsidy.

As the table on page 77 shows, the consumption of flour per head of the civilian population increased decidedly after the introduction of general rationing; for the years from 1941 to 1943 it was running at around 19 per cent above the levels of 1934–8.

THE MAIN PROBLEMS OF THE INDUSTRY

Perhaps the main problem with which the flour-milling industry has been confronted in past years—one which was already becoming apparent before the First World War, is declining or, at best, stable consumption. Here is a trade which caters almost exclusively for the home market and has no hope of extending its production in the export field. In the short run, perhaps, its prospects may be fairly favourable, for the general lowering of the national standard of living is likely for some years to force up bread consumption. Or, at least, to force it up so far as supplies permit; for it is by no means certain that the world supply position will allow even war-time levels of consumption in this country to be maintained. But in any case, in the long run, as standards of living recover and projected increases in the supply of dairy and market-garden produce in this country materialize, there is little doubt that flour consumption will fall still further. Absolute consumption may not show a decline for many years, since the *per capita* figures will be masked by a rise in the adult population; but once the population reaches its peak a cut in output is likely to be necessary. With this prospect before it, the validity of the trade's arguments for maintaining the co-operation existing since 1929 is undeniable. 'The "mutual" spirit,' as one spokesman of the trade said during the war, 'must be kept alive.'

In contrast to the outlook for flour-milling itself, there is every prospect of an increase in the demand for the products of the pro-vender-milling industry, to cater for the requirements of the poultry and cattle industries, both of which are likely ultimately to expand. It has been seen that most of the large mills comprise provender-mill sections as well as flour-milling departments, and this may enable any future slackening off of flour output to be taken up without any great disturbance by increasing production on the other side. It seems reasonable to expect that production in the two industries will be to a large extent complementary.

Another problem which was already looming up many years before 1939 was the decline of freedom in world wheat markets. The years between the two wars saw a number of attempts on the part of the surplus wheat-producing countries to regulate production or distribution so as to maintain a reasonably steady price-level; and in each of these countries the State was forced by the extreme depression in world market prices to come to the aid of its wheat producers in some form or other. The respective Governments became the spokesmen for their wheat producers, and the war saw an enlargement of the part they played in world wheat affairs. Increasing State influence on wheat production in individual producer countries and increasing collaboration between them may bring as a natural corollary a demand for State purchase in the consumer countries. State purchase is, of course, far from a new idea. Advocates of State trading in wheat and other foodstuffs gave extensive evidence before the Royal Commission on Food Prices in 1924, which was carefully weighed. The Commission made clear (Paragraphs 328 to 333) its objections on economic, political, diplomatic, and administrative grounds, and though they said that 'in view of . . . the tendency towards greater combination on the part of producers and distributors the question is still to some extent an open one and calls for more scientific and dispassionate inquiry than it has yet received', they could not recommend such a 'hazardous experiment'. The question again came into prominence in the later 'twenties, State Import Boards being advocated by the Labour Party for the bulk purchase of staple commodities in order to eliminate short-term fluctuations of price and to protect the home producer by the regulation of imports. The earlier proposals for assisting the home wheat-grower also threatened the miller with undue interference with his freedom

4

in the wheat market, though, as has been seen, the final arrangements imposed in practice no such restrictions. All these straws showed which way the wind was blowing. State purchase of wheat would mean the limitation of the miller's activities to processing and distribution, the costs of his materials being known and controlled. It was stated in evidence before the 1924 Royal Commission that a substantial part of millers' earnings were derived from judicious wheat-buying, and that manufacturing profits were often negligible or even negative. This was, of course, at a time when the trade was going through an extremely difficult period; but throughout the inter-war period the wheat market was undergoing continuous and often wide fluctuations, and the prosperity of individual millers could not fail to be closely associated with the success or otherwise of their operations on the future markets.

Another difficulty which confronts the industry in relation to its supplies of raw materials lies in the future production of home-grown wheat. This question will also affect the relative importance of port and country mills. There is a general recognition that home agriculture will assume a greater importance in the supply of wheat to millers than it did in pre-war years, and the importance of retaining the country mill is clear. Nevertheless, it is the opinion of many port millers that even if home-grown wheat is used to a greater extent, the comparative advantages of a port location will not be significantly lessened, and that the division of output between port and country mill is not likely to be greatly changed. The trade is firm in declaring that there is no case for a 'coddled system of protection' for the home wheat-grower. There is a danger that if too much home-grown wheat is produced and its use forced on the milling industry the quality of the flour produced will be unable to compete on level terms with flour manufactured by millers in the surplus wheat-producing countries, and that the home miller will have to receive some kind of protection as compensation for his compulsory use of English wheat. Any uneconomic encouragement of home wheat production of this kind will tend inevitably to lead to the adoption of artificial and rigidly controlled systems of flour and bread production and prices, such as were in operation between the wars in many European countries.

If home wheat production is to be increased, the long-advocated improvement in grading and marketing should also be undertaken. The belated provision of drying plants and storage silos in the main wheat-growing areas during the war was a beginning. Such plants should enable the home crop to be marketed more uniformly throughout the season and to reach the buyer in better condition than formerly. But the fifteen silos built during the war have a combined capacity which can deal with only about one-eighth of the quantity of home-grown wheat used by the milling industry before the war, and clearly much more needs to be done.

Before 1939, as has been seen, the importance of the home crop increased from 9 per cent in 1932–3 to about 16 per cent in 1936–7 of the total quantity of wheat used for flour manufacture, while during the war the proportion increased to over 50 per cent. The latter figure can obviously not be maintained indefinitely in the post-war period: it is far too high for satisfactory milling results. In seeking to estimate the maximum proportion of English wheat which could be taken up by the milling industry without unduly lowering the pre-war quality of flour—other things, notably price, being equal —perhaps the best guide is the fact that from 1934 to 1937 an average of 6 per cent of total wheat supplies was obtained from European countries growing wheats of similar strength to those in Great Britain. These imports might well be replaced by home-grown wheat without any prejudice to the quality of the flours produced. This would bring up the contribution of English wheat to about a fifth of total supplies.

Another question which must vitally affect the trade in the future is the type of flour which the public will demand and the possible regulation of its nutritive content. On the score of public taste, what evidence exists points to an overwhelming desire to return to white bread and flour as soon as circumstances permit, and in milling circles it is confidently assumed that in the absence of any counter-regulation the demand for white flour will not be significantly different from what it was pre-war. The need for increased supplies of wheat feed for cattle-feeding will also involve a return to a lower extraction rate. During the war a great deal of experiment and research was carried out in regard to the vitamin content of flour, and it was established that 70 per cent of the total B_1 content of the grain remains in its germ end even when the germ itself has been removed. These researches point to the possibility of producing a flour which would have the necessary nutritional qualities while retaining the keeping and baking qualities and the good colour associated with white flour. The evolution of such a method is regarded as a major field for research, and already during the war much was done along these lines; certain changes in technique were put into practice and minor modifications of plant made in a number of mills. Even if there is to be no public regulation on this score, it is likely that public consciousness of food values and competition from vitaminized North American flours will force certain vitamin standards in home-milled flours. The M.M.A. had already arranged before the war for the manufacture of synthetic B_1, but whether this will be needed in the flours made in future is not certain.

A further issue which confronted the industry between the wars, though at no very close quarters, is that of the nationalization of flour-milling. It is to be questioned whether the main purpose of nationalization of an industry—ultimate benefit to the consumer— would in this case be achieved. The trade has already organized itself on technically efficient lines, and achieved this without noticeable help from protective duties or subsidies. While milling profits have been high, they have been based first and foremost on a high degree of efficiency in machinery and organization and through experienced buying in world wheat markets. If they are to be lowered, it can be done as effectively through direct control of millers' margins as through transfer to public ownership. State control of home and imported wheat prices and supplies may also give the Government a hold over the industry's policy even under private ownership; though the experience of a number of European countries in recent years hardly suggests that such measures are likely to prove desirable in themselves, or to reduce the cost or improve the quality of service offered to the public. Whatever the means, it is at any rate clear that measures other than nationalization can be found to safeguard the public against monopolistic exploitation: and, so long as private enterprise in flour-milling continues to provide its present high level of technical efficiency, it is difficult to see what further case for nationalization remains.

CHAPTER II

THE WHITE FISH INDUSTRY

Introduction and conclusion by R. K. KELSALL: sections on Aberdeen by Professor H. HAMILTON: on Grimsby and Fleetwood by Dr. F. A. WELLS and K. C. EDWARDS: and on Hull by R. K. KELSALL.

GENERAL INTRODUCTION

IT is customary to divide the fishing industry of Great Britain into two main branches, concerned with herring and white fish respectively. The present chapter only relates to the latter; nor does it attempt to cover, even in general terms, the whole of the white fish industry. Inshore fishing (which in 1935 accounted for about 1 per cent of the total weight of white fish landings in England and Wales, and about 15 per cent in Scotland) is not discussed; while, within the category of deep-sea fishing, attention is concentrated on the fishing based on the four main ports—Hull, Grimsby, Aberdeen, and Fleetwood. A separate section of the chapter is devoted to each of these centres, and the introductory and concluding sections relate very largely to that part of the industry which they represent. The broad justification for such a policy lies in the fact of the heavy concentration of the white fish industry in these particular centres, the four ports between them accounting for over 83 per cent of the total weight of British landings of white fish in this country in 1935.

The industry with which we are here concerned is one the importance of which, relatively to other British industries, it is extraordinarily difficult to assess. Population Census and Ministry of Labour figures do not form a suitable basis of comparison in this case, and fishing is not an industry from the point of view of the Census of Production. In fact, despite the excellence of the statistical material relating to the fishing industry as a whole provided annually by the Ministry of Agriculture and Fisheries and by the Fishery Board for Scotland, no really satisfactory index of the relative importance of the white fish industry exists. Even the Sea-Fish Commission was unable to discover the approximate numbers of fishmongers and proprietors of fish-and-chip shops in Great Britain, far less the amount spent by the British public on white fish in its various shapes and forms.

Some comparisons between the white fish industry's position in the last years of peace and in the years before 1914 can, however, be made, and the main points of change are generally agreed upon. The total weight of landings of white fish in Great Britain had risen by over one-third between 1913 and 1938. The proportion of the total represented by fish caught in distant waters had, however, risen from about 20 per cent at the earlier date to about 52 per cent at the later date; and this 52 per cent was shared by Iceland and by still more distant grounds in the ratio of 3 : 5. This change in the relative significance of the various fishing-grounds was inseparably connected, either as cause, as symptom, or as effect, with most of the other major changes experienced by the industry during the inter-war period. A brief catalogue of such closely related changes will make this clear.

(1) The decline in the weight of catch per unit of fishing power, already noticeable in the pre-1914 period but becoming much more obvious (except during the first post-war years) later on, led both to improvements in gear and to increasing resort to more distant grounds not yet over-fished.

(2) In the exploitation of the more distant grounds Hull trawler-owners played a predominant part. Hence the spectacular increase in the proportion of total British landings of white fish credited to Hull, from 12½ per cent in 1913 to 37 per cent in 1938.

(3) The fish landed from these distant waters tended to consist of the commoner and rougher species. Hence cod from forming 31½ per cent of the weight of British white fish landings in Great Britain in 1913, came to form 46 per cent in 1938; in fact, while the weight of cod caught showed a substantial (99 per cent) increase, the weight of plaice, halibut, whiting and most other kinds of white fish (the principal exceptions being haddock and hake) showed a decline.

(4) These increased landings of cod were partly disposed of through fish-and-chip shops, and were largely instrumental in bringing about a very large increase in the number of such undertakings.

(5) This new, or at any rate greatly enlarged, outlet for the cheaper kinds of fish only, however, absorbed part of the increased landings, the repercussions of which were necessarily felt throughout the industry. Thus it was said that the flooding of markets with fish of inferior quality and freshness was bringing fish in general into disrepute with consumers of discernment; and the increasing unprofitableness of the 'producing' side of the industry was widely believed to be associated, in part at least, with the exploitation of the newer fishing-grounds. Long-distance trawler-owners claim, however, that they have tapped new markets and brought fish within reach of the poorer consumer. Their product, they say, does not compete to any serious extent with better quality fish.

(6) The increasing unprofitability of fishing in the early 1930's led to the passing of the Sea-Fishing Industry Act, 1933, one of the results of which was the promulgation of several Orders, one regulating and restricting landings of white fish from other countries,

while another made compulsory a restriction of fishing in far distant waters during the summer months which had already been arranged voluntarily amongst Hull trawler-owners.

(7) Many of the implications of increasing concentration on distant-water fishing were at first local (i.e. restricted to Hull and, to a smaller extent, Grimsby), but resulted in tendencies which seemed bound in time to become more general. These included the tendency to fillet fish before sending it inland, thus reducing the transport costs of an article of low value in relation to its weight, making it more readily marketable amongst fish-friers, and releasing larger and larger quantities of waste for conversion into fish manure; and the tendency to build larger and faster vessels, resulting in a marked rise in the initial capital required by would-be trawler-owners.

These, then, were some of the changes which had taken place in the industry during the inter-war period. Yet when the Sea-Fish Commission made a study of it in 1935, there were still many features dating from an earlier period. Excluding Hull, 88 per cent of the trawlers were more than fifteen years old, and 35 per cent were actually over twenty-five years old (by including Hull, the corresponding percentages are reduced to 79 and 31 respectively). No less than 28 per cent of all trawlers were owned by persons owning less than five apiece, nearly 12½ per cent were owned on a one-man-one-vessel basis. The share of the net earnings of fishing voyages, which formed the bulk of the remuneration of skippers and mates and part of the remuneration of other members of the crew, was still supposed to be determined in part by those sections of the Merchant Shipping Act of 1894 laying down rules for ascertaining the profits of such voyages; in practice many of these provisions were apparently often ignored, and gross earnings were commonly reduced in ways not envisaged in the Act before the sharing took place, with the result that 'settling sheet' grievances were widespread. Before reaching the final consumer the fish had still normally been the subject of dealings in a market at the port of landing attended by port wholesalers, in an inland market attended by other wholesalers, and in a retail shop. Though in these and other essential respects the structure of the industry had often not fundamentally changed, the Sea-Fish Commission, by securing more accurate information than hitherto, made possible a closer examination of certain features of the industry. This was especially so in matters of accountancy, and some of the broad results of the investigations of their honorary accountants may usefully be summarized here.

Of the main items of expense involved in the actual catching of the fish, coal tended, for voyages in near and middle waters, to absorb 27 or 28 per cent of gross earnings (22 per cent in the case of

Hull); remuneration of the crew 25 to 31 per cent; upkeep 22 to 25 per cent; and other expenses 20 to 23 per cent. In long-distance voyages coal absorbed a smaller proportion of gross earnings (19 to 21 per cent); so did upkeep (19 per cent), presumably partly because the vessels were newer. The most striking difference between voyages in near and middle, by comparison with those in distant waters, was, however, the greater profitability of the latter. Thus in Hull, vessels engaged in voyages of the former type showed, on an average, a net profit forming only 5 per cent of gross earnings, as against 14 per cent in the latter case, in 1934; while the corresponding percentages for Grimsby were nil and 6. The average annual net profits per vessel of Hull and Grimsby boats trawling in distant waters, though showing the same general trend over the period 1929–34 (a sharp fall, followed by a recovery in the last two years, but not to the 1929 level) were invariably smaller in the case of Grimsby; over the six-year period as a whole they sufficed, in the view of the Commission, to yield a reasonable return on capital sunk in Hull vessels, but not in Grimsby ones. The corresponding position for vessels trawling in near and middle waters was a good deal worse; over the six-year period as a whole only Hull and Fleetwood showed a net profit, Grimsby and Aberdeen showing a net loss.

Investigation by the Commission's accountants suggested that those performing the merchanting function were not making large profits either. Thus port wholesalers had increased considerably in numbers; the average volume of fish handled by such a wholesaler had declined in Aberdeen and Grimsby, but risen in Hull; and net profit expressed as a percentage of turnover was only, in 1934, 0·1 for the major ports excluding Hull, and 2·3 for Hull. Little capital was required to set up in the business; and this was regarded as a factor contributing towards the general instability of the port markets. In the main inland wholesale markets, Billingsgate merchants dealing as principals showed, in 1934, an average net profit of 0·7 per cent of turnover, those dealing partly as principals and partly as commission agents 2 per cent, and those dealing only as commission agents a net loss of 0·5 per cent; while Glasgow merchants in the first two of these categories showed net profits averaging 1 per cent of turnover. The average volume of trade transacted by wholesalers in inland markets was very much greater than in the case of port wholesalers; and, at least in the provincial markets, the stances had apparently tended to remain in the hands of particular families for long periods, and the number of wholesalers to remain fairly constant. In retail business, an apparent decline in the number of fishmongers, and an increase in the number of fish-friers, had taken place in recent years; both were, on the whole, fields of small-scale business; the net profit of fishmongers whose accounts were examined averaged 2·4 per cent of turnover in 1934, but it did not prove possible to secure adequate figures for fish-friers.

To many people, an even more alarming feature of the merchanting situation was the wide and increasing margin between fish prices at the opposite ends of the chain of distribution. Despite the qualifications they attached to it, the statement in the Sea-Fish Commission's report that white fish, unheaded, roughly doubled in cost, and trebled when headed, on its way from the port to the consumer, seemed to suggest that the most urgent reforms needed in the industry were on the marketing side.

Here, then, was an industry in which no section seemed able to secure reasonable profits; in which the failure to secure an adequate return on capital made it impossible to modernize a fleet in large part superannuated; in which prices showed wide day-to-day fluctuations, provided an inadequate margin over expense to entrepreneurs and merchants at all stages, and yet were high enough to make fish seem, on the whole, an expensive commodity by comparison with its rivals. Expenses were clearly destined to go up rather than down, at least as far as the catching of the fish was concerned; for coal formed a very material element in cost, and, as over-fishing became more serious, the catch per unit of fishing-power at least in near and middle waters was bound to decline further. Moreover, the only people who had found a way out of these difficulties—the long-distance trawler-owners of Hull and Grimsby—had done so by means which, it was widely believed, had themselves contributed towards the general deterioration in the fortunes of the industry. The Sea-Fish Commission's main recommendations to meet this situation were that existing Orders regulating foreign imports, restricting fishing in northern waters, prescribing size limits of fish for sale, and regulating mesh sizes should, with certain modifications, be continued; and that reorganization of the industry should take place along certain lines. The main features of the reorganization were to be the setting up of a Development Commission, consisting of three persons independent of the industry, with powers to register the units operating in each section of the industry; to licence port wholesalers and possibly fishing vessels also; to consider schemes put forward by approved organizations representing different sections, and forward them to the Ministers with a view to their being made compulsory; to initiate other schemes; and to make grants from the proceeds of registration fees for approved purposes. Existing associations within the industry, both local and national, were to be approved and encouraged to extend; and a Central Board, representative of the different sections of the industry, was to be set up and ultimately to prepare a marketing policy.

The Sea-Fish Industry Act which finally became law in June 1938 provided for the reorganization of the White Fish Industry much on the lines suggested by the Commission. A permanent White Fish Commission was to be established with suitable powers in the matter of registration, of submitting marketing schemes to poll, of setting up a marketing board and of initiating special co-operative arrangements for inshore fishermen who could not readily be brought within the scope of schemes intended for trawler-owners. The Munich crisis and subsequent outbreak of war prevented these arrangements from coming into operation, except in one respect. The Act provided for the establishment of a Joint Council for assisting and advising the Commission in the discharge of its functions. This body, the White Fish Industry Joint Council, was set up and continued until 1943 with its task of bringing together the various sections of the trade and attempting to formulate a common policy. The Council included representatives of the trawler-owners, merchants and processors, fishmongers and fish-friers, and the difficulty of reconciling their conflicting interests soon became apparent. There were conflicts even within the sections. For instance, the Hull trawler-owners held themselves aloof, feeling that they had little to gain and perhaps much to lose by pooling their interests with those of less progressive people. There was dissension, too, on the question of marking fish according to origin, the proposal being favoured by Grimsby but opposed by Hull. Disagreement also arose over the policy of restricting sailings to northern waters during the summer months; the fishmongers and fish-friers regarded this as contrary to their interests and were supported in their attitude by some of the trawler-owners. The Council did, however, show a united front on one occasion: they protested vigorously when the zoning scheme was introduced for economizing transport under war conditions. Nobody liked zoning, which interferes with normal trade connexions; but the fishing industry, like others, was forced to accept it.

It must, of course, be recognized that the Council was severely handicapped by war conditions. The whole fishing industry experienced a large measure of disorganization incidental to the loss of personnel, the requisitioning of the best and most modern trawlers and the introduction of a Government plan (subsequently abandoned) altering the normal channels of distribution. War-time conditions were, however, so abnormal, involving as they did the virtual elimination of long-distance trawling from Hull and Grimsby, that there is probably no need to discuss them here, beyond mentioning that control of the prices of most classes of fish was, after considerable delay, introduced by the Government in 1941.

Before proceeding to the separate sections on individual ports, some account of labour conditions can be given. Before the recent war, the sea-going personnel of the trawling fleet numbered about

20,000. Conditions of employment at Grimsby and Fleetwood were similar to those to be described in the Aberdeen section, and the same grievances were expressed. Hull, as in other respects, was more progressive. One of the main complaints was of fluctuations in earnings, which in the case of skippers and mates depended largely on the net earnings of the voyage; other members of the crew got a basic wage and a share in net earnings, but the men were anxious to secure an increase in the former so that their wages would become more stable. Irregular employment was a serious problem. The best boats were always fully employed, but others were often laid up, and since the engagement of skipper and men is terminable at twenty-four hours' notice, employment for many was precarious. The trade also fluctuates seasonally with consequent repercussions on employment. Besides offering worse prospects of continuous employment the old trawlers have poor accommodation for the crew. Under war conditions the industry was forced to rely on these old vessels, so that the fishermen who remained, besides being exposed to greater risks, had to live under conditions that were being condemned before the war.

Trade unionism has made considerable progress (e.g. in Grimsby) among trawler-men in recent years through the efforts of the Transport and General Workers' Union, and it is interesting to note that many of the skippers and mates are members, as well as their crews.

Besides the fishermen, the trawler-owners employ a considerable amount of labour on the docks, mainly for unloading the boats. The men so engaged are called fish lumpers and form a class of labour distinct from the ordinary docker, who deals with general cargo. Lumpers are engaged by the day, and though rates are fairly good (10s. to 20s. pre-war), the worker, in normal times, can never be sure of making a full week.[1] The men turn up at the fish dock in the early morning and wait about on the chance of getting a ship. Before the war the Union was rapidly increasing its membership among the lumpers and was trying to improve conditions of employment and especially its regularity. It is claimed that as landings can now be forecast three or four days in advance it would not be a difficult matter to determine the labour required, also in advance. This system would at least obviate much waste of time. Registration would also help in eliminating the fringe of casual workers from the occupation. Hull had done much to reduce casual labour in the trade before the war. But it was not until 1942, when the need to economize labour had become so urgent, that a registration scheme was adopted at other ports. It is administered by the trawler-owners, the Union,

---

[1] Where pooling arrangements have been introduced during the war, this position has, of course, been altered. In Hull, for instance, the minimum weekly wage is at present £4.

and the Ministry of Labour. This war-time experiment may provide the experience for organization on a bigger scale later on.

The Act of 1938 contained provisions for the protection of fishermen paid wholly or in part by a share in the catch. But what the fishing industry appears to need for dealing with its labour problems successfully is a joint industrial council. The indispensable conditions for making such a body effective are now much nearer to being realized than was the case a few years ago. The workers have greatly strengthened their organization and the employers in the various sections are showing signs of greater cohesion too. Fishing will probably always be a risky trade, economically as well as physically; but everything should be done that can be done to diminish the risks of both kinds. If the problems involved in this task are not met, the industry may well have difficulty in the future in maintaining an adequate supply of efficient labour.

ABERDEEN

The White Fish Industry occupies a major place in the economic activities of Aberdeen, and indeed of that whole area of North-east Scotland. Before the war the trawler fleet of the port employed 2,834 men and boys, and if one includes fish merchants, coopers, gutters, packers, and others directly concerned in the industry, the total employment reaches the figure of 9,065. This is the highest employment figure of any industry in Aberdeen. The importance of white fishing to the city, however, does not end there, for besides the ancillary occupations many other trades like grocers, and shopkeepers of all kinds, as well as many professional people, are indirectly connected with the industry. It is difficult to give any estimate, but it would be no exaggeration to say that the fortunes of close on half the population are bound up with the prosperity of this industry.

The extensive trawling industry of Aberdeen is comparatively new, dating from the eighties of last century, when steam trawling was introduced. In March 1882 Aberdeen's first steam trawler—a second-hand wooden paddle-boat of 28 tons and 50 h.p., purchased in Dublin for £1,500—commenced to fish in Aberdeen Bay, thus inaugurating one of the most important eras in the history of the port.

This event indeed marks the commencement of a period of fundamental change in the organization of white fishing in Scotland. Hitherto, white fishing had been conducted entirely by sail boats, and with the exception of a few sailing trawlers the method employed was 'lining'. At first, steam trawling made little headway, partly because of the inadequacy of the boats and partly because of the lack of fishermen skilled in trawling and with knowledge of the fishing-grounds. But by 1888 these difficulties had been more or less surmounted, and thereafter progress was rapid and continuous. In 1892 there were 118 steam trawlers working in Scottish waters and of that number 86 landed at Aberdeen; in 1902 the figures were 233 and 156; and in 1912, 322 and 230 respectively.

The introduction of steam power into the fishing fleet effected a complete revolution in the organization of the industry. Specialization and concentration were the most obvious results. White fishing became a highly organized business carried on by steam trawlers and liners. Moreover, it became concentrated at Aberdeen. The reasons for this are not far to seek. Being larger and of greater tonnage than the old sailing-boats, steam trawlers required suitable harbour accommodation, which the many small creeks around the coast were incapable of providing. Aberdeen was the only port on the east coast with such accommodation. Moreover, the port had good railway facilities, and this was of great importance to the expanding fresh fish trade.

Nearness to the fishing-grounds, and good harbour and railway connexions were doubtless the initial advantages possessed by Aberdeen, but suitability for this industry was enhanced year by year. In 1889, the New Fish Market was opened. The increasing number of trawlers frequenting the port soon made it necessary to extend the accommodation thus provided, and these enlarged and up-to-date facilities were in turn a cause of a further increase in the trawler fleet fishing from Aberdeen. The city authorities, quick to appreciate the potentialities of their town as a fishing port, carried out from time to time extensive improvements. Buyers and fish salesmen made Aberdeen their headquarters, and the increase in the fresh fish trade encouraged the railway companies to devote special attention to it. The attracting power of the port was further magnified by the establishment of subsidiary industries—like fish-curing, ice manufacture, box-making, net manufacture, ship repair and engineering. Coaling facilities were established and Aberdeen's shipbuilders concentrated on the special problems of trawler construction.

In the ten years ending 1902, the number of trawlers fishing from the port increased from 75 to 198, and the quantity of fish landed from 290,893 cwt. to 1,104,399 cwt. Aberdeen had become the largest fishing port in Scotland, and the third largest in the United Kingdom. More than three-fifths of the total weight and about two-thirds of the value of white fish landed in Scotland were brought to Aberdeen in 1902. The port was not only the headquarters of most Scottish trawlers and of a large number of English ones, but, especially after 1896, of Danish and German ones too.

Capital was readily forthcoming for the new industry because of the handsome profits to be obtained. Many of those who invested in trawlers were also interested in the supply of coal or ice or stores to them. The interlocking of directorates as between trawl companies, ice or coal companies and the like became the order of the day. The actual fishing was now only part of the industry—the provision of capital, the supply of stores and coal, the marketing of fish, the building and repairing of trawlers became equally important branches. To these one must add the curing industry which expanded rapidly before the First World War.

Despite the tremendous increase in catching-power, the market for fish expanded rapidly. The introduction of filleting for many of the coarser kinds of fish and the growing popularity of fried-fish shops all over the country provided a welcome outlet especially after 1903. At the same time the landings of German and other foreign trawlers were giving a great impetus to the curing trade. How important this branch of the industry was is shown by the fact that in 1913 almost one-quarter of the whole catch landed at Aberdeen was by foreign trawlers. They worked the more distant grounds and the main fish landed were cod and ling, the bulk of which were dried and exported to Spain and South America. Thus, at the outbreak of the First World War the Aberdeen white fish industry consisted of two branches. The first and by far the most extensive was the landing of fish by British trawlers, the bulk of which were sold fresh, and the second the landing by foreign trawlers of coarser and less palatable fish which were cured and exported.

Already Aberdeen, far removed from southern markets and coal supplies, was beginning to feel the effects of the competition of such English ports as Grimsby, Hull, and Fleetwood. Her proximity to the best fishing-grounds in the North Sea and the Shetlands, and the fact that her trawlers could land their catches about two days earlier than, say, those of Grimsby, were very great advantages indeed. It gave Aberdeen the lead in quality fish which has been her speciality down to the present time.

The twenty-odd years separating the two World Wars constituted a period of great difficulty for the white fish industry. It was not, of course, a period of unrelieved gloom; there were ups and downs, but on the whole it could not be regarded with any satisfaction by trawler-owners or merchants.

The First World War was different in one or two important respects from the recent one in so far as white fishing is concerned. During hostilities the Admiralty steadily added to the trawler fleet by construction, so that when the end of the war came more ships were available for fishing than ever before. Though prices were high and building costs almost prohibitive, there was a big demand for trawlers, and the fishing industry, like other industries after the Armistice, looked forward to a period of high prosperity. In 1920, however, it was evident that a difficult period of readjustment lay ahead. The trawler fleet fishing from Scottish ports numbered 385 vessels (including 31 English), the highest figure ever reached. The Aberdeen fleet alone numbered 260 vessels, including 11 new or second-hand ones acquired by trawler-owners from the Admiralty or from English ports. The productive capacity of the industry was thus greater than at any time in its history. There were indeed signs that it was over-capitalized. The amount of fish landed had practically reached the 1914 level, but costs were much higher. Moreover, the fall in wholesale prices, at first not fully reflected in retail prices, widened the gap between costs and price and made fishing unremunerative. By 1921 it was clear that the white fish industry was to share in the general depression which was then settling on the economic life of the country. In that year the price of fish fell almost to pre-war level, but costs of production, though somewhat lower, were still excessive. Yet no fewer than 418 trawlers were at work in Scottish waters—33 more than in the previous year—though only one-third covered expenses. The unprofitable nature of the industry was reflected in the cost of trawlers which were now selling at one-third of 1918 prices.

It was not until 1927 that prospects brightened, and the industry appeared to have reached a satisfactory economic basis. In the interim, the trawl fleet fishing from Aberdeen had decreased and working expenses had been considerably reduced. In 1928 the Fishery Board declared in their Annual Report that the white fish industry had reached a phase of comparative stability and that the trawl fleet was now running on a 'sound economic basis'. The improved prospects of the trade were shown in the rise in value of second-hand trawlers and in the renewal of building.

The Fishery Board were indeed too optimistic, for by 1930 the industry was once more in the throes of depression—a depression not confined to any one industry in the country. Prices reached their lowest in 1932. By 1935, however, they had regained a level higher than in any year since 1924. The upward trend of prices was reflected in increased numbers of trawlers fishing from Aberdeen. The rising demand for fish of prime quality encouraged the Aberdeen fleet to concentrate on the near grounds. For example, no less than 78·8 per cent of the total landings in Scotland were derived from the North Sea and only 10·4 per cent from the Faroes and 2·2 per cent from Iceland. Almost all fish brought from distant grounds were landed by foreign trawlers. These landings had reached their highest point in 1930; thereafter there was a decline and by 1935 they amounted to no more than 39 per cent of the pre-1913 landings. It is striking to notice, however, that in 1935 the average price for foreign-caught demersal fish was 11s. 5d. per cwt, while for landings by British vessels it was 22s. 11d.

The recent war started at a time when the Aberdeen white fish industry was recovering from a long period of depression and when prospects seemed brighter than they had been for many years. For the people in the industry this growing prosperity was, of course, not checked. In fact, some regarded the war as the salvation of the industry. Skippers and crews were soon making large incomes and trawl companies found their deficits turned into profits overnight. Merchants, too, found no difficulty in making large gains—at least down to the time when control was imposed. This artificial prosperity is not to be attributed to the successful surmounting of the difficulties which had previously hampered the white fish industry. It was due entirely to war conditions which restricted the fishing fleet, neutralized Aberdeen's competitors in Grimsby and Hull, and for a time created boom conditions on the fish market.

The immediate effect of the war was a reduction in the number of the fishing fleet. This was not regarded, as might be imagined, as a bad thing for Aberdeen. On the contrary, it was welcomed, for it was believed that in pre-war days unrestricted fishing was one of the chief causes of the economic difficulties experienced by the industry. Before the war any substantial increase in prices was followed by a disproportionate increase in the fishing fleet, thus leading to over-production, whereas under war conditions, so far from the fleet being increased by the rise in prices, it was decreased by the demands of the Admiralty. This meant that the fleet then in commission could fish to its fullest capacity on grounds which were more prolific, thus resulting in a reduction in real costs. Moreover, Aberdeen had now a clear field in the home market since her two main rivals, Hull and Grimsby, had in the meantime practically ceased to operate as fishing ports. All these factors combined to strengthen Aberdeen's position in the trade and to give her top prices for her fish.

The effect of this was to turn trawling into a profitable business. Trawler-owners, of course, complained that through the operation of the Excess Profits Tax practically all this profit disappeared, as they had no pre-war standard to take as a reasonable basis. This argument applied to companies, but not to the individual owner who could earn up to £1,500 without being liable to Excess Profits Tax. The trawler-owners naturally felt that this would result in the impoverishment of the industry when the war was over, for the reconstruction and re-equipment of vessels then would involve a heavy capital charge. One of the obvious effects of the war was to increase the price of vessels; for instance, a trawler costing £15,000 in 1939 was sold in 1942 for £30,000.

The profitable nature of fishing and the high prices of trawlers led to some change in ownership. One or two firms sold their vessels at good prices, thus, they said, recouping themselves for losses incurred in less prosperous times. Some, who had only a secondary interest in trawling, also sold out, while others, like skippers and people outside the industry, bought shares in ships so that they might participate in the profits. Trawl crews and skippers shared in the good times which the war brought to the industry. The latter clearly stood to gain since their remuneration depended on a share of the profits. Many were reputed to be making incomes of £2,000 and £3,000 per annum. In spite of the high earnings of the crews difficulty was experienced in securing the right personnel. Large numbers, of course, were withdrawn from the industry for war service, leaving a less satisfactory type to man the trawlers.

The distributive side was affected in many respects by war conditions. Up to the establishment of control prices, profits were excessive and there was little change in general organization. Thereafter various innovations were introduced. Price control (maximum prices) restricted the operation of auction sales, and the allocation of supplies to merchants restricted competition. This had a serious effect on the business of some merchants who dealt in good-quality fish, since they had to take their share of coarse fish and much smaller supplies of the best quality than they would like. Some declared they were ashamed of the condition of the fish which they handled. Indeed, one prominent fish merchant said he welcomed the zoning scheme on the ground that he would be relieved from the ignominy of supplying stale fish to his customers. He believed that when the war was over he would have no difficulty in regaining his old customers. Another important war-time measure widely welcomed by responsible merchants was the registration of buyers. They would be glad of the permanent adoption of this arrangement, for all agreed that there were too many merchants in the trade. Another war-time change, enthusiastically received in Aberdeen, was the uniform transport charges made by the Ministry of Food on their purchases.

The main respects in which drastic improvements will have to be introduced in the Aberdeen industry, if it is to compete effectively with its rivals now the war is over, relate to the obsolescence of the fleet, the inefficient organization of subsidiaries, wasteful organization of distribution, labour conditions, and high costs of transport. In what follows something will be said on each of these in turn. Certain other questions, common to the whole industry (e.g. over-fishing), are discussed in the concluding section of the chapter.

(a) Aberdeen's fishing fleet is owned by a large number of units, unlike Hull, where the local fleet is concentrated in the hands of fifteen to twenty companies. At one extreme there is the large company, like the Aberdeen Steam Trawling and Fishing Company, a branch of Mac Fisheries and a subsidiary of the Leverhulme group, owning twenty-six vessels in 1939; at the other extreme there is the skipper-owner or private owner or small partnership with a single vessel. Altogether in 1942 there were between sixty and sixty-four owners in Aberdeen, but 75 per cent of the fleet was owned by limited companies. In 1934 no less than 41 per cent of the Aberdeen fleet was held by concerns owning less than five vessels, and almost 70 per cent was held by concerns owning nine or fewer vessels. The position had changed but little by the beginning of the recent war.

Intermediate between the company, owning its dozen or half-dozen ships, and the single owner, there are a number of vessels in which various individuals own shares. The capital is divided into sixty-four shares or parts, this denomination being a relic of the days of sailing-vessels. Those who hold such shares may be 'outsiders', anxious to participate in the profits of the fishing industry in good times and as anxious to transfer their capital elsewhere in bad. People in the industry object to this, believing that such outside interests bring neither credit nor stability to an industry which demands so much specialized knowledge and experience. More often one finds the shareholder is interested not in trawling as such, but in the provision of the trawler's needs, as in supplies of coal, oil, stores, paint, nets, repairs, etc. One hears much criticism of these people who sacrifice the productive side of fishing to their own interests. More will be said of this later when the subsidiary industries and the complicated system of interlocking are discussed.

The diversity of ownership makes concerted action difficult if not impossible. It is true that the owners are organized in the Aberdeen Steam Fishing Vessels' Association, which is federated to the British Trawler-owners' Federation; but, so far as Aberdeen is concerned, this organization is not particularly effective. It cannot control building or fishing or indeed take any concerted action to secure economies in the general organization of the trade.

It is well known that a large part of the Aberdeen fleet is obsolete. In 1934 no less than 60 per cent of the vessels were over twenty years old, and only 11 per cent were less than fifteen years old. At the outbreak of war the position was no better. The last ship built for Aberdeen was launched in 1936.

There are perhaps two reasons why Aberdeen has got into this unenviable position. In the first place, those concerned with the industry have shown a lack of enterprise. It is difficult to say whether this is due to the large profits made during and immediately after the war of 1914–18 or to the replacement of the generation which had built up the industry by men content to live on the wealth accumulated by their enterprising and hard-working fathers. The history of most industries displays this characteristic development—the first phase of rapid expansion when great vigour and enterprise is shown by the personnel, followed by a period of relative stagnation when a generation apparently incapable of sustained hard work and lacking initiative and enterprise takes the wheel. Anyhow, the fact is that after the war of 1914–18, Aberdeen did not advance in white fishing. It is true that during that war the Government built trawlers, and these were utilized for fishing when peace was established, but no further building programme was embarked on. A few German trawlers were secured by one of the largest Aberdeen firms, but others were content to make do with what they had. The Aberdeen trawler-owners, if they had to replace ships, bought second-hand ones, believing that they were just as efficient for fishing as new ones. Quite the opposite view is held by the crews who sail such ships. A well-known skipper, who is regarded as one of the most competent in Aberdeen, declared that Aberdeen trawlers are in a disgraceful condition. He said he would refuse to put to sea in many of them. 'They are,' he said, 'ill-equipped, they have poor and often scandalous provision for the crews, and sometimes they are rat-infested. So long as they can bring a catch to market,' he declared, 'the owners are satisfied, but,' he added pungently, 'they haven't to sail in them.' This state of affairs is contrasted with the Hull fleet or the German trawlers which in pre-war days used to frequent the port. In both cases conditions for the crew were infinitely superior to those in the Aberdeen-owned trawlers. This failure to equip these boats must be attributed in part at least to the lack of initiative among trawler-owners, but this is perhaps not the only factor involved. A further reason for Aberdeen's unenviable position, so far as the condition of the trawl fleet is concerned, is found in the long period of depression already discussed which followed the collapse of prices shortly after the end of the First World War.

A solution of the vitally important problem of the obsolescence of the fleet will depend on several considerations. By far the most urgent is the cost of building. The cost of replacement by 1942 had increased by over 100 per cent, and this was certainly not the end of the rise. It is true that a certain proportion of Excess Profits Duty collected from trawler-owners was earmarked for reconstruction and that a further pool was created by Admiralty compensation for lost vessels, but producers are convinced that no owner will be in a position to face unaided the cost of rebuilding. Moreover, the position is radically different from 1918 when considerable numbers of trawlers built by the Government during the war years were returned to the industry. Practically no serviceable trawlers were built in the recent war, and many of those commandeered have been so radically altered for war service that their re-adaptation to fishing will be a costly business.

The provision of capital, however, is not the only consideration. Before embarking on any scheme of building, some policy must be formulated as to the type of vessel most suited to the requirements of the Aberdeen industry. Hitherto Aberdeen has concentrated on the near fishing-grounds, and until modern scientific methods of preservation are adopted, it is probable that this will remain the most profitable field for her trawlers. The view is held by some prominent owners that this should be supplemented by some participation in the more distant fishings. The merchants, it should be noted, are strongly in favour of this extension because a good part of the curing and export trade depends on large quantities of cheap fish brought from the more distant grounds, such as Iceland and the Faroes. The question for the trade is whether they should embark on the building of vessels specially adapted for distant fishing, as Hull did after the 1914–18 war, or whether they should concentrate on building vessels equally suited to fishing near and distant grounds. The consensus of opinion in Aberdeen seems to favour the latter. Believing that they cannot compete with Hull on account of the difficulty of marketing a cheap product, Aberdeen trawler-owners favour the building of what they term 'utility trawlers', which could fish the distant and middle waters, like Iceland and the Faroes, and the near waters like the North Sea and the Shetlands. Moreover, this type of trawler could also be adapted to trawling for herring during the season. The importance of this is that this all-purpose ship could be profitably employed all the year round, according to the seasonal nature of fishing. The employment, in a well-planned rotation of grounds, of such vessels, larger than the ordinary run of Aberdeen trawlers, would make for a reduction in running costs and for a steady flow of fish to the market throughout the year, a consideration of immense advantage to the consumer.

Closely bound up with the type of vessel is the motive-power employed. Whether Diesel or steam should be used is debatable. Some argue that the reliability of steam-engines and the convenience of steam for winches and heat outweigh such advantages of oil as cleanliness, ease of handling, lower costs, and so forth—at least so far as trawlers are concerned. Until recently this was the general view. It is worth noting that in the case of drifters and Seine-net boats, there was much initial opposition to motors, but once their efficiency had been demonstrated, the fleet rapidly turned from steam to oil. In the last few years trawling has had a somewhat similar experience. Since the end of the war a number of owners have converted their ships to oil, and the success thereby achieved is likely to encourage others to follow suit.

A further matter which must be considered when plans for rebuilding are formulated is the possible improvement in methods of fish preservation aboard ship. This is a highly technical subject which has been investigated by several bodies and is continuously under review by the Department of Scientific and Industrial Research at their Torry Research Station, Aberdeen.

Some trawler-owners have tested out at least in part the improved methods thus demonstrated, but little real progress has been made. The importance of this matter is too obvious to be emphasized. It is of special value on long-distance voyages such as are undertaken by the Hull trawlers to Bear Island, but its value even for Aberdeen trawlers fishing in the Faroe and Icelandic waters or in the Shetland waters is immense. Such voyages present greater difficulties than in the case of fishing in the near waters, but if Aberdeen decides, now the war is over, to engage on a larger scale in Faroe and Icelandic fishings, the whole question becomes one of immediate practical importance to her trawler-owners. It is also of great consequence to the wider interests of the fishing industry of Aberdeen in so far as her credit has hitherto depended on quality. It has been shown by research at the Torry Station that the supplies of palatable fish could be vastly increased, and what is equally valuable, could be more evenly spread over the year by proper methods of preservation. It is not simply a matter of installing proper plant in trawlers as well as of ensuring hygienic conditions on the ships themselves, but of making adequate provision for preserving fish in the port itself, in the handling of the fish on the market and in the fish-houses, as well as in the proper provision of cold storage.

In view of the high degree of obsolescence of the Aberdeen fleet and of the rather experimental nature of the methods proposed, little has been done to face up to this urgent problem, but quite clearly it is one to which special attention should be directed. So much attention is now being paid to the preservation of food that it is all the more imperative that an industry which handles such a perishable commodity as fish, and whose fortunes are so closely bound up with quality, should give a prominent place to this question of preservation in any programme of post-war reconstruction.

(b) An industry like white fishing is naturally dependent on a number of subsidiary industries, and the port which can provide them efficiently strengthens its hold over the major industry. Of these subsidiaries, the supply of coal and equipment, the manufacture of ice, and ship repairing are among the chief. It was in fact Aberdeen's ability to provide these necessary services that gave her white fishing industry its initial impulse.

The close relationships existing between trawling and these subsidiary industries has resulted in a high degree of financial integration. It is illuminating to examine the position as it existed in Aberdeen in 1943, for the extremely involved character of organization with its high degree of interlocking in fact militates against the rehabilitation of the fleet and the reconstruction of the industry.

One or two companies are more or less complete units in themselves. The Aberdeen Steam Trawling and Fishing Company, a branch of Mac Fisheries, for instance, are trawler-owners, fish-salesmen (i.e. they sell fish in the market to buyers, or merchants as they are usually called), ice manufacturers, net manufacturers, engineers and ship repairers, and coal merchants. The Leverhulme group, which controls this concern, secured this position in Aberdeen by acquiring the Strath Fishing Company, the Strath Engineering Works, the Aberdeen Ice Manufacturing Company, etc. Since each part is a financial unit it is possible for the trawling company to show a loss while the subsidiaries show profits. Another company—the Walker Steam Trawl Fishing Company—has a fleet of trawlers; they sell their own fish and act as fish-salesmen for other owners both in Aberdeen and at Hull and Grimsby; they have their own net factory and engineering works, and they do their own storing of vessels. In 1943 the managing director was a director of Ellis and McHardy (coal), Isaac Spencer and Company (Aberdeen) (oil and paint manufacturers and leather merchants and belt and leather hose manufacturers), and of the North-Eastern Ice Company.

Some of the smaller companies confine their activities to trawling and selling, but their managing directors may sit on boards of firms in the subsidiary industries. The manager of the North Star Steam Fishing Company, for instance, was a director of the Aberdeen Coal and Shipping Company, the North-Eastern Ice Company, the Harrow-Baxter Steam Fishing Company, the Enterprise Ship Stores Ltd., and the Aberdeen Mutual and General Insurance Company. A director of Richard Irvin and Sons (a firm which engages in trawling and herring fishing and curing) was also a director of the North-Eastern Ice Company, Isaac Spencer and Company (Aberdeen) (paint), and Ellis and McHardy (coal). Sometimes a firm is mainly engaged in selling, like the Don Fishing Company (fish salesmen and shipstore merchants) but here too one finds interlocking. A firm like this may have shares in trawlers, and they in turn may be expected to sell their fish through it and obtain supplies from its store. The managing director of this concern was a director of the Aberdeen Coal and Shipping Company, the Bon Accord Ice Company, and Isaac Spencer and Company (Aberdeen).

Doubtless trawler-owners who sit on the boards of firms in the subsidiary industries are mainly interested in the supplying of their vessels, but there are others whose main interest is in the subsidiaries. There is much criticism of the latter and there is a general feeling amongst producers (i.e. those engaged in trawling) that this is putting the cart before the horse. A favourite expression in the trade is that 'everything comes out of the cod end', and so it is maintained that extra profit and expense entailed in the duplication and overlapping

SAMPLE ILLUSTRATION OF INTERLOCKING

(Based on Aberdeen Directories, *Stock Exchange Year Book* and the *Directory of Directors*)

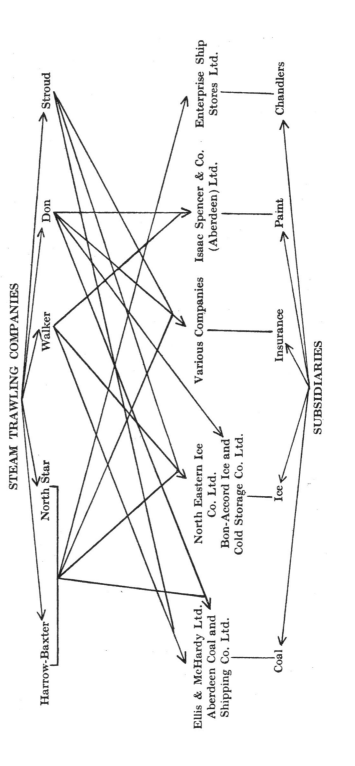

STEAM TRAWLING COMPANIES

SUBSIDIARIES

of services must eventually come out of trawling. Men who sit on the boards of subsidiary firms draw their directors' fees and profit, and so may make quite a good income, while the actual trawling firm is returning a loss. Thus it is maintained that many interests thrive while the productive side languishes.

Probably those who suffer most are the crews, for they are paid on a share basis. When the catch is sold a Settling Sheet is drawn up, showing all the various items of expenditure on the trip, such as coal, gear, baskets, oil, carting, wireless, provisions, and even water for the boiler. All these come out of the gross receipts as well as all wages paid to the crew. A company, therefore, supplying coal, gear, provisions, etc., from its own subsidiaries is in a strong position to make what charges it likes. Even the carting of coal and other supplies to the quay is a charge on the ship, although the carts belong to the company. Only after all these and other charges have been met do the crew participate in the profits of the voyage. Naturally skippers resent a situation which thus safeguards the interests of trawler-owners and subsidiaries and leaves those who have done the work and taken the risks of fishing as a last charge on the industry. In ordinary times this often results in meagre payments or none at all.

The fact appears to be that the subsidiary industries have been the paying end of white fishing and that the actual trawling has been put last in order of importance. This is a very common complaint. Instead of the subsidiary industries being owned mutually and run for the benefit of the trawling section of the industry, they have been the happy hunting-ground of those not directly interested in fishing. It is true that in the long run these subsidiary industries would suffer if trawling remained unremunerative, but even before the war there was no sign that they were being seriously affected. This is one of the major problems that will have to be faced now the war is over. At the present time there are three ice companies; six box-making firms, four privately owned, one large company and a fish merchant's mutual company; there are three firms concerned with fish-meal, one of which is a fish merchants' mutual; there are several coal companies large and small; many supply concerns (ships' stores); and several engineering and ship-repair companies. Though there are one or two mutual concerns, as, for instance, the Enterprise Ship Stores, most of these firms are dominated by outside interests. Even the 'mutuals' are not well supported by those for whom they have been created.

The absence of efficient organization of the subsidiary services involves the White Fish Industry of Aberdeen in heavy charges. For instance, there is no modern coal-loading plant. The various companies serve coal in their own way. If brought to Aberdeen by ship, the coal is unloaded and filled into bags and carted to the company's depot, where the bags are emptied. When a ship requires coaling, the bags are filled again, carted to the quay-side, and emptied into the hold of the ship. All this is done by hand. When one remembers that there are some half-dozen largish firms and a good many smaller ones carrying on activities in the same way, one sees how utterly wasteful the whole system is. Yet the coal companies are said to have made most of their profits out of the supply of bunker coal. In the handling of ice the same inefficiencies are observed. The supplies of ice for ships have to be carted to the quay-side and once again the loading is done by hand. There are three ice companies where one would be sufficient if it were so situated that ice could be loaded on to trawlers by chute instead of the laborious handling and carting that is the present practice.

The provision of supplies to trawlers and the repair of engines and ships and other related matters could with advantage be rationalized. Indeed, some trawler-owners declared that they would willingly submerge their own subsidiary services in a large undertaking to be run co-operatively for the benefit of the trawlers. This would be an advantage to the industry as a whole and would eliminate some of the discreditable features of existing organization. There is little doubt, however, that this rationalization could not be effected by the industry as at present constituted. Interests are so varied that it is impossible to secure agreement on any of these major points without the weight of Government authority. These proposed reforms are by no means visionary, but are of immediate practical importance, for one of the fundamental problems in the reconstruction of Aberdeen's fishing industry is a reduction in the real costs of production. And it is certain that considerable economies could be effected if a bold policy were carried out with determination and vigour.

Closely related to the foregoing is the general planning of the layout of the industry. Perhaps more than in any other, the various parts of the white fish industry of a port like Aberdeen hang to-gether. Trawler-owners, fish-salesmen, and buyers, find the fish market their forum, and all the subsidiary industries, including the transport facilities at the port, are closely bound up with one another. Thus it is apparent that the economical working of the industry depends to a large extent on the general layout of the fish market and all other services with which it is associated.

On the credit side, Aberdeen possesses a first-class fish market with adequate rail facilities on the quays. It is commodious and well-planned for the handling of the large fleet which fishes from the port. At the moment, and for some years past, these rail facilities have not been used, and buyers have been content to load their fish in lorries and have them carted away to their respective fish-houses, the majority of which are some distance outside the harbour area. Wastage in the transport and handling of fish is thus extensive, since there are so many merchants and each handles his own supplies whether large or small. A greater concentration of fish-houses beside the fish market would eliminate a great deal of this unnecessary transport, contribute to the maintenance of quality, make possible the boxing of fish on the market ready for final dispatch, and so result in a considerable saving of time. The harbour as at present constituted could easily provide for one or two up-to-date coaling berths, for example at Point Law, as well as a modern ice factory so that the ice could be loaded direct into the trawlers.

To sum up, the layout of the interdependent parts of the industry in the most efficient and economical way should present no serious difficulties if all concerned would tackle the matter in a co-operative spirit, believing that this might make the biggest single contribution to lowering costs in Aberdeen and putting the fishing industry of the port on a satisfactory economic basis. No advances in methods (except in the case of trawling) or in organization have been made for a generation, and a period of post-war reconstruction would seem to present a splendid opportunity for a drastic modernizing of the whole industry.

(c) The distribution of fish is in the hands of quite different firms from those engaged in the producing side. This is unlike the practice of the herring industry where firms combine buying, curing, and export of herring with extensive interests in drifters. In white fishing an occasional buyer may own a trawler, but this is quite exceptional. This may be due either to the divergent interests within the industry, which places trawler-owners and distributors in different camps, or to the economic impossibility of combining in one unit two operations demanding different abilities and experience. Certainly most merchants who have owned trawlers have been forced to sell out. Similarly, the trawler-owners have in their turn made several attempts to break into the distributive side, but on every occasion these have been abortive, and the premises of the Aberdeen Trawl Owners' Fish Curing Company long languished in a disused state. Besides the reasons quoted above, the bitterness existing between trawler-owners and distributors on this question no doubt contributes to this result. Indeed, a striking fact of the Aberdeen industry is the hostility existing between these two main sections of the trade. It is certain that some of the most important problems calling for solution arise from the failure of the two key sections to co-operate and see that in fact they constitute two interdependent parts of a single industry. Failure to make progress in methods and organization in the last twenty years is due, in part at least, to these bitter relations based on the irreconcilable attitudes of trawler-owners and merchants. They have been so busily engaged in waging guerrilla warfare against each other that they have failed to see that their actions, far from strengthening their position or that of the industry, are indeed detrimental to their long-term interests and to the future of the port.

The merchant commences his operations in the fish market, where he buys his fish from fish-salesmen, who in general are the paid officials or agents of the trawling companies. In 1942 there were 227 buyers or merchants handling the catches landed at the port. This number is unusually high; it had increased from 146 in the year 1920.

The main reason for this large number of merchants is found in the ease with which one can enter the trade. It is possible, in fact, for a man with no more equipment than a box, a pocketful of nails, and a hammer to enter the fish market as a merchant. Even the person who wishes to commence on a somewhat more elaborate scale requires little capital and can easily secure sufficient credit from his bank. He can do this all the more readily if he has been previously an employee of a larger merchant, for then, under the competitive conditions which appear to prevail at the port, he can proceed to quote at lower prices to the clients of his former employer. Though these are the lesser fry, the small man with no more than two or three employees represent a high proportion of the 227 merchants. At the other extreme there are, of course, a number of large firms, eight of which handle about 70 per cent of the catch landed at Aberdeen.

Like the trawler-owners, these merchants are organized into the Aberdeen Fish Trade Association, but again, the organization is not particularly effective owing to the large number of small people in the trade who do not readily agree to any regulation proposed by the Association. In fact, the great mass of small people act as if they were a law unto themselves. Though the Association is not in a position to enforce control over prices in normal times, groups of merchants constitute themselves into what one might call unofficial rings.

When the fish is landed from the trawlers it is laid out on the market floor, and the merchant or his manager passes round, note-book in hand, in order to obtain a general idea of the state of supplies. Meantime some estimate has been received of the landings at other ports and contact has been made by telephone or telegraph with numerous wholesale and retail dealers throughout the country. Thus, when the fish is being landed, the buyer knows what type of fish he wants and what prices he can offer. So equipped, the merchant is ready to buy the fish by auction. Despite the number of merchants engaged, competition to buy is not so general as might be imagined, because it is a common practice for groups of merchants to act collectively in their dealings with fish-salesmen. For instance, when a certain lot of fish is put up for auction only one merchant will bid, thus securing a low price, but the actual lot which is marked down to him is then divided among perhaps twenty different merchants who compose the ring. This very general practice is naturally condemned by the trawler-owners, as they obviously do not get the price for their goods that could be secured if the merchants operated singly. A high quotation for Billingsgate, or some other inland market, is not necessarily reflected in the prices obtained by the trawler-owners. The general criticism is that the merchant always stands to gain, while the actual producer must accept the price offered to him. Because of the perishability of his article he is unable to withhold his goods from the market until a better price can be obtained. He has only two options, either to accept the merchant's price or to send his fish to the fish-meal factories. In a short market the trawler-owners' position is naturally stronger, but even then rings may operate to his detriment. He is all the more critical of this state of affairs because of the large amount of capital involved in the catching side as compared with the meagre resources of many of those who hold the whip hand in the market. It is true that, even from the point of view of the merchant, these rings are not necessarily an unqualified advantage. For example, it may happen that on occasions a merchant who could use, say, twenty boxes of halibut, is allowed only one box. In the long run, however, such disadvantages must be outweighed by the advantages, otherwise he would cut himself adrift from the ring.

Though, on the face of it, it may appear that the merchants have interests in common, yet, on closer investigation, it is seen that there is often a clash between those who handle good-quality fish and those whose main business is in the cheaper varieties. For example, a large merchant who deals in the former class of article may be willing to pay more in the fish market to secure the fresh supplies on which his credit depends, but when he sells in the inland markets he may find that the price he can obtain is depressed through the action of those who can offer large supplies of inferior fish at lower prices. Thus the fish merchant who handles prime fish is compelled to lower his offer to some extent in order to meet this competition in the inland markets. So once again it is the trawler-owner who suffers. Another factor making for depression of prices on the fish market is the bad debts incurred by merchants who supply fish friers and retailers. As in every other industry there are racketeers in the fish trade, who open premises, make what they can on a few deals, and then leave debts unpaid. These men, by virtue of a bank reference and the usual trade references, are in a watertight position legally. Fish merchants hesitate to go into court as the legal expenses outweigh the financial return of a successful case. Thus, they simply register the account as a bad debt, and to recoup themselves again buy at a low price. This is not, perhaps, a vital factor in the depression of prices, but it does operate to the disadvantage of the producer.

After the fish has been sold, it is put into boxes and carted away by motor- or horse-lorry to the merchant's fish-house. On arrival the boxes are unpacked and the fish gutted and cleaned. Those to be sold are repacked in boxes with ice and then carted to the railway station and dispatched by passenger train. The fish to be cured is treated by smoking or drying on the premises of the merchant, who usually combines freshing and curing, and then boxed and dispatched to the inland markets. Fish for export are usually stored in the cold storage provided by two firms in Aberdeen, until arrangements are completed for their transit overseas. When shipped from a port other than Aberdeen they are usually sent south in refrigerating vans on goods trains.

There is considerable wastage of transport, since the great majority of fish-houses are outside the harbour area. The fresh fish could be dealt with entirely in the fish market itself and dispatched direct to the railway station, instead of time, labour, and transport being wasted in the unnecessary carting from market to fish-house and then to the station.

Before the war, there was a considerable drift of fish traffic from rail to road because of the cheaper rates offered. Fish was sent by road as far as Billingsgate and the great inland markets of England, like Birmingham, Liverpool, and Manchester. Though fish merchants declared that there were abundant facilities for the transport of fish to the inland markets, they were all agreed that rail transport was far better for long distances, but lack of co-operation and high rates made them switch over to road transport, which was cheaper but less satisfactory in view of the fact that the drivers had to cover the ground at a reckless pace in order to reach market in time. For the nearer markets road transport was highly satisfactory. For instance, a lorry could serve a number of villages and towns on the way to, say, Fife or Perth and deliver fresh fish in time for it to be served the same day as it was landed in Aberdeen.

In pre-war days all the Aberdeen merchants had their own customers throughout the length and breadth of the country. Indeed, it was a common experience for several merchants to serve the same village and sometimes indeed the same customers. One merchant carrying on business in a fairly small way (the number of his employees in Aberdeen being no more than a dozen) sent fish daily to such varied places as Golspie, Dornoch, Oban, Inverness, Lamlash, Glasgow, Dunoon, Gretna Green, Inverary, Girvan, Sheffield, Carlisle, and Wales, and these are only a small selection of the places where he had customers. A map showing the distribution of fish from Aberdeen to inland markets would consist of innumerable lines crisscrossing in all directions in the most chaotic fashion, radiating from the port to almost every village in the country.

Of much less importance than the inland market is the export trade, at least when considered in terms of quantity. As compared with the home market the export is comparatively small. In 1935 only 91,974 cwt. were exported out of a total landing of 1,831,880 cwt. On the whole it is the larger firms that engage in the export trade, and they feel that now the war is over this should prove a promising field for expansion.

Most merchants are fish curers as well as fresh fish buyers and distributors. Since there are so many fish merchants in Aberdeen, it is clear that there is a considerable number of curing establishments. They vary in size from the small place with half a dozen employees to the large firm, like the Scottish C.W.S. with 120 employees. In 1939 there were 232 fish curers and fresh fish buyers employing 1,443 gutters, packers, and kipperers; this being a drop from the 1935 figures of 11 and 44 respectively. Because of the combination of freshing and curing, it is impossible to give figures relating to curing only. A striking fact of this side of the industry, however, is the large number of extremely small units, often with ill-equipped and indeed insanitary premises. It is surprising that in the production of an important food, conditions such as exist in scores of Aberdeen curing-houses should be allowed to continue. The buildings are usually wooden structures with cement floors and long wooden tables where the fish-girls work side by side with the vats of dye for kippering and the kilns for smoking the fish. The cement floors are satisfactory, but the runnels or gutters they are provided with make the daily cleaning at best an unsatisfactory operation. The filleting tables, which are of wood, are also difficult to keep in a hygienic condition. In the opinion of the more enlightened merchants many of the places are really wrecks and require drastic overhaul. Many of the fish-houses and curing establishments are close to one another, making expansion of premises difficult if not impossible.

Trawler-owners and merchants do not always see eye to eye as regards the type of fish to be landed in Aberdeen. Trawler-owners whose ships are adapted for the near grounds naturally are interested in maintaining supplies of best-quality fish; the curers, on the other hand, though in their capacity as freshers also interested in good-quality fish, want supplies of distant fish, coarser in quality, but very saleable when cured. For this reason they welcomed the landings of German trawlers in the years following the war of 1914–18, and were gravely perturbed by the fall in these landings during the few years before the recent war.

Aberdeen trawler-owners, though anxious to stop the imports of foreign fish, have been reluctant to replace them by entering into distant fishing themselves. A prominent member of the Aberdeen fishing industry declared that 'a man who puts a ship to Iceland is out of his senses'. On the face of it this may appear a decidedly conservative opinion, but it is based on some experience in landing coarse fish which will not bear the cost of transport to England, where it comes into competition with the same but cheaper commodity marketed by Hull. It is probable that the demand of the Aberdeen curers is insufficient to make economic the fishing of distant grounds by local trawlers. However, the fact at the moment is that Aberdeen trawler-owners generally are unwilling to embark on distant fishing to any great extent. Some are prepared to tackle Iceland fishing, but not to go so far afield as Bear Island. The merchants and curers naturally feel aggrieved at this attitude, for, they declare, their export trade depends on such supplies.

The distributive side of the industry also comes into contact with the subsidiary industries. Merchants require ice, use boxes for fish, and send their fish offal to the fish-meal factories. Here, however, the situation is considerably simpler and few of the interlocking relationships, already seen on the trawling side, exist. The merchants, on the whole, are satisfied with the services of the subsidiaries and have little complaint. They have a Mutual Association for the manufacture of boxes and one for fish-meal, in which many of the merchants have shares, though no one is allowed to gain control, as the maximum holding of shares by an individual is fixed. There is a feeling that these associations are not patronized as they should be and also that they are not truly co-operative.

The need for reform on the distributive side of the industry is very urgent. The registration of merchants is clearly a first step towards securing better organization of the marketing side, and proper control of freshing and curing. The unnecessarily large number of establishments, the uneconomic size of the majority, the primitive methods and the unhygienic conditions prevailing, are all matters which have been widely criticized. The fish that passes through the market could well be handled by as few as four or five large concerns, but a reduction of the present number to 150 licensed merchants would be a feasible and constructive reform. This is a view that is widely accepted by the merchants themselves, but the impossibility of effecting these reforms without the aid of Government authority is self-evident. This reduction in the number of merchants would lead to larger and more efficient establishments, and the warren of ramshackle buildings owned by the small concerns would in time disappear, giving way to more permanent and satisfactory structures, such as are at present owned by the few large firms. This telescoping of the distributive side would automatically lead to greater concentration in the layout of the industry.

Greater control should be exercised by the sanitary authorities over conditions obtaining in fish-houses and curing establishments, and merchants, with considerable advantage to themselves, could pay much more attention to the important matters of preservation and methods of curing, upon which the Torry Research Station has for some time been experimenting. These experiments aim at improving the quality and freshness of fish. While it is believed that the new methods will in the long run prove economical, the capital outlay involved is obviously too great for the small business.

(d) On the labour side of the industry there are two outstanding matters which require attention, namely, living conditions on board trawlers, and remuneration of the crews. On this latter point the charges made in settling sheets seem to be still the chief bone of contention. A reconstructed fishing industry will naturally depend on an adequate and satisfied labour supply. Before the war there was already a drift away from the fishing industry which for the time being was made good by the movement of fishermen from Morayshire ports to Aberdeen. It is extremely likely that unless a fair deal is now given to the men a serious shortage of labour will occur. The nature of the work is such that unless a great deal more is done by the employers to make the career of fishermen more attractive, a serious problem for the industry will arise.

(e) The cost of transport is a matter of great importance to all concerned in the fishing industry in Aberdeen. On the productive side, coal has to be shipped or railed from the collieries in the south, and since coal is the chief item in the running costs of trawlers, heavy transport charges are necessarily a handicap to the Aberdeen industry as compared with ports like Hull, more conveniently situated with reference to the mines. On the marketing side, transport is of even greater importance because Aberdeen trawlers save forty-eight hours of steam-power as compared with ports in the south, while merchants sending fish to London or the large inland markets of England have to meet added transport costs without any similar factor of compensation. The remedy for this high charge on industry favoured by people in the industry in Aberdeen is a flat rate of transport, such as operates at the present time when the Ministry of Food makes a levy (varying from time to time) on every stone of white fish to cover transport charges. Naturally such a proposal does not commend itself to consumers or to Hull fishing interests; but the whole question of transport charges for a place like Aberdeen does certainly call for serious consideration. The view is widely held locally that Aberdeen is refused transport concessions since her harbour is not owned by the railway companies, as is the case at Hull and Grimsby, her main competitors, and also that these competitors have always used their influence to prevent Aberdeen fishing interests from securing favourable treatment from the railway companies. This problem, however, raises wider issues than those of the fishing industry, for it might be argued that in the transport of food flat rates should operate everywhere.

GRIMSBY

Grimsby claims to rank as the premier fishing port of the country, indeed of the world; but her title to that status can be challenged. It is true that Grimsby has maintained her lead in total value of fish landed and has more trawlers than any other port; but in the 1930's Hull landed by far the bigger weight of fish and her fleet contained a higher proportion of modern large trawlers.

The Hull fishing industry has shown a rapid advance in recent years; but Grimsby's earlier expansion was more remarkable. For centuries Hull had been one of the leading ports of the country, while Grimsby, though an ancient borough, stagnated. Its first dock, an enlargement of the natural haven, was not made until the beginning of the nineteenth century when the population of the place was about 1,500. This enterprise brought little increase in trade, however, and thirty years later Boston, Gainsborough, and Spalding had considerably more shipping than Grimsby. The port was too remote, in the days of slow inland transport, from the more important agricultural districts and manufacturing centres, while fish could not be distributed outside the immediate neighbourhood, which offered but a poor market.

This condition was transformed by the coming of the railway. Already in 1844 the Sheffield and Lincolnshire Railway Company had penetrated into the county and prominent landowners were negotiating with them for an extension to Grimsby and the building of a new dock there. Two years later a great scheme was promoted for the amalgamation of five railway undertakings into the Manchester, Sheffield, and Lincolnshire Railway Company which would also absorb the Grimsby Dock Company. With the completion of the line to Grimsby the port secured rail connexion with the Yorkshire coalfield and the manufacturing regions of the Midlands and Lancashire as well as with the rich agricultural districts of Lincolnshire. The complementary enterprise, the building of the new dock, was immediately begun, in the belief, apparently, that the provision of facilities would bring the traffic. At the time there were only two vessels of any size using the port, sailing-brigs bringing timber from Norway, and if the M.S. & L.R. had plans for the development of Grimsby's trade so had the Lancashire and Yorkshire for that of Hull.

Soon, however, the M.S. & L.R. began to foster the Grimsby trade by more direct means. In 1856 the Anglo-French Shipping Company

5

was formed, the board consisting mainly of railway directors, and this concern employed nine steamers taking Yorkshire coal to French ports. The railway company also organized the Grimsby Deep Sea Fishing Company. The fishing trade was stimulated by the arrangement of favourable rates of carriage and Grimsby began to benefit by the migration of enterprising fishermen from other ports. Among the first arrivals was Harrison Mudd, destined to play a leading part in Grimsby's industrial and civic life. Mudd came from Manningtree, and others followed from Ramsgate, Barking, and Brixham. Many also went to Hull, for the rich fisheries of the Dogger Bank had lately been rediscovered and the Humber ports were the most convenient base for operations. But the Dock Company at Hull was slow in providing for the increasing traffic, and eventually many of the Hull trawler-owners came over to Grimsby.

Expansion was by no means rapid during the 1850's, however; the population of Grimsby, 8,638 in 1850, was only 11,067 ten years later, though in the previous decade it had more than doubled. But the next twenty years saw remarkable progress. By 1870 there were 500 smacks using the fish docks, giving employment to over 2,500 men and boys, besides those engaged in landing and packing the fish ashore. Landings of fish had reached 30,000 tons a year, most of this being dispatched by rail; by 1880 the railway was handling 45,000 tons a year. It was a period of very active enterprise when many fishing companies were formed. One grandiose project had a proposed capitalization of £200,000; it did not materialize, but its very contemplation suggests the optimism that prevailed in the fishing industry. Two of Grimsby's most notable enterprises, the Ice Company and the Coal, Salt, and Tanning Company, date from this period. Both were intimately associated with the fishing industry. In 1879 more new docks were opened, for the coal and timber trades were rapidly expanding. Everywhere building was going on, especially house-building, for Grimsby's population grew more than fourfold during these twenty years.

The fishing industry was now on the threshold of revolutionary changes. So far the expanding market for fish, reached by the railway, had been supplied by sailing-vessels. Now the transition to steam trawling began. Already in the 1870's sailing trawlers had small steam plants installed for shooting and hauling their gear, in place of the hand-worked system. Steam carriers had also been introduced for taking fish from the North Sea fleet to London. Experiments had been made in the application of steam-power to fishing vessels, though with no great success. But in 1881 the Grimsby and North Sea Steam Trawling Company was formed with a capital of £50,000; it is interesting to note that its directors included smack-owners, fish and coal merchants, and the secretary of the M.S. & L.R. The

Company had two steam trawlers built, at a cost of between £3,000 and £4,000 each, in its first year. By this enterprise Grimsby claims to be the pioneer of steam trawling. A few years later the North Eastern Steam Fishing Company was established with a capital of £30,000.

Once the advantages of steam had been proved the transition proceeded steadily, though less rapidly than might have been expected. It was in the next decade, 1890 to 1900, that the revolution was accomplished. The following figures give a striking illustration of the process:

Year	No. of Sailing Vessels	No. of Steam Vessels	Fish Dispatched by rail
1890	769	35	1,427,640 cwt.
1900	61	471	2,680,000 ,,
1909	29	608	3,519,300 ,,

These figures show, also, the great increase in productivity of the industry with the substitution of steam for sail, and how heavily the increased trade depended on the railway. Moreover, the railway was equally essential for the cheap transport of coal to the port. Thus the transition to steam trawling further strengthened the concentration of the fishing industry at ports like Grimsby, well served by railways and with suitable dock accommodation for steamers.

A further stage was reached in the development of the modern fishing industry with the great extension of the fishing-grounds. By 1890 the danger of over-fishing was already apparent in the North Sea, and the Grimsby and Hull trawler-owners were conferring on the problem. Legal restriction was proposed, but international agreement would have been necessary to make such a scheme effective. Enterprising trawler-owners, however, were already exploring the more northerly waters, which were within the range of the new steamers. The new fishing-grounds they discovered proved extremely rich, and as more and bigger vessels were introduced to exploit them, pressure in the North Sea was relieved.

The curtailment of trawling during the 1914–18 war gave the North Sea fisheries a chance to recover their productivity. But it was not long before intensive fishing again began to reduce the catch per voyage. The industry then had to choose between supplying a strictly limited quantity of prime fish, possibly at high prices (though that would depend on the degree of competition among producers), and going for the big low-priced market in fish of inferior grade. It was essentially a choice between quality production and mass production.

To say that Grimsby has chosen the former alternative and Hull the latter is misleading, without qualification, but it is broadly true. Before the recent war about 30 per cent of Grimsby's catch came from the North Sea and about 45 per cent from Iceland; only a small proportion came from the extreme north. Hence, Grimsby's claim to the status of premier fishing port came to depend on the variety and high quality of its fish. Hull, in contrast, has shown great enterprise in developing the distant fishing, which yields mainly the coarser qualities necessarily landed in a less fresh condition.

The contrast in the progress of the two ports between the wars is striking. Before the 1914–18 war Grimsby's annual landings, measured by weight, were more than double those of Hull. But from 1920 onwards, while Grimsby's quantity remained almost stationary at the pre-war level, that of Hull rapidly increased; it overtook Grimsby's total in 1930 and came greatly to exceed it during the next few years. Moreover, the expanding trade of Hull was decidedly more profitable than Grimsby's. This was not entirely due to Hull's development of distant fishing, for even in near and middle waters Hull owners did better than those of Grimsby in the 1930's. The Hull owners appear to have succeeded by virtue of their enterprise and efficiency; in particular, they realized the importance of keeping the fleet up to date. At the time of the Sea Fish Commission's investigation in 1934, 47 per cent of the Hull trawlers were less than ten years old; Grimsby had only 12 per cent in this category.

Hull did not gain at the expense of Grimsby. Her expansion was based on a new class of trade, which was equally open to Grimsby. With all her advantages Grimsby had been steadily falling behind in the leadership of the fishing industry. She had not fully adapted her resources to the changing conditions, which were becoming evident even before the 1914–18 war. This was the more serious in that Grimsby, as we have seen, has been built up on the fish trade and is pre-eminently a fishing port. It is not easy to discover why, with so much at stake, the spirit of enterprise should suddenly have flagged. But this historical sketch at least reveals the springs of past enterprise and also shows that these springs are by no means exhausted, for there was a distinct revival in the years just before the recent war which promises well for the future.

Grimsby stands on the south bank of the Humber estuary less than 8 miles from the open sea. Spurn Point actually lies due east of the port at a distance of 7 miles. Hull is situated some 16 miles farther from the sea, a disadvantage which to-day appears to be of little account. Unlike Hull, the port of Grimsby is not located with reference to the natural deep-water channel of the Humber, for the only stretch where this channel swings close to the Lincolnshire shore is about 5 miles farther upstream. Instead, Grimsby is founded on the site of a small creek where the little River Freshney reached the Humber, the modern port having been extended out into the tidal zone of the estuary. The original harbour, like the Alexandra Docks of to-day, ran canal-wise into the town which grew up some distance behind the shore. Later on, neglect of the approaches and the silting of the creek brought decline and stagnation, and, as mentioned earlier, no serious attempt at harbour improvement was made till the beginning of the nineteenth century. Now the Humber above Grimsby is not an easy estuary for navigation, for tides require careful negotiation and the periodic shifting of sandbanks necessitates the frequent alteration of mark-boats. There can be little doubt therefore that from this point of view the port is more favourably situated than places farther up the estuary.

Most of the existing docks, including the fish docks, in view of the absence of deep water at the Freshney outfall, have been excavated from the broad inter-tidal flats, and thus stand out from the shore for a distance of three-quarters of a mile. The older Alexandra Docks, however, lie behind the shore, one branch still serving as the outlet for the river. Tidal water is admitted to all the docks by means of locks.

The fish docks occupy the eastern portion of the port and form three contiguous basins having a combined quay length of about 3 miles. No. 1 Fish Dock (1856) encloses a water space of 13 acres, and is the oldest of the group. There are two entrance locks, the larger of which has a length of 143 feet and a width of 34 feet 9 inches —some of the largest up-to-date trawlers have a length of 160 feet— and a depth of 22 feet 9 inches M.H.W. spring tides and 18 feet 3 inches M.H.W. neap tides. No. 2 Fish Dock (1870) has a water space of 16 acres and its locks a depth of 22 feet 8 inches M.H.W. spring tides and 18 feet 2 inches M.H.W. neap tides. No. 3 (New) Dock, opened in 1934, marks the latest extension of the port, and its extent of 35 acres has more than doubled the previous water space. It is provided with specially devised slipways for carrying out repairs to trawlers, and is fitted with three hydraulic coal hoists for bunkering. The fish docks thus provide a total water surface of 64 acres, an immense area compared with that of the St. Andrew's Dock and its extension at Hull, which is barely 20 acres. Further, though Grimsby is mainly concerned with demersal fish, there is a considerable herring trade which finds accommodation in the tidal basin forming the entrance to the harbour. Here the drifters and luggers can land their catch at almost any time of day or night.

With regard to communications with the interior Grimsby is well provided. Railway routes serve all parts of the country with excellent services to London and the South. Hull may appear to be better placed to service the North, since many of the industrial districts lie close at hand, but, in point of fact, fish is distributed from Grimsby to some 3,000 railway stations in all parts of the country, delivery being either on the same day or the day following dispatch. It is true that until lately handling facilities left something to be desired.

Before the 1914–18 war there was some fear that the Grimsby fish trade might lose to other ports if more dock accommodation was not provided. But at the time the railway company were building their new docks at Immingham (opened in 1912) to provide mainly for the coal and timber trade. The conditions following the war did not encourage further developments, and it was not until 1934 that the New Dock was made available. This delay in improving facilities can hardly be regarded as a major cause of the relative stagnation in recent years and may well have been as much the effect of it. In any case a similar problem arose at Hull and the scheme for improvements at that port has still to be realized.

Communications are also important for the supply of materials used in the fish trade, especially coal and, to a lesser extent, salt. For coal, Grimsby draws from the collieries of South Yorkshire, largely from the Doncaster area, the haulage distance being little more than 40 miles. In this respect Hull is similarly well placed. An idea of the quantities required may be gained from the fact that North Sea trawlers need 40 to 50 tons per trip of three to four weeks. Salt is no longer required in the trawling industry, though some quantities are used in the salt fish-curing trade.

Not unnaturally there is a concentration of activities connected with the fish trade, including subsidiary and dependent industries, in the vicinity of the docks. The manufacture of ice is carried on close to the quays, and from one factory, which claims to be the largest in the world, ice is loaded ready crushed direct to the trawlers by means of overhead conveyors. Fish-curing establishments, as well as those producing fish-meal and fertilizer, are also found adjoining the docks, though the largest salt fish-curing works are at Pyewipe to the west of the harbour. Efficient arrangements exist for the repair and refitting of trawlers, and various marine engineering firms are equipped to undertake major repairs, many parts including propellers being made on the spot. A vessel can be given a considerable overhaul, including the fitting of a new propeller and painting within thirty-six hours. Such expeditious work is invaluable, for the majority of trawlers are only in port for thirty-six to forty-eight hours between trips. Although shipbuilding is not normally carried on nowadays, small wooden craft were being constructed under war conditions, and one engineering firm at least considers that Grimsby could well undertake to build its own trawlers. Though a certain amount of congestion results from the focusing of these activities around the older docks, the New Dock and the adjoining reclaimed land offer scope for great extension.

As a modern fishing port Grimsby is particularly well situated in relation to the rich grounds of the southern North Sea, above all, the Dogger Bank and the Silver Pits. It is easily the nearest port to the

Bank, which is only 100 miles away. With the extension of deep-sea fishing many trawlers now work at much greater distances, the principal areas being the waters around the Faroe Islands and Iceland, around Bear Island and in the White and Barents Seas. The remotest of these grounds lie up to 1,500 miles distant, involving three weeks or more at sea. Before the war attempts were made to fish the Newfoundland and Labrador cod-banks, but this necessitated a three months' voyage with running expenses so high that trawler-owning companies were obliged to discontinue the experiment. The North Sea, however, remains one of the richest grounds, especially for prime fish, and as a rule involves only seven days away from port. Quite one-half of the Grimsby trawlers are therefore employed in the Dogger Bank region and home waters.

When landed, the fish is sold by auction on the quay-side where the merchants have their stands. The quay, known as the Pontoon, is really a wharf, market, and packing shed combined, and continues round the dock for over a mile. Railways run alongside, the level of the platform being flush with the floor of the wagons. On an average in pre-war years forty trawlers landed their catch daily, the fish being disposed of by about 500 wholesale merchants, many of whom represent only very small businesses. The principal types brought in are demersal prime fish such as cod, haddock, and plaice. More than half the total landings are of cod—approximately 2 million cwt. per annum—the rest, in order of weight, consisting of haddock, plaice, skate, catfish, herring (pelagic or non-demersal), dogfish, whiting, ling, dory, and hake. Small quantities of halibut, turbot, and sturgeon are also landed. Independent of the regular traffic is the herring trade. The local herring season is brief, lasting from mid-August to early October when drifters from Yarmouth, Lowestoft, and Scottish ports bring in their catch, a large proportion of which is converted into kippers.

The bulk of the demersal fish, after being cleaned and some of it filleted, is put on the railway for immediate dispatch inland. A considerable quantity, however, is conveyed by lorry to the various drying, salting, and curing works. Some 75 per cent of the country's consumption of smoked haddock and codling and more recently fillets originated from Grimsby, there being nearly fifty curing-houses which normally give employment to 1,500 men and women. The salting of cod, ling, and various smaller fish, in connexion with which 100 acres of open land are used for drying, provides for an export trade to Latin countries. Besides these sections of the fish trade, Grimsby has exceptional facilities for cold storage, one store alone having a capacity of 2,000 tons of fish and another of 1,800 tons.

Most of the Grimsby trawling firms, though corporate concerns, are small in size. Five of them had over 250 workers each in 1939, and another six firms had between 100 and 200 workers, but most of these are merchants as well as trawler-owners. The private company is the usual form, and many are family businesses, founded by skilful and enterprising skippers, who accumulated capital out of their earnings. There is a tendency in such firms for the ownership to be divided and subdivided through succeeding generations and for increasing claims on the profits to leave the business denuded of liquid resources for replacement and expansion.

The relatively small-scale organization at Grimsby is illustrated by the statistics given in the Sea-Fish Commission Report. In 1934 two-thirds of the Grimsby trawlers were owned by concerns with fewer than nineteen vessels each. At Hull less than half the total number were in that class of ownership, and this fact largely explains why Hull had the more modern fleet.

It must, however, be emphasized that much has been done since 1934 to improve the condition of the Grimsby fleet. The following list shows the number of new trawlers introduced in each of the years 1930 to 1940:

Year	No. of Vessels	Length in Feet
1930	9	122–143
1931	6	140–157
1932	1	150
1933	9	155
1934	9	157–160
1935	10	100–164 including 1 Diesel
1936	16	101–166 ,, 1 ,,
1937	15	101–173 ,, 1 ,,
1938	5	175
1939	—	—
1940	2	142–178 including 1 Diesel

The general increase in size will be noted. From 1936 the minimum length for steam trawlers was 158 feet; the motor ships, which require less engine space, were smaller, but the latest vessel of this type was 142 feet in length.

In addition to the new trawlers listed above, Associated Fisheries Ltd. bought in 1938 fifteen very large trawlers from Mac Fisheries, who had had the vessels built in Germany. The former owners had tried to operate them from Fleetwood, but without much success, and Associated Fisheries brought them to Grimsby, where they made a big difference to the balance of supplies between that port and Hull.

Associated Fisheries Ltd. is the biggest of the small group of public companies engaged in the Grimsby trawling industry. It was established in 1929 with a capital of £500,000, and has acquired three trawling companies as well as merchanting interests. It appears to have been conspicuously successful. The other members of the group are much smaller concerns. They include Consolidated Fisheries Ltd., formed in 1905, with £100,000 capital, to take over a number of existing businesses, and Trawlers Grimsby Ltd., which has an issued capital of £102,000, and dates from 1920.

The burst of enterprise which is illustrated in the table given above appears to have been stimulated by the opening of the new fish dock, an important undertaking carried out by the L.N.E.R. with financial assistance from the Grimsby Corporation. This has placed Grimsby definitely ahead in the facilities it offers for the fish trade; but local opinion is by no means confident that the industry will be capable of seizing its opportunities. Apparently the criticisms underlined in the Commission's Report are still valid.

The highly specialized character of the trawling business has hitherto forced it to depend largely on its own resources not only for managerial personnel, but also for capital. In the past there was no difficulty in securing the capital for corporate enterprise on the scale then appropriate, and the supply of managerial ability seems to have been fully equal to the demand. Personal leadership is still important, for trawling demands personal knowledge and experience, and where those qualities are not allied with business ability of a high order the operating unit necessarily remains small. But on the other hand, the large business provides opportunities for division of functions making for increased all-round efficiency.

In the large trawling concern, responsibility for the technical side of operations can be delegated, as indeed it must be, to the man on the spot—the skipper; but the operations of the fleet as a whole, the purchase of equipment and stores, decisions about laying up vessels and about replacements and additions, present problems that are similar to those met with in other businesses. It may happen that the personal qualities required for managing operations on the large scale will be found in men brought up in the fishing industry. But there appears to be no reason why the industry should have to depend on this, provided there is faith in its future. There is at least one example of a large and successful concern at Grimsby managed by a man who came into trawling after experience gained in other fields of business.

Some of the bigger companies have a wide range of interests. As already mentioned, Associated Fisheries have a merchanting side. Consolidated Fisheries Ltd., besides owning trawlers, are proprietors of dry docks and cold storage; they undertake ship-repairing and ice manufacture and are also fish merchants and curers. Another firm is an amalgamation of two trawler-owning concerns which has developed engineering and ship-repairing; they buy coal direct for their own vessels and supply others; they also make nets. There are other firms which, besides operating their own trawlers, undertake the complete management of trawlers belonging to outsiders. It is for this reason that the number of operating concerns is less than that of ownership units.

These examples are interesting illustrations of the scope for administrative ability in trawling and its related trades. But on the merits of direct linkage between the various sections opinion is divided. Experience proves that it can succeed, especially where ability of a high order and adequate capital resources have been available. But there is also evidence to the contrary. At one time it was fairly common for fish merchants to invest some of their accumulated profits in trawlers. But many of these mixed concerns fell into difficulties; it was found that trawler-ownership absorbed too great a part of the firm's energies, and even when the interest was retained it was sometimes found expedient to operate the trawler branch as virtually a separate business.

Grimsby trawler-owners, even when organized as joint stock companies, apparently still rely largely on their own capital resources, though shares are, of course, held by investors in the allied trades, just as the latter have attracted share capital from the trawling section. But it is declared that, taking the fishing and allied trades as a group, there is no lack of capital. What is complained of is the dearth of business leaders capable of undertaking operations on the scale demanded by modern technique. This is the explanation generally offered for the flagging of enterprise, with the consequent deterioration of equipment and the failure to develop the trade of the port. All this would be less noticeable, of course, but for the vivid contrast presented by Hull; indeed, when compared with Aberdeen, Grimsby appears progressive. It is true that the economic environment has been less favourable to enterprise since the 1914–18 war. With the comparative exhaustion of the nearer fishing-grounds the industry came to require bigger trawlers capable of long voyages. This meant the investment of more capital in an industry risky at all times, and with dubious prospects in the 1920's and 1930's. It is hardly surprising that many trawler-owners declined to take the risk. Yet the experience of Hull shows that the risk was well worth taking.

Another factor that militated against enterprise in the later 1930's when Grimsby, as has been said, showed some signs of revival, was the growing risk of war. Owners knew that in war-time it is the best boats that are requisitioned. When war actually came Hull lost most of its trawlers; at Grimsby at least a nucleus of the fleet was kept together and considerably more trade was being done than at the neighbouring port. The most progressive owners at both ports were the most heavily hit by the war. They took the risk of sinking capital in new boats, for the Admiralty, though approached, gave no assistance, and it was just these boats that were taken immediately war broke out. In so far as this was anticipated there was naturally some hesitation in undertaking responsibility for additions to the fishing fleet.

It is difficult to make any statement about post-war prospects for the trawling section. Ultimately they depend on the future of the fishing industry; more immediately they depend on the conditions under which the replacement of the fishing fleet will have to be undertaken. The latter problem will be more serious for Hull than for Grimsby, but Grimsby will have to decide about modernization as well as the replacement of lost vessels. She will have to decide whether to continue to concentrate on the nearer fishing-grounds or to follow Hull's example. This raises a further question: will policy be determined through the unco-ordinated decisions of individual owners, or will the organization of the section be so strengthened that it becomes possible to adopt an agreed line of action? Hitherto the existence of so many small units at Grimsby has prevented this. There is a representative body, the Grimsby Trawler Owners' Exchange, which has increased its strength in recent years, and is affiliated to the British Trawler Owners' Federation, but the lack of team spirit and leadership is a general complaint at Grimsby.

Besides the general question of the type of trade which Grimsby is to undertake there are several technical issues that will have to be decided in relation to the general problem. For instance, some trawler-owners are becoming oil-minded. The motor vessel has definite advantages over the steamer; its engines are more compact, it is cleaner, and requires less fuel space. On the other hand, electric power has to be provided for working the landing gear, and the problem of heating the ship, an important matter when fishing in northern waters, presents special difficulties. Then there is the question of fuel cost. The price trend was favourable to oil before the war, but it is by no means certain that that condition will be re-established. Another interesting problem concerns the method of fishing. Continental fishermen have been very successful with smaller boats using the Seine-net in preference to the trawl; they make frequent journeys to port to unload the catch, and it is claimed that the method makes for economy in fishing as well as yielding good-quality fish. As against this technique there is the method formerly favoured by some of the Hull firms, and at one time used by some Grimsby owners, of keeping the trawlers at sea for longer periods and using carriers to take off the fish, already boxed, and transport it direct to the London market. More speculative is the possibility of introducing the factory ship, as in the whaling industry. Already many trawlers have boiling-plants for extracting liver oil; but how far the development of processing at sea is likely to go is a question upon which owners are reluctant to venture an opinion at the moment.

Grimsby had, before the war, about 560 fish merchants who bought fish by auction on its arrival and distributed it, fresh or cured, either to inland wholesalers or direct to retailers. It is surprising to learn that 418 of these merchants were still operating under the restrictions of war-time trading. Of these 418 only eighty-one each employed a staff of four workers or more, and the operations of many, even before the war, were on an incredibly small scale. Cases were mentioned of merchants with only one customer, perhaps in a distant town, doing a high-class trade and requiring a good assortment of the prime fish for which Grimsby is famous. Others have all their customers in one town.

The success, such as it is, of operations on this scale, apparently depends on the personal attention which the small man can give to the requirements of his customers. Entry into this class of trade is easy; little capital is needed, since business is conducted on weekly terms, and an enterprising man who has acquired a knowledge of the market and made contacts with customers as an employee of a fish merchant can easily set up on his own account. These conditions naturally foster keen competition and keep margins very moderate. Indeed, the market is so unstable at times that many of the merchants favour the establishment of a scale of minimum prices. The price of fish is bound to fluctuate with seasonal variations in supply. But the fluctuations, it is argued, are much greater than they need be. Moreover, a price slump in the primary market, detrimental to trawler-owners and merchants alike, has little effect on the ultimate retail market. Here demand tends to be inelastic and fishmongers order much the same quantities whether the price be high or low. It is suggested that the cost to the final consumer of organization for steadying prices in the primary market would be no more than $\frac{1}{2}d.$ a pound.

It might be expected that war conditions, which forced concentration on so many trades, would have had a similar effect on fish merchanting, especially in view of the great curtailment of supplies and the introduction of zoning and distribution. But the great majority of merchants continued to trade. Quotas were apportioned through an Allocation Committee consisting of six trawler-owners and six merchants. The extent to which the pre-war organization was preserved is evident in the fact that one-half of the merchants still in business did less than 20 per cent of the total trade. Transport was, of course, economized by the zoning scheme, which, however, was decidedly unpopular. Grimsby's zone included Lincolnshire, the Eastern Counties, Kent, Surrey, Sussex, Hampshire, and London, which was open to all the zones. But these arbitrary boundaries cut across many of Grimsby's normal connexions; for instance, those with Sheffield and Doncaster, Nottingham, Derby, and Leicester, Leeds and Bradford.

The survival of the small fish merchants now the war is over would seem to depend on conditions in the retail market. So long as specialized fishmongers exist, especially those having a high-class trade in fresh fish, there is a place for the small merchant, able to give close personal attention to his customers' requirements and ensuring a reliable supply of the right kinds of prime fish. But, as with so many foods, the nature of the demand for fish is changing, and if, as seems likely, the pre-war tendency is re-established, the distributing organizations will change too.

One notable aspect of the change is the growth of the fried-fish trade. This trade seems likely to expand further with the growing preference for ready-cooked food and the possible removal of fish-frying from the list of obnoxious trades, as recommended by the Sea-Fish Commission. If Grimsby goes more into this market, it is the bigger merchants who are likely to undertake the trade, which requires bulk supplies of cheaper kinds of fish filleted before dispatch. There is even a possibility of linkage between fish-merchanting and fish-frying; one Grimsby merchant is reported to have set up a chain of twenty fried-fish shops in the London area.

The development of fish processing and packing, involving mechanization, is also likely to benefit the bigger merchant who is able to undertake the work. Curing is, of course, an old-established process, filleting is now very general, and quick chilling is undertaken by some merchants. Sometimes the fish is cooked before sale. One or two firms have experimented with standard packets of fish, sealed with paraffin wax, and have tried to popularize their sale through grocers. They believe that the fishmonger is doomed and that in the future most of the fish will be sold, after factory processing and packing, through grocers and chain stores, except, of course, for the fried fish trade. Another possibility is fish-canning; experiments in the canning of white fish have been made by at least one firm, though so far without much success. The manufacture of foods in which fish is a main ingredient has also been extensively developed.

In these ways fish seems likely to become more and more the raw material of manufactures. There are other developments that emphasize the same tendency, such as the extraction of oils and isinglass and the making of fish-meals from offal and stale fish. There have even been experiments in making leather from fish skin: it is claimed that the material could be used for the uppers of women's shoes and for handbags.

These developments may profoundly influence the whole organization of the fishing industry. They will enhance the advantage of the big merchant who is able to branch out into manufacture. They may also affect the relations between the trawling and merchanting sections. For instance, one of the important manufacturers of fish foods who also supplies fresh fish to large buyers such as cafés, hotels, and shipping companies, buys from all ports. The firm has also built up an important trade in the import of fish from Iceland. Small boats fishing the fiords of that country deliver their catch to processing stations where the fish is prepared for export. This firm controls thirty-two such plants in Iceland, and before the war imported 95 per cent of Icelandic fish brought to this country. It employs 350 workers in fish processing at Grimsby, and is now planning an expansion which will eventually raise its labour force to 1,000.

The extension of manufacture should certainly make for greater stability of prices. Any student of the fish trade must be struck by the similarity of its marketing problems to those of milk. The peak of white fish production occurs in the early summer, when conditions are not favourable for a corresponding increase in retail sales of 'fresh' fish. Even at lower prices fishmongers apparently are not prepared to take the risk of buying much bigger quantities, which they would be forced to sell cheap to their retail customers. Consequently prices at the port fall heavily in the summer season. This has been partially remedied by the prohibition of landings of fish caught in distant waters during the summer months; but the processing of fish, making it less perishable, also helps to regulate the flow of supplies through the retail market. Whether the trawler-owners secure their due share of benefit from steadier prices depends on the strength of their organization. Before the war Grimsby trawler-owners were trying to establish a scale of minimum prices for sales to merchants, the surplus going to the fish-meal factories. But the prices paid by the latter are necessarily low; greater benefit would be received by regulating the sale of fish for human consumption, and there seems to be a good prospect of this in the development of the trade in fish foods.

At the same time something could be done to improve the trade in prime fresh fish, which is so important for Grimsby. The first essential is a guarantee of quality, enabling the retail customers to buy with confidence. At present the customer must trust to the reputation of the fishmonger, who in turn relies on the merchant. The typical Grimsby merchant sells direct to the retailer rather than to inland wholesalers, which is the more usual method in the Hull trade. But the direct system of trading, although better adapted to the requirements of the high-quality trade, apparently still falls short of the conditions necessary for securing the most profitable development. A scheme for marking fish has been proposed by Grimsby merchants; but the difficulties of ensuring that all fish sold under the

mark was of the implied quality are obvious; a very strong organization would be needed to ensure the success of the scheme.

The provisioning of the fishing fleet is itself an important trade at
Grimsby. Coal is the main item, accounting for an annual expenditure
of nearly a million pounds. The demand for stores, especially ice, is
also considerable, and nets and gear of all kinds need frequent replacement. The connexion between these supply trades and the fishing
industry is so close that they may be considered as forming part of
its organization.

As early as 1873 many of the owners of fishing vessels at Grimsby
had realized the advantages of combination for direct buying of coal,
salt, and other supplies. The enterprise for which they supplied most
of the original capital, the Great Grimsby Coal, Salt, and Tanning
Company Ltd., is a remarkable organization. Well-established and
with an increasing trade before the advent of steam trawling, its
great period of expansion coincided with the revolution in the fishing
industry. The supply of coal to the trawling fleet became a major
undertaking in which the Company played a leading part, while at
the same time developing its business as general coal merchants and
importers. But the Company also extended its activities into several
branches of manufacture. These include net-making (or 'braiding',
as it is called), twine-spinning, and rope-making, the manufacture of
oilskin clothing and knitted goods, sheet-metal and tinplate work.
At one time ship-repairing was also undertaken, but it was given up
after a few years. The Company now has branches in most of the
British fishing ports and has several establishments abroad.

The Company has striven to preserve its character as a co-operative
undertaking. On its reconstruction in 1884 it was decided that all
profits remaining after the payment of a 7 per cent dividend on
capital should be distributed to each shareholder in proportion to
purchases. Ten years later, when the M.S. & L. Railway Company
had improved the facilities for delivering coal at the docks, the Great
Grimsby Coal, Salt, and Tanning Company made an arrangement
whereby the leading trawler-owners were formed into a coal syndicate,
which operated as part of its organization.

But it would be misleading to suggest that there is complete
identity of interests between the Company as suppliers, and the
trawler-owners as consumers. A good deal of the share capital is
now held outside the industry, and some consumers prefer to deal
with other suppliers of coal and stores. One firm buys its coal direct
from the colliery and supplies other trawler-owners; but this is
exceptional. It also has a net braiding works and undertakes ship
repairs. Mixed concerns like this are not easy to manage, however;
in any case, direct buying of coal is only possible for big consumers.
For those who feel that direct buying offers advantages, co-operation

is the obvious method, and there is some tentative discussion of a new project for this purpose at the present time. But all such schemes require considerable capital, and even if, as is contended, the trawler-owners have the capital for such ventures, it would appear to be the sounder policy to concentrate their resources in improving the efficiency of the trawler fleet, whose standards had, before the war, fallen so much below those of Hull. This point is further emphasised by the great increase in replacement costs.

The important business of supplying ice is mainly undertaken by one concern, the Grimsby Ice Company Ltd. This enterprise began in a small way as long ago as 1865; twenty years later it was reconstructed with a capital of £250,000 and absorbed two other firms. At that time the Company had a fleet bringing ice from Norway, and also carrying fish, but it now went in for ice manufacture. To-day its factory, with an output of 300,000 tons of ice a year, is said to be the biggest of its kind in the world. At Hull the ice manufacture is a co-operative undertaking owned by the consumers, but this is not the position at Grimsby. Much of the capital of the Grimsby Ice Company, however, is held in the various sections of the fishing trade, the connexion with the Coal, Salt, and Tanning Company being especially close. It seems to be agreed that the cost of ice, as of coal, is about the same at Grimsby as at Hull.

Besides these major enterprises there are many smaller firms supplying the needs of the basic industry. The engineering activities of the port have already been mentioned. Nets, ropes, and other fishing gear as well as clothing are made in a number of factories. Box-making is done by several firms who supply not only the large requirements of the fish trade, but also those of fruit and vegetable packers.

The statistics of insured employment for the immediate pre-war years show that about one-third of Grimsby's population normally depends on fishing and these related trades. The sea-going personnel of the fishing fleet was about 5,000. Grimsby was not a prosperous town in the inter-war period. There was a serious decline in the general trade of the port; and although certain industries, particularly food, paper, and chemical manufactures, expanded, there are not many industries that will fit into the peculiar pattern of local resources and at the same time encounter no marked disadvantage in being located on the Lincolnshire coast. Two new enterprises for the manufacture of chemicals and fertilisers which will be appropriately located in Grimsby are now to be established; and the clothing trade, attracted by the supply of female labour available, is being expanded. The local engineering firms are also in a prosperous condition, having been kept busy during the war on Government contracts. But the industrial pattern of Grimsby is essentially that of a port with the emphasis on fishing, and it is evident that the tempo of economic activity in this town of 92,000 people will continue to be determined largely by the state of the fishing industry.

The revival of Grimsby's basic industry thus presents an urgent problem. Revival has already begun; although the fleet is far below pre-war strength more fish is being landed than in 1938, owing to the re-stocking of the nearer fishing-grounds. But this is a temporary condition and before long more extensive fishing will have to be resumed. That will require more trawlers and more men. Building costs are more than double the pre-war figure (£69,000 was recently quoted for a large trawler); but it is believed that the necessary capital could be obtained within the industry, which has made good profits in recent years, if there were sufficient confidence in its future. The industry is now looking to the Government for a statement of policy, and in the meantime the British Trawlers' Federation is not prepared to support a rebuilding programme. Labour supply also presents difficulties. Grimsby alone lost over 600 trawler men killed during the war and for some years previously the labour force had been declining. Young recruits must now be secured in the face of keener competition from other occupations; and this requires that the industry be made more attractive, with probably a consequent increase in operating costs.

HULL

For a long time prior to the whaling industry's establishment there, Hull had been one of the leading ports in England, with a mercantile and sea-going community eager to try out new possibilities of profit.[1] From the very beginning of British attempts to enter the northern whale-fishing (at the end of the sixteenth century) Hull merchants are to be found fitting out vessels for this purpose; and when the fishing was extended some years later, from Iceland and the North Cape to Spitsbergen, Hull whalers were in the forefront of this movement also. Little is known of what happened between the middle of the seventeenth century (when the Dutch wars brought the English whaling trade to an end) and the middle of the eighteenth century. But in 1753 a group of Hull merchants and shipowners is found forming a company, with a capital of £20,000 to engage in Greenland fishing, and for nine years or so after that date similar ventures, with a marked degree of success in most cases, were launched. And, despite periodic setbacks, the Hull whaling fleet steadily increased in size thereafter, particularly after bounties were revived and improved in 1786. From the 1770's, ships from other

---

[1] The historical account given here is partly based on Mr. E. Jacobs' unpublished Leeds University B.A. thesis on the Hull Fishing Industry (1931).

ports started bringing their oil and whalebone to Hull. The first twenty years of the nineteenth century was the most prosperous period in the business, and Hull people owned about two-fifths of the English industry's ships at that time. In the peak year of 1818 no fewer than sixty-four whalers left Hull. Thereafter, a decline set in, though Hull, with a steadily decreasing number of whaling vessels, still remained the most important whaling port in England; Hull's participation in the whaling trade finally came to an end in 1869.

Meanwhile, however, significant developments were taking place in the rise of a deep-sea trawl-fishing industry which was ultimately to make Hull the most important fishing centre (in terms of weight of catch) in Britain. The circumstances in which this began are of some interest. One story is that in 1850 some small fishing-smacks from Brixham, Devonshire, which were in the habit of sailing into the North Sea and fishing off the North-east Coast during the late summer and early autumn stayed there later than usual, and, after being blown inland during a gale, found some large soles in their nets. They had accidentally discovered what have since been named the 'Silver Pits'. It was not long before a small fleet of Brixham and South Coast trawlers came north to exploit this discovery, and the obvious place to land the big catches made was Hull; particularly as it was reasonably near the new grounds, and had a population sufficient to absorb the fish landed. It was only a question of a year or two before the obviously greater profitability of this winter fishing in the North Sea led some of the Brixham families (including that of Hellyer, probably still the most enterprising fishing family in Hull) to move permanently to Hull.

Despite the advantages of Hull as a port for the purpose, the increasing number of vessels specially built to work the relatively unfished Dogger Bank had no adequate facilities there for unloading, for lying-up when discharged, or for refitting. In time part of one dock was allocated to the fishing industry, but it was not until some time after many of the Hull trawler-owners had been induced to move to Grimsby by the better facilities offered them there by the Manchester, Sheffield, and Lincolnshire Railway Company, that the Hull Dock Company began to recognize the importance of the fishing industry. The Albert Dock gradually came to be devoted almost exclusively to fish, and merchants and trawler-owners built ice-houses, store-houses, and markets there, with smoke-houses nearby. But the growth in the number of fishing vessels (well over 400 in the 1880's) made even the Albert Dock insufficient, and vessels often had to lie off the entrance to the dock, their fish deteriorating the while, for lack of accommodation. The Hull and Barnsley Railway Company prepared plans for the building of a special fish dock at Saltend, nearer the mouth of the Humber; had these plans gone through, it is probable that Hull would have been better able to compete with Grimsby in later years in short-voyage fishing, including fresh herrings; the proposal, however, fell through. Instead, the newly completed St. Andrew's Dock, originally meant for the coal export trade which failed to come up to expectations, was, in 1884, allocated by the Dock Company to the fishing industry. This meant a still longer journey from the sea, as well as the scrapping of all the storage and other facilities erected at Albert Dock by merchants and owners and their re-erection at and around the new dock. Shortly afterwards the Dock Company sold the dock to the North Eastern Railway Company; and ultimately the railway company proved more willing than the old Dock Company to provide the modern equipment which the growth of the industry, and the steady replacement of sail by steam, demanded. The dock was extended in 1897, and equipment provided enabling coal, ice, pure water, and stores to be taken on by trawlers by the most modern methods, as well as slipways for painting and minor repairs. But in the period of congestion before these various improvements were made, many Hull fishing people went elsewhere (e.g. Grimsby, Aberdeen, and Milford Haven) and lent their skill and experience to the building-up of rival fishing industries.

In the meantime, of course, the area fished from Hull had been steadily widening, so that first the whole of the Dogger Bank (and not merely the Silver Pits and the southern edge of the Dogger) was included, and then in the 1880's the east coast of Scotland and the west coast of Denmark were brought in. Over-fishing in the North Sea, and the greater range made possible by the changes in vessel construction, led Hull trawler-owners to start fishing around the Faroe Islands and Iceland from 1889 onwards (though, to begin with, fishing in these distant waters was by line). And this, coupled with the general substitution of the otter-trawl for the beam-trawl, led to enormously increased landings in the last years of the nineteenth century. Hull's more rapid adoption of steam trawlers than some of the other British ports is no doubt partly to be explained by its favourable bunker position arising out of quick and easy rail communication with the South Yorkshire coalfield.

Hull trawler-owners continued, in the twentieth century, to pioneer new fishing-grounds, and in 1905 they got as far as the White Sea, from which medium-sized plaice were brought; and this new area soon showed signs of replacing Iceland in popularity and productiveness. During 1914–18 this movement towards going farther and farther afield for fish naturally received a check, since war conditions made it necessary to concentrate once more on shorter-distance fishing, and the North Sea came into its own again. By the 1920's the previous trend had been resumed, and Hull trawlers were again going to

Iceland, as well as the White Sea and the Barents Sea. The industry experienced numerous difficulties (e.g. disputes with foreign governments about the limits within which fishing might take place, bunker shortages owing to coal strikes, a glut of fish in British markets, over-hasty buying by trawler-owners of expensive and unsuitable Admiralty trawlers after the war, building of new trawlers when building costs were excessive, and so on), and numbers of trawler-owners went out of business. White Sea fishing was discontinued, as the Government could not guarantee protection for British vessels in that area, but the majority of Hull trawler-owners still continued to fish off Iceland, the Murmansk coast, and the Barents Sea. Hellyer's, in the late 1920's, had two large vessels built and specially equipped for halibut-fishing off the Davis Strait; a regular service of carriers brought the halibut from these two ships to Hull in prime condition every day; while in winter the ships, loaded with halibut, remained in port, and discharged over a long period.

But though North Sea fishing had ceased to be of great importance to Hull as a port (now that a high degree of concentration on more distant waters had taken place), some Hull trawler-owners were still interested in it, but took their catches direct to London. From 1918 to 1930 the extent and nature of this by-passing of Hull, as it were, was as follows. Two fleets of Hull trawlers, comprising together about seventy-five small trawlers and eight 'carriers', were run by Kelsall Brothers and Beechings Ltd., and the Hull Steam Fishing and Ice Company Ltd., respectively. Haddock, plaice, cod, and whiting (with soles and turbot when in season) were sent direct to the London market daily in the carriers. The fleets (each of which was under the general direction of an 'admiral', who changed the fishing-ground each day) fished off the German and Danish coasts in the summer and the Dogger Bank in the winter. Hull's facilities for refuelling, overhauling, provisioning, and providing ice were used by both the fleeters and the carriers under this arrangement, but the port's facilities for handling and sending the fish to where it was wanted were not, of course, made use of. As a means of supplying the London market with fresh fish, the arrangement (which was peculiar to Hull) was something of an historical relic. The decline in the number of fleets and fleeters in the post-1918 as compared with the pre-war period is said to have been due partly to the prohibitive cost of rebuilding a fleet after the war. However that may be, the system was naturally unpopular with other Hull trawler-owners, and with the L.N.E.R.; it is said to have originated partly because the L.N.E.R.'s predecessors between them charged excessive rates for carrying fish from Hull to the London market.

The fish-curing industry in Hull was not dependent entirely on imported foreign-caught herrings, though they undoubtedly formed its mainstay. During the Icelandic cod season (March, April, and May) some of the cod and haddock landed from Hull trawlers went to the curers and driers to be converted into smoked fillets. June to November tended to be a slack season for Hull curers, who therefore took to importing English herrings during that period from Peterhead, Mallaig, Yarmouth, and Lowestoft. Another branch of the curing industry was concerned with the salting and drying of cod, ling, and haddock by sun and wind or by artificial heat, mainly during the Icelandic season. It is probable that about half the fish landed here in that period was treated in this way. Were it not for the existence of this salting industry, the quantities of fish landed in Hull could hardly have been disposed of at remunerative prices at all. Much of the salted and dried fish was exported to Southern Europe and South America. Most of the curing-houses were conveniently situated near St. Andrew's Dock so that, whether the final product was for export or for home consumption, freight charges before the boxes reached the cargo vessels or fish-wagons were reduced to a minimum. The labour employed was, of course, mainly female.

It will be clear from the historical account given above that certain fairly obvious features characterized Hull fishing in the period after the 1914–18 war. The bulk of the fish was caught in distant waters, a factor certainly not unconnected with Hull's early interest in whaling in that area; with the tendency to go farther and farther afield for fish there developed a tendency to work with larger, faster, and better-equipped trawlers; the fish caught tended (as it apparently generally does, in waters hitherto unfished) not to be of first quality, much of it being dried and salted for export and much going to fried-fish shops throughout Britain; while the dock equipment and facilities for treating and carrying the fish, either abroad or to the home market, were modern and highly efficient. By comparison with the fishing industry of other British ports, Hull's industry was obviously more highly organized, was equipped—particularly after the early 1930's—with a very much more modern fleet (nearly half of which was, in 1934, less than ten years old), and the unit of trawler-ownership was very much larger in Hull than elsewhere (52 per cent of the Hull vessels were found in 1934 to be owned by concerns possessing more than nineteen trawlers apiece).

There were, however, certain other features of the industry at that time to which attention ought to be drawn. (1) The great rise in the amount of fish landed and forwarded by rail in the period would probably not have been possible but for the increasing development, in the late 1920's, of the filleting system. Hull merchants, instead of sending their fish with bone and skins, saved transport charges by filleting, which reduced the weight very substantially. In time the bulk of fish transported inland by rail from Hull came to be prepared

in this way before consignment. (2) Partly arising out of this development, the industry in Hull which was engaged in making marketable
products out of fish offals, and which had previously mainly depended
on fish unsold or unfit for human consumption (as well as fish residues
from the curing-houses) for its supplies, now got the residue from the
filleting process, and had to be very greatly expanded. As far back
as 1891 the Hull Fish Meal and Oil Company had been formed on a
co-operative basis, virtually all the local trawler-owners, fish-curers,
and fish merchants taking shares in it. By the late 1920's this company was operating three large factories, capable between them of
dealing with about 80,000 tons of offal a year. The Company produced fish manure, fish-meal, and fish-liver oil (most of the latter
only being suitable for industrial use), and exported a fair proportion
of the product. Other concerns of similar type, but smaller in size,
were also located here. (3) Another important and successful venture
was the manufacture of ice on a large scale. Following on the import
of ice to Hull from Norway in the last years of the nineteenth century,
some of the Hull trawler-owners started a joint venture to produce
ice by the brine system of freezing. The Hull Ice Company, formed
in this way, soon extended its operations, and as it opened more and
more factories, so the imports of Norwegian ice declined; by 1914
six such factories were in action, with a combined output of nearly
90,000 tons a year, and imports virtually ceased. By the late 1920's
two more factories had been opened and the previous output had
been more than doubled. Large storehouses had been built in the
meantime, mechanical crushers were in use, and the crushed ice was
conveyed to the trawlers by means of covered conveyor-belts.

Many of the tendencies already noted were carried a stage further
in the years immediately preceding the recent war. Distant-water
fishing was continued; trawlers became still more elaborate and
expensive, and now that the newest of them had their own ice-
producing plant as well as numerous other improvements, the term
'floating factories' (often applied to them locally) seemed not inappro-
priate. No one could deny that the trawlers of the Hull and Grimsby
long-distance fishing business were the largest and most up to date
in Britain. At the same time, the old 'fleeter' system, with its direct
delivery to London, died out; the trawlers involved had been small
and old-fashioned, and it apparently did not pay to sink further
capital in the business when they became unseaworthy. More sur-
prisingly, Hellyer's experiment with two large vessels solely devoted
to prime halibut was discontinued in this period, apparently through
poor fish prices. Imports of foreign-caught, fresh, or frozen fish other
than herrings began to appear, but foreign landings as a whole never
reached large proportions—in the three years 1930–2 they only
formed about 2 per cent of total landings at Hull. Nevertheless,

even a small proportion, in these difficult years of record high landings and low prices, was a cause of ill-feeling amongst Hull trawler-owners, who were glad when, by the Sea-Fishing Industry Act of 1933, restrictions, in the form of quotas, were imposed on foreign landings and imports. The Order, under the same Act, prohibiting the landing by British trawlers of fish from Bear Island and the Barents Sea during the four months June to September (later reduced to three, and then to two, months) was received with mixed feelings in Hull, which inevitably felt the immediate ill-effects of such a measure to a greater extent than other ports, whilst sharing with them the beneficial results. Hull trawler-owners had already, on a voluntary basis, done something to restrict the months of their own distant-water fishing in 1932, as an emergency measure to meet an abnormal situation. A revival of the North Sea trawled herring fishery from Hull had taken place since 1929 or so, the season being late July to October; and increasing numbers of Hull trawler-owners used the trawlers they were no longer allowed to employ in the summer and autumn in northern waters for this purpose. The emergence of Hull as the principal centre for herring trawling in the North Sea area can, indeed, be regarded as an important new development of the period under review, and naturally led to an extension of curing-house capacity in the port.

Nevertheless, Hull trawler-owners found the position becoming more and more difficult as the 1930's progressed; landings increased, 'first sale' prices declined, costs (particularly bunker coal) moved upwards. It was this sort of situation which led the trawler-owners of Hull and Grimsby to adopt a voluntary scheme of regulation of their own, as a result of which a substantial decrease in landings of cod from distant waters was secured. The main feature of this voluntary scheme was the laying-up of about 20 per cent of the long-distance trawlers of the two ports (representing, as they naturally were not the newest ones, perhaps 15 per cent of fishing capacity), and the spreading of the cost of this over the whole group. In addition, permitted landings were restricted to a proportion of each vessel's cubic capacity, and this led to an improvement in the quality of the fish sold.

Preliminary discussions regarding the complete reconstruction of the Hull fish dock also took place in the years before the war; the cost, estimated to be about £750,000, was to be borne in agreed proportions between the railway company and the various interests concerned. The fishing industry's prospects did not at that time seem sufficiently bright, however, to secure the implementing of this plan. Greater willingness to invest capital in a venture which would take some years to show any return was evidenced by the trawler-owners of the port when they jointly, under the name of British Cod Liver

Oil Producers (Hull) Ltd., built a very large factory for refining cod-liver oil by the latest methods. The erection of the new plant brought with it changes in the methods of handling the livers and in the remuneration of the trawler-hands. Thus, instead of the livers being boiled down in Hull when, because of the length of their journey, they were in poor condition (which, taken in conjunction with the old-fashioned methods employed, meant that the product of the Hull Fish Meal and Oil Company was unsuitable for medicinal use) oil is now won from them initially on the trawlers themselves, so that the new Hull plant can concentrate on the further refinement by stages. And the trawlermen have surrendered their traditional rights in respect of livers in return for half the value of the oil kept fresh under the new arrangements.

Before the recent war, then, Hull had reached the position of being the British port where the greatest weight of white fish (or, indeed, wet fish as a whole) was landed. Grimsby ranked higher in terms of value of fish landed, and also in terms of number of trawlers operating from the port; but this last comparison is misleading unless it is remembered that the Hull vessels tended to be both larger and more modern than those elsewhere. That fishing was more efficiently conducted at Hull than at other British ports was clear from the comparison of profits per vessel made by the Sea-Fish Commission's honorary accountants. It is probable that the merchanting function was more efficiently performed there, too, if we are to judge by the quantity of fish handled by each wholesale merchant.

Though the prosperity of its fishing industry is of great importance to the town and port of Hull, and though it formed, along with transit trade and shipbuilding, one of the three key activities of Hull in recent years, it is clear that it does not dominate the town's life to the extent of its counterparts in other ports (e.g. Aberdeen). This is, perhaps, a healthy feature, since undue concentration on one activity has obvious drawbacks; and it has been to some extent an unfortunate coincidence that the three key activities mentioned have happened to experience serious difficulties at roughly the same times.

Hull, with 4,500 insured workers in the fishing industry proper in 1939, had fewer than Grimsby with 5,000; but they only formed 4 per cent of the non-agricultural insured males in the former case, as against $12\frac{1}{2}$ per cent in the latter. In an industry of this kind, where many of those engaged are working on their own account, figures of insured workers are not as helpful as they might be; but it is not without significance that Hull was able to land a greater weight of fish, brought from a greater distance, with fewer insured workers than Grimsby. In Hull, as in other fishing ports, there was a wide range of persons who, though not going to sea, were directly or indirectly dependent on the industry for their livelihood; no satisfactory guess can be made at their numbers in Hull, for to do so would involve such difficulties as specifying the proportion of railway workers who should be regarded as ancillary to fishing. It is only possible to record that the range includes dealers and merchants both wholesale and retail, both in Hull and inland, some of those engaged in dock and railway work in the area, as well as in the engineering, shipbuilding and repairing and paint industries, and those concerned in the fuelling and provisioning of the trawlers.

It may be worth while to list some of the factors which, it is generally agreed, have contributed towards Hull's success as a fishing port, without attempting to assess their relative importance.

(1) The existence in Hull of a community long experienced in the fishing industry is obviously of very great importance. The successful completion of fishing ventures in the distant waters to which Hull trawlers normally go necessitates not only a high degree of skill, ability, and experience on the part of the owners, skippers, and men, but also presupposes an adequate supply of fishing-men of all the types required who are prepared to live, both so far as their life ashore and afloat is concerned, under the conditions which distant-water fishing necessarily involves. It can safely be said that so far as Britain in 1939 was concerned there were only two places which fulfilled this condition necessary to the operation of a large fleet of trawlers in distant waters; those two places being Hull and Grimsby. An increasing amount of distant-water fishing was being done from Fleetwood; the amount from other British ports was relatively insignificant. A long-distance trawling tradition, the attitude of mind required in those who take part in it, cannot be built up in a year or two. If Britain is to continue now the war is over to get white fish in the sort of quantities landed before 1939, it can only be with the help of Hull and Grimsby people; and those people will not lightly uproot themselves and their families and move to other fishing ports. There is a sense, of course, in which the trawler-owners and skippers would be more easily persuaded to move elsewhere than the men; Fleetwood itself has quite largely been built up by the enterprise of Hull and Grimsby owners. But in the normal course of events only some highly unfavourable elements in the situation at the Humber ports would lead them to do so.

(2) Closely related to the first factor is the ability to co-operate successfully shown by trawler-owners and others in Hull. The importance of the willingness of Hull trawler-owners, fish-curers, and wholesalers to set up jointly owned and operated concerns for their mutual benefit, ranging from ice factories, fish-meal and manure factories, and cod-liver oil plants to mutual insurance companies, can hardly be overstressed. The same feature is noticeable in the appointment in the 1930's of an economic adviser to the Hull trawler-owners'

federation, and in the 1938 voluntary restriction scheme amongst the Hull and Grimsby long-distance trawler-owners. The benefits accruing from this policy of co-operation have been obvious and far-reaching.

(3) Hull has been something of a pioneer in the improvement of conditions for the workpeople in the industry. Now that methods of remuneration are fairly closely controlled by the Merchant Shipping Acts, this may not seem important, though there is reason to believe that 'settling-sheet' grievances are less acute here than at other ports; but the increasing modernity of Hull's fishing fleet has naturally brought with it very greatly improved conditions afloat. Moreover, the greater success of Hull trawling has naturally brought increased 'shares' not only for skippers and mates, but also for other members of the crew, in whose remuneration, at Hull in recent years, the sharing element has bulked more largely than the minimum-wage element; and when the new cod-liver oil plant was set up, the arrangement whereby the crews commuted their traditional liver rights was by no means unfavourable to them. Nor is it an accident that Hull was the first British port to try the experiment of setting up local Conciliation Boards. Co-operative arrangements amongst the Hull trawler-owners are of benefit to the workpeople in other respects also. There is, for instance, a non-profit-making store to supply fishermen with clothing and equipment. Medical facilities of various kinds are available; and arrangements are made for disabled fishermen to be employed in basket-making.

(4) The natural advantages of Hull's situation are worth noting too. It is not merely its position on the broad estuary of the Humber, giving shelter and safety all the year round, that is involved here, but also Hull's trading connexions with the Continent, its nearness to the great agglomeration of population represented by the West Riding and North Midland towns, as well as to the South Yorkshire coalfield and the cheap bunkering possibilities opened up thereby. As against this, it is true that Aberdeen, for example, is a good deal nearer the grounds that Hull trawlers fish, but Aberdeen trawler-owners have not taken advantage of this situation; in any case, it is probably cheaper to bring fish in trawlers along the Scottish and North English coasts than to send it the corresponding distance by rail.

(5) To reinforce Hull's natural advantages, very large amounts of capital have been, at different times, sunk in the building of port facilities and railway connexions, so that Hull trawler-owners, wholesalers, and others connected with the fishing industry are well served in these respects. In any assessment of the relative advantages of different British fishing ports, the importance of the very large capital investment in Hull port 'fixtures' (most of which are of comparatively

modern construction, and capable of economical operation) must be put side by side with the factories and plant for producing ice, fish-meal and manure, and cod-liver oil, as well as the curing-houses and other ancillary equipment, and given due weight.

(6) Sufficient emphasis has already been laid on the size and up-to-dateness of the trawlers themselves, which clearly constitutes an important advantage over the industries of other ports. Unfortunately, under war conditions this proved to be a positive disadvantage, since the Government naturally requisitioned the best and fastest trawlers first. Indeed, Hull probably owed its recent unenviable position, in which trawling had in large part ceased, to the superior efficiency of its vessels. For, on the outbreak of war, Hull's entire fishing fleet was taken over by the Admiralty; and though the Government later agreed to allow a small part of the fleet to be used for fishing, it was understood that, should a further emergency arise, these few vessels would also be taken over; and Dunkirk constituted such an emergency. By comparison with this, most other ports were allowed to retain skeleton fleets with which to engage in a limited amount of fishing; and the owners of these vessels were able, despite E.P.T. and maximum price arrangements, to build up out of war-time profits financial reserves which will stand them in good stead now.

(7) Finally, in this list of advantages possessed by the Hull fishing industry, some mention must be made of the existence in the area of units of the shipbuilding industry which have specialized in the building of trawlers for the Hull and Grimsby fishing fleets. The presence of these two industries in the same district, fishing and trawler-building, is probably of considerable mutual benefit. One small instance which may be given is that during the period when both shipbuilding and fishing were experiencing very bad times several Hull trawler-owners kept some of the yards supplied with work by ordering new trawlers, even though there was no immediate prospect of being able to operate them at a profit. No doubt the owners who placed these orders had in mind the desirability of keeping their fleets up to date and of buying when building prices were low and hard bargains could be driven; but there was also the element of keeping local people employed and local friends in business, which would not have been as strongly felt had the trawler building taken place outside the area.

In assessing the future prospects of the Hull fishing industry, due weight must be given to the factors mentioned above, which would seem to ensure that the port will always have a major part to play in the success of the British white fish industry as a whole. The position in Hull will obviously be greatly influenced by the considerations to which attention is drawn in the concluding section of this chapter; but there are one or two additional matters to which reference can conveniently be made here.

(1) The requisitioning of Hull's entire trawling fleet is still having serious post-war repercussions. For one thing, losses have been heavy, and only something like half of Hull's pre-war fleet is available at present. No doubt compensation for requisitioning, loss and damage is, and will be, adequate in the ordinary sense; adequate, that is, to enable the owners to maintain reasonable standards of living and to rebuild eventually. Yet their post-war position, from the point of view of being able to tide themselves over a difficult period of (probably) unremunerative prices, is obviously likely to be much less favourable than that of their counterparts in other ports, who have been able to 'get some wool on their backs' during the war period of operating skeleton fleets under favourable first-sale price conditions. Moreover, Hull owners have a clear recollection of the course of events after the 1914–18 war, when many of them bought ex-Admiralty trawlers at inflated prices, or had trawlers built when costs were high, and then found that they had hardly started to use them before fish prices slumped. Many of them, even with the financial reserves they had built up from war-time fishing (for Hull maintained a skeleton fleet during that war), were forced out of business; and it seems probable that they will be chary of being caught by the same sequence of events after the recent war.

(2) It is still too early to judge how far the habits and preferences of the British public in regard to the consumption of fish will prove, once existing food shortages have been overcome, to have undergone a permanent change. Some observers believe that fish will regain its popularity in the end; but it is equally possible to find reasons justifying the opposite conclusion. The Hull industry's future prosperity clearly might be seriously prejudiced if the public ultimately became less fish-minded (and, particularly, less fried-fish-minded) than it used to be before the war. There is a sense, as has been pointed out earlier, in which the interests of Hull differ materially from the interests of the white fish industry in the rest of the country.

(3) It has often been claimed that the inland marketing of fish landed at Hull was made more difficult and more expensive by the restrictions on the use of road transport which the ownership of the docks by a railway company has involved. It remains to be seen whether these restrictions will cease to operate when inland transport as a whole is nationalized. Just as Hull's prospects would be improved by the removal of such restrictions, so also they would clearly be made worse if it became part of Government policy to fix uniform rates, disregarding distance, for the inland transport of fish.

(4) With regard to the two Humber ports, some further consideration should clearly be given to their relative dock capacity and

handling facilities if a rational policy of development is to be sought. The facts are that before the war Grimsby's extensive accommodation, which included the New Fish Dock opened in 1934, was not utilized to full capacity, whereas the old St. Andrew's Dock at Hull suffered much congestion. This is not to say that further expansion should be discouraged at either port, but it would seem advisable to ensure the full use of the existing facilities at the one port before embarking on major dock building schemes at the other. Thus some of the congestion at Hull might be relieved by landing a proportion of the prime fish at Grimsby, especially as the Yorkshire port is not so dependent upon that section of the trade. At any rate, co-ordination between the various sections of the trade and between the principal centres should be a primary objective of post-war policy.

FLEETWOOD

Fleetwood, now a municipal borough with a population of some 25,000, stands fourth among the British trawling ports, and is easily the chief fishing port of the West Coast. The quantity of white fish landed there was, in 1938, about 23 per cent of Hull's total and about 32 per cent of Grimsby's. It must be remembered, however, that comparison on a quantitative basis exaggerates the relative importance of Hull, where the average value of the fish landed is very low. In this respect Fleetwood is in the same class as Grimsby and Aberdeen; its landings include a wide variety of fish in which the higher grades, especially hake and haddock, bulk largely. Fleetwood is more dependent than the east coast ports on the nearer fishing-grounds. A large part of the catch is taken from the Irish Sea, where, as in the North Sea, over-fishing has become a serious problem; but most of the hake, which is such an important item in Fleetwood's trade, comes from the east Atlantic, towards the edge of the Continental Shelf. Fleetwood trawlers also fish in the more northerly waters of the Atlantic from North-west Ireland to North-west Scotland and make regular visits to the Icelandic fisheries, which are nearer to Fleetwood than to Hull. So far, however, Fleetwood owners have not shown much interest in the more distant fishing-grounds, and they do not undertake the long voyages to Bear Island and the Barents Sea.

The history of Fleetwood as a fishing port is similar in some respects to that of Grimsby. The latter, it is true, is a far older town, but it owes its development as a port almost entirely to the railway. Fleetwood owes its very existence to the railway. Little more than a century ago its site was a sandy waste like the rest of the Fylde coast, except where Blackpool had already made a beginning. The site had natural advantages, for the Wyre mouth, on whose west bank the town now stands, is connected by a deep channel with

Morecambe Bay. A port here could provide a useful connexion between industrial Lancashire and the ports of Northern Ireland and West Scotland when linked up with the railway which had already reached Preston. A Fylde railway would also provide the farmers of the district with a wide market. These advantages were recognized by Sir Peter Fleetwood, lord of the manor, and it was chiefly through his efforts that the Preston and Wyre Harbour and Dock Company was formed. In 1835 the Company secured Parliamentary powers to construct a railway from Preston to Fleetwood and to establish a harbour and dock there.

During the next few decades Fleetwood expanded steadily as a well-planned town, and there is evidence of its prosperity in the substantial scale of many of the buildings belonging to this period. By 1875 the population had reached 5,000. As yet fishing from the port was on a moderate scale, employing about eighty smacks as compared with Grimsby's 500, but a fair amount of trade was done with Belfast, especially in cattle, while flax and timber were imported from Russia and the Baltic countries, and cotton from America. The town was also becoming popular as a holiday resort.

It was in the 1890's that Fleetwood began to assume a more definite status as a centre of the fishing industry. There had already been a considerable development of fishing off the Lancashire coast, for supplies were abundant and the market was near at hand; hundreds of sailing-craft, mostly of small size, operated from various ports and landed between 50,000 and 60,000 cwt. a year. The introduction of steam trawlers rapidly transformed this organization; as in other fishing districts, it made for concentration, and on the north-west coast the point of concentration was Fleetwood.

Various factors contributed to the selection of Fleetwood as a centre of the steam-trawling industry; its natural advantages had been capitalized by the construction of railways which gave ready access to a large inland market, and with the change to steam the proximity of the Lancashire and Yorkshire coalfields was of cardinal importance. The discovery of a rock salt bed at Preesall, two miles to the east, gave a further stimulus to the fish trade and brought a new industry to the town when the United Alkali Company set up their works in 1885. About the same time the Lancashire and Yorkshire Railway Company provided improved accommodation with coaling facilities on their Wyre Dock estate and another essential enterprise, the Fylde Ice and Cold Storage Company, was established.

The pioneers in steam trawling at Fleetwood were a Hull firm, Beeching and Kelsall, who came originally from Milford Haven. They started in 1892 with eleven ships, and by the end of the century the number had grown to forty-five. Fleetwood's main attraction was the hake fishery, but intensive working by the steam trawlers produced such a glut of hake that the price fell to a very low level and eventually the fleet returned to Hull. This setback, however, was only temporary and in the decade before the 1914–18 war expansion was remarkable; in 1913 landings at Fleetwood were more than ten times the total for the whole Lancashire coast before the advent of steam trawling. But the episode illustrates a characteristic feature of the Fleetwood fishing trade; it has continued to depend on the enterprise of outside firms to an extent that is detrimental to its steady progress.

Reference is made in the Grimsby section of this survey to the relatively small-scale organization of the trawling industry. This characteristic is still more marked at Fleetwood, which in this respect stands between Grimsby and Aberdeen. In 1939 the fishing fleet numbered 112 vessels and their ownership was distributed among forty-one companies and individuals. It is important, however, to distinguish between ownership and management, the latter determining the size of the operating unit. There were twenty-one managing concerns and the distribution of the vessels under their control is shown in the following table:

No. of Firms	No. of Vessels
1	24
1	19
1	18
1	14
1	11
3	8
1	7
2	5
3	3
3	2
4	1
21	112

This table is based on information supplied by the Fleetwood Fishing Vessel Owners' Association.

During the war the size of the fleet was substantially maintained. As at other ports, the best trawlers were requisitioned by the Admiralty, and a number of others were lost while fishing, but war conditions encouraged the transfer of vessels from the east coast, some being purchased by Fleetwood owners and others placed under their management. Several foreign trawlers, Norwegian, French, Dutch, and Polish also found a temporary base at Fleetwood.

These changes appear, however, to have had little effect on the structure of the industry. Even before the war, when many of the trawler companies were in financial difficulties and the fleet was shrinking in size, there was little evidence of any tendency towards consolidation of ownership. A few owners have sold out at prices two and even three times those ruling in 1939, but most have preferred to profit by the higher earning-power of their vessels while the war lasted. There are still no more than six firms with more than ten boats each, and at the other end of the scale there are several one-vessel concerns, though it is now very unusual for boats to be owned by their skippers.

The Sea-Fish Commission stressed the advantages of large units in trawling, and by this criterion the structure of the industry at Fleetwood appears to be out of date and inefficient. But there are several factors to be taken into account in assessing the position. In the first place, the number of vessels owned or managed is not an altogether satisfactory basis for measuring the size of firms. In so far as the bigger firms tend to have the larger and more modern trawlers their relative importance is greater than is indicated by the table given above. Again, some of the firms owning only a few boats are fish merchants with considerable financial resources. Further, a number of the Fleetwood trawling companies are linked by common directorships while some have subsidiaries in other ports or are themselves subsidiaries of outside firms. Another complication arises from the practice of buying and selling trawlers, which sometimes takes place on a considerable scale with variations in the prosperity of the different fishing ports. One large Fleetwood firm had at one time some fifty trawlers under its control; at another time its fleet was down to eight vessels. It must be realized, too, when comparing Fleetwood with Hull or Grimsby, that what is the most efficient size of trawling unit, as of the trawler itself, is related to the type of fishing in which it is engaged. Fleetwood trawlers usually go out for between ten and fourteen days, and so long as they can secure full catches from the near fishing-grounds, comparatively small fleets of medium-sized vessels can be quite profitable. On the other hand, the absence of really big concerns tends to restrict operations to the nearer waters even when fishing there becomes less profitable.

On one point, however, there seems to be no doubt. Except for inshore fishing, the very small independent concerns with only two or three vessels cannot hope to succeed under modern conditions. Opinions differ as to what is the minimum size of unit for economical operation. The large owner puts it as high as twelve vessels of the usual Fleetwood type, but it seems to be agreed that perhaps half that number of up-to-date trawlers make an effective unit for fishing in the nearer or middle waters, that is, as far as Iceland. Here, as at other ports, owners emphasize the point that the bigger firms with the best boats can get the best skippers, which is the main condition of success. They can also provide more regular employment, buy stores more economically and secure the advantage of interchangeable equipment.

Looking to the future, there appears to be a strong case for the rationalization of the Fleetwood trawling industry. Before the war, owing to intensive fishing from the port, it was quite common for trawlers to come in only one-third full. It has been estimated that forty good trawlers would have sufficed for the range of operation then covered. In any case, a large proportion of the present fleet will cease to be available now the war is over. With the reopening of the North Sea, east coast vessels will, it is assumed, return to their former ports and the foreign trawlers will go home. A few vessels will return from war service, but, on the other hand, many at present in use will have to be scrapped. The Sea-Fish Commission found that in 1934 56 per cent of the Fleetwood trawlers were over twenty years old; and only two new vessels have been added since that time. The average age of the present fleet is put at thirty years. Replacement can, of course, be undertaken at comparatively small cost by buying slightly more modern ships from other ports, but this can only mean that in the long run Fleetwood will fall even further behind its east coast rivals.

The alternative policy, aiming at a smaller fleet of first-rate vessels, would require concerted action by the trawling section as a whole, and even then new capital would be needed. In the days of Lancashire's prosperity outside share capital was readily forthcoming and the banks were prepared to advance as much as half the purchase price of trawlers. But the experiences of the inter-war years have made investors chary of taking risks, and fishing must always be a risky trade in every sense of the word. Moreover, the amount of capital required to operate on an efficient scale will be much higher for the future, for it is estimated that building costs will be about double the pre-war level. Another factor which in the opinion of some critics has acted as a deterrent to new investment is lack of confidence in the quality of management. There have been managing directors, it is alleged, who thought more about personal commission or profit on supplies for their trawlers than of keeping down the cost of stores in the interests of their fellow shareholders. It is also said that when the management gets a commission on the gross value of the catch it will be tempted to look at that figure alone, irrespective of costs.

The importance of personal leadership in this industry has already been stressed in reviewing the position at Grimsby. There seems to be some doubt as to whether those who could exert the most influence have a sufficient faith in the future of Fleetwood to give the lead that is required. There was a period in the 1930's when a powerful stimulus was supplied by Mac Fisheries, a subsidiary of the Lever combine. This concern introduced fifteen new trawlers of the latest type, which had been acquired from Germany in settlement of debts owed in that country to the parent company. These vessels were employed in the Icelandic fisheries and might have been the salvation of Fleetwood had they remained; but in 1938, as mentioned in the Grimsby section, they were sold and transferred to the east coast port. The reasons for the transfer are somewhat obscure; but some believe that under suitable management the fleet could have been successfully operated from Fleetwood. Another experiment by the same concern was also abandoned. This was a project for converting a large disused grain elevator into a canning factory; the building is now being demolished.

The interests of the trawling section are not entirely confined to the catching of fish. As at other ports, several of the Fleetwood trawler-owners are also fish merchants. One of the advantages of having a stake in merchanting, they claim, is that it enables them to combat any monopolistic tendencies that may develop in the market. The largest firm in the section, the Boston Deep Sea Fishing and Ice Company Ltd., is especially interesting in view of its wide range of operations. Originally established at Boston, Lincs., the firm is now a public company with a share capital of £68,000; it has subsidiaries at Aberdeen and Hull, though these are operated as autonomous units. Besides acting as fish merchants, the firm has an engineering department for servicing its trawler fleet, it produces nets and much other equipment and has developed fish-processing on a considerable scale.

This example illustrates the possibilities of vertical organization with a moderate-sized trawling fleet. The main advantage in undertaking maintenance work appears to be not so much in a saving on the cost of the work itself as in the convenience of being able to get it done just when it is required. The firm can readily adapt its vessels for the different types of fishing, which at Fleetwood have a wide range and require a great variety of gear. Direct supervision also provides a check on the quality of repair work and equipment. There is no other Fleetwood firm comparable with the Boston concern in its range of operations.

The representative organization of the trawling section is the Fleetwood Fishing Vessel Owners' Association. Besides acting for the owners in negotiating with other sections of the trade and with Government Departments, the Association has introduced some useful co-operation schemes. It provides all the boxes and baskets into which the fish are loaded before sale; it invoices the fish and collects from the merchants, supplying its members with a weekly statement of money due. It also engages crews and organizes the supply of labour for unloading the trawlers; this begins at midnight and must be completed in time for the market, which opens at 8 a.m. Before the establishment of the National Dock Labour Corporation the Association assumed responsibility for paying the dock labourers or lumpers as they are called. Fishermen's stores are also supplied by the Association.

The marketing of fish is organized at Fleetwood in much the same way as at other ports. The trade is distributed among 225 wholesale merchants. Some of these are linked with trawling concerns, but on the whole there is a distinct cleavage of interest between the two sections. Many of the merchants represented at Fleetwood have a stake in other ports, and some are branch establishments of inland wholesalers; but the great majority, and especially the smaller firms, are entirely dependent on the Fleetwood market. As at Grimsby, the number of small merchants is remarkable. Under the war-time scheme for allocating supplies, seventy-two firms handled two-thirds of the total landings and the remaining third was distributed among 153 merchants. The inshore fishermen have a Co-operative Society, established about twenty-five years ago, for selling direct to local consumers.

The fact that Fleetwood has concentrated to an even greater extent than Grimsby on the prime fish trade helps to explain the existence of so many small merchants. In this trade the need for careful selection and close attention to the requirements of inland buyers gives the small merchant a certain advantage. There is, however, less direct selling to retailers than at Grimsby, most of Fleetwood's trade being with inland wholesalers. It was the latter who developed the market in the early days, sending their representatives to buy direct from the trawler-owners, but most of them now prefer to deal with independent merchants established in different ports and able, collectively, to maintain regular supplies of a wide range of fish. Inland wholesalers, and even retailers, are, however, always potential, if not actual, competitors of the port merchant.

The tendency, very marked at Grimsby, towards the development of fish-processing by the larger merchants is less noticeable at Fleetwood. One reason for this is the comparatively small proportion of cod in the landings. Fleetwood looks to the trade in prime fresh fish for its prosperity. Even in this trade, however, there is some scope for processing. The war, emphasizing the need for transport economy, has given a great stimulus to the practice of filleting fish at the port; practically all Fleetwood fish which is suitable for filleting is now distributed in this form. But fish deteriorates rapidly when taken off the bone; hence filleting implies quick freezing of the fish if it is to reach the consumer in good condition. This process is now being extended. There is no doubt about the popularity of filleted fish, and merchants say that there would have been more filleting before the war if the railway companies had supplied more refrigerator vans. The railway companies, on the other hand, contend that the initiative in improving technique should come from the trade and that transport facilities would then be adapted to traders' requirements. This illustrates a tendency that is met with only too often in the fishing industry, though it may be observed in other trades too: each section seems concerned to pass on the blame for inefficiency or lack of initiative to another section or to some outside interest.

Apart from filleting, there has been some development of more elaborate forms of processing at Fleetwood. About twenty merchants undertake fish-curing, especially kippering and the smoking of haddock. The herrings for kippering are trawl-caught, the season extending from June to November. Fleetwood kippers are the biggest in Britain and have a high fat content; many are exported, especially to U.S.A., and there is also some export of salted fish.

The manufacture of fish by-products is naturally less important than at the larger ports of Hull and Grimsby. It is concentrated, at Fleetwood, mainly in one concern: Isaac Spencer and Sons Ltd., who are also represented at Hull, Grimsby, and Aberdeen, though by separate companies. Spencers' main products are fish-meal, fertilizers, and cod-liver oil. The cod livers and the oil extracted from them at sea are bought from the trawler-owners, while most of the fish offal comes from the merchants. The existence of a market for offal and stale fish is an important factor in enabling the trawler-owners in agreement with the Fish Merchants' Association to establish minimum prices. Spencers have also endeavoured to secure the co-operation of owners and merchants on a profit-sharing basis, while some owners and merchants have a more direct interest in the firm as directors and shareholders. The firm has the further advantage of being linked financially with the Lever Combine. There is, however, a feeling among some members of the trade in favour of collective enterprise in the manufacture of by-products such as exists at Hull. On the other hand, the Boston Deep Sea Fishing Company have shown that a concern whose primary interest is in trawling can develop the manufacture of certain by-products with success. It is claimed that the quantity and quality of by-products and the supply of material for research depend primarily on the fishermen, whose interest in this side of the industry can best be encouraged by those who employ them.

There is clearly much scope for experiment in the organization of the manufacture of by-products. Success demands a wide knowledge of sources of supply, technique, and markets. Conditions change so rapidly that a profitable trade in some particular line may at any time be jeopardized by the appearance of a competitive commodity.

For instance, before the war the trade in cod-liver oil was being threatened from several directions; other fish oils, especially tunny and halibut, proved far richer in the essential vitamins, and the competition of synthetic vitamins was growing; further competition among the six British manufacturers for control of the cod-liver oil trade was driving down prices to an unremunerative level.

The future prospects of Fleetwood as a fishing port may now be considered. One outstanding feature of the fishing industry is the comparative ease with which operations can be transferred from one base to another. This flexibility has its advantages, enabling the industry to respond to changes in fishing conditions and to keep the consumer supplied at minimum costs. But it can be detrimental to the prosperity of ancillary trades such as fish-processing and marine engineering, which have considerable fixed equipment; it may result in loss on capital sunk in the development of a port; it may mean at least temporary loss of livelihood for many workers and increase the difficulties of local authorities in planning for future development.

It is true that Fleetwood is by no means entirely dependent on the fishing industry; its attractions as a holiday resort have been appreciated for many years, and since the 1914–18 war the local authority have spent large sums in laying out the foreshore; a great deal of residential building has been undertaken and there are plans for further extensions. But Fleetwood's industrial structure is based on fishing, which provided employment, directly or indrectly, for between 5,000 and 6,000 people before the war. There is very little general cargo trade, the port having lost to Manchester and Preston, and though there is at present a daily passenger service to the Isle of Man, the former service to Belfast was removed to Heysham by the L.M.S.R. following the railway amalgamation.

The dock facilities for the fishing industry at Fleetwood are, it is generally agreed, of the first order. The fish dock of eleven acres can accommodate the largest trawlers. Coaling arrangements were much improved a few years before the war by the installation of six electric belt conveyors, and ice is delivered directly to the trawlers by chutes. The market accommodation at the quayside has recently been extended in area by about 50 per cent, and the owners' and merchants' offices, curing-houses, and engineering works are compactly grouped near the dock. The efficiency of the railway organization is evident in the great expansion of traffic which has been possible under war conditions; before the war the biggest quantity of fish dispatched from Fleetwood was 72,000 tons in a year; in one war year as much as 160,000 tons were handled, and, it is claimed, not one box has ever been left over.

As regards the inland distribution of fish, the railway company claims that Fleetwood's facilities are about equal to those of Hull and Grimsby; besides the facilities for distribution to the nearer markets of Manchester, Liverpool, and Birmingham there are three services daily to London; one train, introduced shortly before the war, covered the 230 miles in seven hours. As a means of further improving the transport arrangements the L.M.S.R. have considered a scheme for radial distribution under which fish would be taken by rail to a number of inland centres, and from there distributed in smaller consignments by road. But the scheme did not find much support among the merchants, who apparently feared that it would interfere with established trade connexions. There is a feeling among members of the trade that Fleetwood is handicapped by having no direct railway connexions with the North, but to overcome this would mean bridging the Wyre estuary, and it is hard to see any sufficient justification for such an undertaking.

On the whole, then, it appears that Fleetwood is well equipped for its function as a fishing port. If there are doubts as to its future prosperity the reasons lie in defective organization within the trade and in the possible failure of the fishing-grounds on which Fleetwood depends. The reopening of the North Sea has naturally given a fillip to the east coast ports. As over-fishing becomes more serious there, however, there may be a revival at Fleetwood. It is believed that there is less danger of over-fishing on the west coast because the rocky bottom provides more refuge for the fish. In the ten years before the war Fleetwood maintained its importance relatively to Grimsby despite its dependence on the nearer fishing-grounds. But a change of great significance was taking place in the nature of Fleetwood's trade; there was a remarkable decline in the landings of hake, hitherto the great speciality of the port. Landings of hake at 401,000 cwt. constituted 40 per cent of the total catch in 1927; in 1938 hake had fallen to 206,000 cwt., about 16 per cent of the total. This decline in the hake catch was experienced by other ports too, especially Milford Haven; indeed, Fleetwood's share of the total, at 32 per cent in 1938, was slightly higher than it had been ten years earlier. The position was made even worse by the fact that the price of hake had declined far more than that of fish generally.

The uncertainties of trade in the better quality fish have already been shown in the case of Grimsby. Fortunately for Fleetwood, landings of almost all kinds of fish, other than hake, increased during the last pre-war decade, especially haddock, which at 236,000 cwt. formed the biggest item in the 1938 total. Some members of the trade argue that it is a mistaken policy to concentrate unduly on hake; it is an expensive fish to catch, liking a rocky bottom, which is destructive to nets and gear. What is necessary to ensure the prosperity of Fleetwood, they say, is to maintain regular supplies of a wide variety of fish so as to make the market attractive to buyers.

The importance of retaining a bigger share in the Icelandic trade, as under war conditions, is also stressed; in this connexion it may be pointed out that Iceland is twenty-four hours nearer to Fleetwood than to Hull and Grimsby.

There appears to be no disposition at Fleetwood to assume that the fortuitous benefits of the war years will secure any permanent advantage to the port at the expense of its rivals on the east coast. On the contrary, it seems to be suggested that the transfer of firms from Fleetwood to Hull and Grimsby may go beyond the return of war-time migrants. It is even suggested that others may follow. The dock extensions at Grimsby will provide accommodation for an enlarged fleet, but a similar scheme for Hull still remains to be undertaken. Yet it is Hull that is generally mentioned when the possibility of transfer from Fleetwood is suggested. Though some extension of facilities at Hull is clearly necessary, it might be bad economy for the fishing industry as a whole if it resulted in redundant capacity at Fleetwood. If Fleetwood were out of date and badly situated in relation to fishing-grounds and markets its decline could be accepted as a concomitant of progress. But this is not the case. Given vigorous leadership and a capacity for effective organization of the sectional interests, there seems to be no reason why Fleetwood should not hold its own. But nothing succeeds like success, and Hull, which has been raised to a dominant position by confident leadership, may continue to attract from other ports where faith is lacking.

CONCLUSION

One of the major uncertainties regarding the future of Britain's white fish industry relates to the possible permanent effects of the war. Will the effects of the war-time unequal requisitioning of trawlers as between the rival ports continue to handicap Hull and Grimsby relatively to other fishing ports, or will the capital equipment—in port installations, plant for making cod-liver oil, ice, and so on—which these two ports possess continue to count in their favour? Will consumers react towards the war-time scarcity and poor quality of fish and the present scarcity of other goods by placing fish higher or lower in their scales of preferences? It was very roughly estimated in 1939 that the consumption of fish per head of Britain's population had risen by nearly 30 per cent since 1918; it was known that the increase of white fish consumption, and particularly of cod consumption, had been partly at the expense of herring; it was guessed that fish-friers, increasing rapidly in numbers, took about half of the total weight of white fish landed in the late 1930's. These trends might, but for the war, have been expected to continue. The war, involving as it has done a good deal of consultation amongst the various organizations claiming to represent sections of the industry—the British Trawlers' Federation and its local associations, the Federations of Wholesale Fish Merchants Associations, of Fishmongers, of Fish Friers, and so on—and between these organizations and the Government, might be expected to lead to a greater degree of co-operation between the different sections.

Amongst the legacies of the war which are most apparent at the present time are the loss of 383 trawlers and of thousands of sea-going personnel which, together with the time taken in the reconditioning of trawlers and the war-time cessation of building and recruitment of personnel, have led to serious shortages in man-power, in vessels and in equipment of all kinds. In addition, the continuance of the war-time abandonment of the quota system for foreign landings has contributed towards making the post-war period of high profits and high trawlermen's earnings of very short duration; crews have taken strike action, and a governmental Board of Inquiry has examined certain aspects of the position, including the system of controlled prices. Owners and men are demanding the reintroduction of the quota arrangements for foreign landings.

Assuming the war were to produce no major permanent change in these and other respects, it might reasonably be argued that the industry would nevertheless be faced with certain general problems, failure to solve which would have grave consequences.

(1) If a particular fishing-ground is fished more and more intensively it naturally follows that the catch per unit of fishing-power eventually falls off. Clearly, what is wanted is, first of all, to determine what is the optimum rate of removal of fish from the ground in question, so that it is neither under- nor over-fished; and, secondly, to ensure that this optimum rate is in fact maintained. In the main areas from which the British white fish industry draws its supplies, the decline in yield per unit of fishing-power has already set in; in distant waters it can only be a question of time before it does so. A good deal of scientific thought has been given to the question of the optimum rate of fishing; but so far the only practical measures taken to improve the position have been the Orders, issued under the Sea-Fishing Industry Act of 1933, aimed at preventing the taking and marketing of under-sized fish, and the Convention of 1937—signed by the representatives of ten Governments—for the regulation of meshes of nets and size-limits for fish. Even if these rules are strictly observed by all concerned, however, over-fishing is still likely to result unless both national and international measures are taken to restrict the total amount of fishing energy expended on particular grounds; for, faced with a declining yield, trawler-owners will endeavour to improve the efficiency of their apparatus by every means in their power. It is, indeed, one of the tragedies of the industry that though in the 'thirties there had been technical progress

in many different ways, fishing was nevertheless less profitable than it had been before the new devices were introduced. There are, to all intents and purposes, no new fishing-grounds to tap. 'Free fishing', as Mr. Michael Graham puts it, 'has failed everywhere.'

(2) Before the war the price that white fish as a whole was fetching at first sale was insufficient to provide for replacement and modernization of the trawlers, except in the case of the coarser types of fish from distant waters and the most efficient units. Yet the final consumer was paying twice or three times as much for the fish, and there was a strong suspicion that the difference was not wholly accounted for by necessary costs of transport, cleaning, grading, sorting, packing, and so on. If the margin between first and last sale could be substantially reduced, it was believed that increased consumption of fish might restore profits to a reasonable level in all sections of the industry. As to how reduction of the distributive margin was to be effected, there were numerous suggestions. (a) A reduction in the number of port wholesalers was recommended by the Sea-Fish Commission, this to be secured by a system of licensing. Mr. Graham has since pointed out that fewer buyers would not normally be expected to make a better market for the trawlers' catch; and has asked whether inland traders would necessarily get the fish more cheaply because it had been sent from fewer consignors. (b) The elimination of inland wholesalers, on the ground that they have no essential duties to perform beyond that of distribution, is called for in a recent Fabian Research Pamphlet; York, Hereford, Plymouth, Huddersfield, and Aberdare are cited as towns which receive much of their fish direct from the port wholesaler to the retailer. Moreover fish-friers, though tending to work on a small scale, generally obtain their supplies direct from the port. (c) The white fish industry would appear to offer considerable scope for securing economies by vertical integration. With a few exceptions (of which Mac Fisheries forms the outstanding case) there seems, however, to have been little attempt to bring all stages from catching to final sale into a single undertaking, though an unsuccessful experiment in entering the merchanting side of the business was made by Hull trawler-owners after the 1914–18 war. If any substantial reduction in the distributive margin is to be secured—and it is obviously vital that it should be—bulk buying and bulk dispatch must play a large part, whether by horizontal integration amongst retailers, by vertical integration, or by co-operative arrangements.

(3) Closely related to the two problems mentioned so far is the failure of the finer varieties of white fish in the best condition to command prices appropriately higher than those of coarse varieties in poor condition. The housewife, it is said, fails to discriminate adequately when buying fish, so that the trawling of near and middle

waters, as well as inshore fishing, becomes even less remunerative than it could be. Here, in short, is a problem of grading; and since this is a function of the port wholesaler, it is not surprising to find the Sea-Fish Commission saying that port wholesalers could support the trawler-owners by a concerted effort to ensure that, on the market, the better-preserved fish fetched a higher price. All sorts of measures to improve the freshness of fish at the time of final sale have been suggested, ranging from an extension of brine-freezing on trawlers to improvements in railway fish-wagons; many of these reforms, though most desirable in themselves, would probably have the effect of still further narrowing the margin between the price of fish from home waters and from more distant grounds. Even were this not so, it can safely be assumed that no probable improvement in fish discrimination amongst housewives will make unnecessary special measures for the protection of inshore fishermen, or reduce the urgency of helping those engaged in short-distance trawling. Conversely, however, if all consumers of fish were as easy to please as those who buy their fish fried, there would soon be no room on the 'productive' side of the industry for any but those engaged in long-distance trawling; in this connexion it is significant that opposition to the ban on fishing in distant waters during the summer months came mainly from fish-friers.

(4) A greater degree of stability in the day-to-day prices at first sale would, most observers agree, be of considerable benefit if it could be achieved, even if the mean of such prices over a period were unaffected. More ordered spacing of the arrival of vessels from the fishing-grounds has been suggested. Port wholesalers, it is said, have not been able to exert the steadying influence they might have done, owing to their numbers and the ease with which casual merchants could drift in and out of the business. In Hull, rather exceptionally, it had become the practice before the war to fix minimum prices of a sort and withdraw fish if bids above these minima were not forthcoming.

These, then, are some of the major problems with which the industry is faced. The modernization of equipment and improvement of methods which are so urgently needed throughout the industry will not be undertaken until a satisfactory return on capital laid out in these ways is assured, so that the key to the whole position is, ultimately, the securing of a satisfactory price structure for the sale of white fish. Until that has been done, not merely will the average level of efficiency and modernization continue to be too far below that which has already been achieved in those sections where circumstances were favourable, but the vast benefits which could accrue to producers and consumers alike by improvements in technique waiting to be applied, will not be forthcoming. It may prove technically possible to improve existing methods of locating fish shoals by the use of Asdic and Radar devices and to improve methods of packing and distribution by plastic boxes, better refrigerator vans and quick freezing methods. The internal combustion engine may be found to be more satisfactory than the steam engine in certain types of trawler, oil may prove better than coal. Yet the widespread introduction of technical improvements of these and other types is unlikely, if not impossible, under the conditions which obtained during the inter-war period.[1]

Legislation to replace the 1938 Act is expected shortly, but it is still not publicly known what the main features of the Government's plan for the reorganization of the industry will be. The reorganization envisaged under the 1938 Act would not, of itself, have solved any of the major problems of the industry. It could, however, by introducing a greater degree of order into some of the more disorderly sections of the industry, have made important improvements possible. Care would have been needed to ensure that the marketing schemes were not of such a character as merely to raise prices all round, without doing anything to reduce costs or margins or to increase efficiency. It should not be impossible, within the framework of the 1938 Act or that of its successor, to provide the encouragement and the means needed for the replacement of obsolete trawlers, to secure the economies of bulk buying and bulk dispatch, to arrange that fish be removed from the sea at the optimum rate, whilst at the same time preserving whatever it is desired to preserve in the way of inshore fishermen and one-trawler businesses. Given the necessary Government help and encouragement towards reorganization on these lines, the industry has shown that it possesses adequate reserves of skill and leadership for its destiny to be left with safety in its own hands.

[1] Another recent development with revolutionary possibilities takes the form of an American fish-filleting machine which is being demonstrated at Hull. It is claimed that the machine 'will fillet 45 fish a minute and give 18% more flesh per fillet than by hand-cutting'. Opposition from those likely to become redundant if such machines were used may well delay their introduction for a time.

SHORT BIBLIOGRAPHY

Aflalo, F. G.   The Sea Fishing Industry of England and Wales. 1904.
Alward, G. L.   The Sea Fisheries of Great Britain and Ireland. 1932.
Anson, P. F.   British Sea Fishermen. 1944.
Atkins, J.   The Distribution of Fish (Fabian Society). 1941.
Graham, M.   The Fish Gate. 1943.
Official Reports: Department of Scientific and Industrial Research.
          The Handling and Preservation of Fish. 1925.
          The Handling and Stowage of White Fish at Sea. 1929.
          Economic Advisory Council.
          Committee on the Fishing Industry. Report. 1932.
          Fishery Board for Scotland. Annual Reports.
          Sea Fisheries. Annual Statistical Tables.
          Imperial Economic Committee. Marketing and Pre-
             paring for Market of Foodstuffs. 5th Report. 1927.
          Ministry of Agriculture & Fisheries.
          Sea Fisheries. Annual Reports.
          Sea Fisheries. Annual Statistical Tables.
          Sea-Fish Commission.   2nd Report.   The White Fish
             Industry. 1938.
Russell, E. S.   The Over-fishing Problem. 1942.
Wood, W.   The Fleeters. 1934.
The Times.   Deep-Sea Fishing. 14th and 15th August 1946.

TABLE 1

AGES OF TRAWLERS IN 1934 AT THE FOUR MAJOR PORTS

Age	Hull		Grimsby		Aberdeen		Fleetwood		The Four Ports Combined	
	No.	%	No.	%	No.	%	No.	%	No.	%
Less than 10 years	156	47	60	12	29	10	9	6	254	20
10 and under 15 years	30	9	3	1	3	1	4	3	40	3
15 and under 20 years	53	16	131	27	82	29	52	35	318	26
20 and under 25 years	37	11	121	24	68	22	44	30	265	21
25 years and over .	54	17	178	36	108	38	38	26	378	30
Total	330	100	493	100	285	100	147	100	1,255	100

From data contained in the Second Report of the Sea-Fish Commission, The White Fish Industry.

TABLE II

OWNERSHIP OF TRAWLERS AT THE MAJOR PORTS IN GREAT BRITAIN IN 1934

Class of Ownership, i.e. No. of Vessels per Concern	No. of Concerns	No. of Vessels	Percentage of Vessels in each Class of Ownership					
			Total	Hull	Grimsby	Aberdeen	Fleetwood	Milford Haven
			%	%	%	%	%	%
Under 5	206	352	28	11	25	41	31	56
5 to 9	39	240	19	15	17	28	20	13
10 to 19	26	326	25	22	25	22	36	31
Over 19	12	362	28	52	33	9	13	—
Total . .	283	1,280	100	100	100	100	100	100

From data contained in the Second Report of the Sea-Fish Commission, The White Fish Industry.

TABLE III
VESSELS TRAWLING IN NEAR AND MIDDLE WATERS

Average Expenses and Net Profits of Vessels, for the year 1934, expressed as a Percentage of Gross Earnings

	Hull	Grimsby	Aberdeen	Fleetwood	Milford Haven
	%	%	%	%	%
Coal	22	28	27	27	28
Upkeep of Vessel, including Stores, Gear, Repairs, and Depreciation . .	22	25	24	25	18(a)
Other Expenses, including Ice, Dock Expenses, Insurance, Selling Commission, Discount, and Miscellaneous . .	20	22	15(b)	22	23
Remuneration of Crew, including Skipper and Mate (c) . . .	31	25	33(b)	25	27
Total Expenses . .	95	100	99	99	96
Net Profit . . .	5	—	1	1	4
	100	100	100	100	100

Notes; (a) The expenditure on repairs in 1934 was considerably below the annual average for the preceding five years.

(b) In comparing the Aberdeen figures with those of the other ports, these two items should be taken together, owing mainly to a different practice in respect of the crews' food.

(c) Excludes perquisites of crew, such as 'stocker', i.e. the money realized by the sale of certain of the less valuable fish.

From data contained in the Second Report of the Sea-Fish Commission, The White Fish Industry.

TABLE IV

VESSELS TRAWLING IN DISTANT WATERS

Average Expenses and Net Profits of Vessels, for the Year 1934, expressed
as a Percentage of Gross Earnings

	Hull	Grimsby
	%	%
Coal	19	21
Upkeep of Vessel, including Stores, Gear, Repairs, and Depreciation .	19	19
Other Expenses, including Ice, Dock Expenses, Insurance, Selling Commission, Discount, and Miscellaneous	22	26
Remuneration of Crew, including Skipper and Mate[1] . . .	26	28
Total Expenses	86	94
Net Profit	14	6
	100	100

[1] Excludes perquisites of crew, such as 'stocker'.

From data contained in the Second Report of the Sea-Fish Commission, The White Fish Industry.

TABLE V

VESSELS TRAWLING IN NEAR AND MIDDLE WATERS

Average Annual Gross Earnings and Net Profits, or Losses, per Vessel for
the Years 1929 to 1934 inclusive

	Hull	Grimsby	Aberdeen	Fleetwood	Milford Haven
I—Gross Earnings:					
1929 . . .	8,657	7,171	6,628	11,042	8,644
1930 . . .	7,690	6,147	5,876	9,445	8,254
1931 . . .	6,741	5,677	5,579	8,112	7,750
1932 . . .	6,115	5,565	5,360	7,901	6,876
1933 . . .	6,011	5,972	5,608	8,552	7,170
1934 . . .	6,342	5,911	5,932	8,398	5,510
II—Net Profits (+) or Losses (−)[1]					
1929 . . .	+ 1,137	+ 344	+ 277	+ 1,284	+ 472
1930 . . .	+ 274	− 279	− 260	+ 164	− 21
1931 . . .	+ 89	− 333	− 459	− 335	− 452
1932 . . .	+ 17	− 170	− 345	− 39	− 294
1933 . . .	+ 376	+ 81	− 176	+ 233	− 311
1934 . . .	+ 345	+ 9	+ 70	+ 71	+ 331

TABLE VI

VESSELS TRAWLING IN DISTANT WATERS

Average Annual Gross Earnings and Net Profits, or Losses, per Vessel for
the Years 1929 to 1934 inclusive

	Hull	Grimsby
I—Gross Earnings:	£	£
1929	15,569	13,132
1930	13,327	12,093
1931	11,894	10,547
1932	11,429	10,292
1933	12,081	10,962
1934	13,070	12,427
II—Net Profits (+) or Losses (−)[1]		
1929	+ 2,601	+ 1,157
1930	+ 1,373	+ 396
1931	+ 957	− 300
1932	+ 816	− 434
1933	+ 1,202	+ 192
1934	+ 1,834	+ 744

[1] In computing the net profits or losses, depreciation of vessels has been allowed
for on a somewhat lower scale, on the average, than that provided by owners in
their accounts.

From data contained in the Second Report of the Sea-Fish Commission, The
White Fish Industry.

TABLE VII

NUMBER OF PORT WHOLESALERS AT THE MAJOR PORTS AND THE AVERAGE QUANTITY AND VALUE OF WHITE FISH (BRITISH AND FOREIGN) HANDLED BY EACH MERCHANT IN 1913, 1924, AND 1934

Port	Number of Wholesalers			Average quantity and value of White Fish handled by each Merchant					
	1913	1924	1934	1913		1924		1934	
				cwt.	£	cwt.	£	cwt.	£
Hull	167	276	319	8,567	5,551	8,167	8,376	15,102	10,328
Grimsby	510	590	729	6,349	5,902	5,206	8,050	4,666	5,518
Aberdeen	146	202	222	16,499	9,239	12,212	11,373	8,236	8,278
Fleetwood	160	160	180	4,241	3,677	5,914	8,424	5,738	6,966

From data contained in the Second Report of the Sea-Fish Commission, The White Fish Industry.

TABLE VIII

BRITISH LANDINGS (IN 100,000 CWT.) OF WHITE FISH IN GREAT BRITAIN IN 1913 AND FOR THE YEARS 1925 TO 1938

Ports	1913	1925	1926	1927	1928	1929	1930	1931	1932	1933	1934	1935	1936	1937	1938
1. Hull	14	23	24	26	26	30	41	42	42	43	48	53	62	64	56
2. Grimsby	32	33	29	31	30	32	37	35	36	34	31	31	35	38	41
3. Aberdeen	19	15	15	16	15	16	16	17	17	17	16	16	15	15	16
4. Fleetwood	7	10	9	11	9	10	11	11	11	10	10	11	13	14	13
5. Milford Haven	4	6	5	6	6	6	7	7	6	5	5	5	5	6	6
Total of 2 to 5	62	64	58	64	60	64	71	70	70	66	62	63	68	73	76
6. All other Ports	35	31	28	29	30	29	29	27	27	27	24	22	19	21	19
Grand total	111	118	110	119	116	123	141	139	139	136	134	138	149	158	151

From data contained in the Second Report of the Sea-Fish Commission, The White Fish Industry; Ministry of Agriculture and Fisheries, Sea Fisheries, Annual Statistical Tables; Fishery Board for Scotland, Annual Statistical Tables.

TABLE IX
AVERAGE VALUE OF ALL DEMERSAL FISH OF BRITISH TAKING LANDED IN ENGLAND AND WALES

Year	Average value per cwt. £ s. d.
1913	0 17 10
1917	2 15 8
1918	4 0 5
1919	2 8 10
1920	1 17 10
1921	1 17 1
1922	1 7 11
1923	1 10 8
1924	1 8 6
1925	1 5 9
1926	1 5 7
1927	1 3 4
1928	1 5 1
1929	1 5 5
1930	1 1 1
1931	1 0 2
1932	0 18 6
1933	0 18 7
1934	1 0 3
1935	0 19 3
1936	0 16 9
1937	0 15 11
1938	0 17 10

From data contained in the Ministry of Agriculture and Fisheries, Sea Fisheries Annual Statistical Tables.

	1906		1913		1920		1924		
	Quantity landed (cwt.)	Quantity per day's absence from port (cwt.)	Quantity landed (cwt.)	Quantity per day's absence from port (cwt.)	Quantity landed (cwt.)	Quantity per day's absence from port (cwt.)	Quantity landed (cwt.)	Quantity per day's absence from port (cwt.)	Qu pe: h fis (
Barents Sea and Murman Coast . .	45,330	40·2	120,455	44·1	4,301	25·4	430,469	42·1	
Norwegian Coast .	—	—	—	—	—	—	—	—	
Bear Island and Spitsbergen . . .	—	—	—	—	—	—	—	—	
North Sea . .	3,988,985	17·6	3,551,756	17·3	4,531,353	25·4	2,254,859	14·5	
Iceland . . .	1,549,502	44·2	1,708,260	46·1	2,137,473	58·5	1,909,314	51·3	
Faroe . . .	536,947	31·2	623,643	28·2	189,871	27·0	891,701	27·3	
West of Scotland .	228,251	21·2	612,756	28·3	407,846	29·2	492,146	22·2	
Rockall . . .	53,942	39·0	36,047	39·3	27,242	49·5	52,767	41·9	
Irish Sea . . .	17,781	15·7	141,850	12·0	110,480	18·8	136,056	13·2	
W. of Ireland and Porcupine Bank . .	7,023	21·5	148,664	30·2	115,781	26·0	277,037	27·1	
English Channel .	10,095	11·4	12,545	10·8	64,882	25·7	45,823	12·7	
Bristol Channel . .	10,825	13·0	55,570	18·1	115,629	40·8	61,727	11·6	
SE. Ireland, Gt. and Little Sole Bank, W. of Gt. Sole Bank .	431,660	27·0	703,853	27·3	1,031,006	27·5	804,910	24·9	
Total from all regions	7,340,696	22·9	7,991,404	23·8	8,948,559	30·3	7,648,665	23·4	

From data contained in Ministry of Agricul

	1929		1934			1937			1938		
y	Quantity per day's absence from port (cwt.)	Quantity per 100 hours' fishing (cwt.)	Quantity landed (cwt.)	Quantity per day's absence from port (cwt.)	Quantity per 100 hours' fishing (cwt.)	Quantity landed (cwt.)	Quantity per day's absence from port (cwt.)	Quantity per 100 hours' fishing (cwt.)	Quantity landed (cwt.)	Quantity per day's absence from port (cwt.)	Quantity per 100 hours' fishing (cwt.)
2	47·7	1,104	926,701	59·5	1,139	2,031,595	82·3	1,548	1,551,916	80·4	1,640
2	48·4	963	87,514	69·4	1,195	664,277	122·4	3,188	354,380	111·7	3,465
7	86·0	2,010	823,993	75·4	1,625	2,156,372	126·2	2,964	2,700,527	114·1	2,709
9	17·1	121	2,177,216	14·6	106	1,597,614	14·7	107	1,464,388	15·5	116
0	49·6	789	3,406,938	58·7	941	3,515,191	58·2	877	3,142,993	71·9	1,133
8	27·7	479	869,951	29·8	397	639,330	30·3	425	661,719	33·9	497
0	25·5	304	716,018	24·1	279	825,817	31·0	337	929,587	34·1	375
5	39·0	436	99,452	24·5	315	111,214	38·2	492	111,206	41·6	469
3	15·7	119	264,333	13·6	100	205,079	14·1	110	311,222	16·7	134
5	24·0	255	224,825	21·4	177	326,325	27·7	216	332,181	28·6	232
8	14·5	99	42,472	12·3	90	39,473	11·2	96	32,004	12·5	101
3	12·5	119	63,636	11·7	95	54,084	12·1	108	48,924	11·9	102
8	21·2	219	533,452	19·7	173	567,704	22·8	200	466,088	23·6	203
5	26·6	255	10,560,280	28·8	272	13,202,884	39·0	392	12,493,461	41·6	427

CHAPTER III

THE GRANITE INDUSTRY

By PROFESSOR H. HAMILTON

HISTORICAL INTRODUCTION

THE granite industry is rightly associated with Aberdeen, for, though quarrying is carried on in Kirkcudbright, North Wales, Cornwall, and Devon, and manufacturing in various towns, like Glasgow, Edinburgh, Dalbeattie, and Penryn, it is in North-east Scotland that the major part is located. Deposits of granite of high durability and beauty stretch along both sides of the River Dee and at certain places on Donside, while large masses are found at the well-known Rubislaw Quarry within the city boundaries, at Kemnay on Donside some 15 miles from Aberdeen, and in the neighbourhood of Peterhead.

The Aberdeenshire industry dates back to the eighteenth century. Long before this, however, isolated instances of the use of granite in building occur, notably in the Castles of Crathes and Drum on Deeside, Midmar Castle, close to the Hill of Fare, and Castle Fraser on Donside, while in Old Aberdeen the nave and west front of St. Machar's Cathedral were built of granite about 1430. In Aberdeen itself there were probably a few granite buildings before the Union of Parliaments, but most houses were built of timber or freestone. Early examples of granite public buildings are the Town House of Old Aberdeen, erected in 1721, and the Grammar School and Robert Gordon's College, erected some years later. A disastrous fire in 1741, when a large part of the city was laid waste, was the occasion of an order by the magistrates that stone or brick should be used in house construction. Attention was thus directed to the durable quality of local stone, and before the close of the century granite was being used extensively for house-building, notably in Marischal Street, Queen Street, and Union Street. The last-named was constructed in the early nineteenth century, an integral part of which was Union Bridge built of granite by Thomas Telford in 1803.

Before 1800 a great stimulus was given to the industry from an unexpected direction. The drive for public health involved paving streets, while the Industrial Revolution demanded improved harbours to handle the produce of the new machine age. For both purposes granite was eminently suitable. At first Aberdeen exported to London sea-washed boulders or granite stones from the fields which at this time were being cleared for improved cultivation. Such a source of supply, however, was unlikely to last, and the increasing

181

demands of road-builders led to the opening of quarries in the vicinity of the city, the most famous being Rubislaw Quarry, which had been worked as early as 1741. The decision of London in 1764 to pave its streets with granite encouraged the local industry. Other towns followed suit, and soon the export of granite for road-making became an important feature of Aberdeen's trade.

The first use of Aberdeenshire granite in large constructional works was for harbours, bridges, and lighthouses. The new profession of civil engineering, headed by men like Telford and Rennie, was not slow to appreciate the value of granite. When Thomas Telford visited Peterhead in 1801 to survey the new harbour, he reported on the great mass of local granite 'very proper for wharfs, piers of harbours and bridges, and for forming tide walls'. When engaged on the Southwark Bridge, Rennie himself went to Peterhead to secure large blocks of from 15 to 25 tons. He caused a local sensation when he moved a 25-ton block four miles to the harbour and had it shipped to London. Other public works constructed of granite at this time were the Portsmouth and Sheerness Docks, Waterloo and London Bridges in London, and the famous Bell Rock Lighthouse, first lighted on February 2nd, 1811. But by no means all the granite for these undertakings was Aberdeen produced. Some of them, like the London and Waterloo Bridges, were almost entirely constructed of Cornish granite. The section of the industry concerned with large public works and the production of street setts and kerbs thus expanded rapidly during the nineteenth century. To-day it is of considerable importance in the economy of Aberdeen.

The manufacture of monuments is the other main branch of the industry. Its origin goes back to about 1820 when Alexander MacDonald, manufacturer of paving-stones, chimney-pieces, and head-stones in Aberdeen, succeeded in evolving a satisfactory method of polishing granite. The traditional story is that MacDonald's interest was aroused by seeing examples of Egyptian polished granite in the British Museum. After many experiments he at last succeeded, and in 1842 the first polished granite monument was sent to London and erected in Kensal Green Cemetery. The process of manufacture was very primitive and was done entirely by hand, but other local people were not slow to follow MacDonald's lead, and soon the monumental branch of the industry was well established.

During this period of experiment and extension the chief Aberdeenshire quarry was at Rubislaw, now within the city boundary, but many smaller ones were being worked in other parts of the county. In 1858 the large Kemnay Quarry, close by the Don, was opened. Stone for many famous buildings, like Blackfriars, Southwark, and Putney Bridges in London, and best known of all, Marischal College in Aberdeen, came from the silver-white granite of Kemnay. Along with Rubislaw, it has remained by far the most important quarry in this area. In the vicinity of Peterhead several quarries have been worked from time to time, producing a stone of a rich red colour. It is said to be the best weathering granite known to the monumental and architectural trade, taking on a brilliant polish which remains undimmed for fifty years. Examples of such granite are seen in the columns of the London Stock Exchange, made by hand in 1882, in the polished pillars in Covent Garden, and in the pillars and pilasters of the Foreign Office, the India Office, and Australia House.

LOCATION OF THE INDUSTRY

Though the extent of granite deposits is determined by geological factors, economic considerations define the areas to be worked. Some deposits, like those in the extreme north of Scotland, may be so far removed from rail and sea transport or manufacturing centres that it does not pay to work them. Or, again, a quarry may contain excellent stone, but if the quantities are small, it is generally un-economic to produce, except for road material or street setts. The constructional and monumental branches demand considerable quantities of a given quality and shade, and so the small quarry, unable to fulfil this condition, is passed over in favour of the large producer. Many such quarries in North-east Scotland have been closed for this reason. On the other hand, quarries producing inferior stone or relatively small quantities of a given quality or colour can find a ready market for their material in road construction or in the house-building industry, where a flaw or a slight break in colour is unimportant. But every quarry, small or large, good or bad, has a certain amount of scrap which may be used for those purposes where quality is not the first consideration.

North-east Scotland has developed an important position in this industry because of the abundant supplies of good granite in the area. The two chief quarries, as we have seen, are at Rubislaw, within the city boundaries, and at Kemnay on Donside some fifteen miles from Aberdeen. Their effectiveness depends on the quality of stone as well as on their large capacity, which makes possible the supply of a given shade of granite in considerable quantities. There are many smaller quarries in the area, as, for instance, in the neighbour-hood of Peterhead, where some twenty were in operation at one time. By 1939, however, all but one had closed down in face of the large importations of red granite from Sweden in the inter-war period. A similar fate awaited other small quarries in the county of Aberdeen —like Correnie, Hill of Fare, Tillyfourie. Where production has continued it has been limited to crushed granite for road-making or dressed stones for street setts. In these cases, however, heavy transport costs have been a material factor. A few minor quarries near Aberdeen, like Persley, Sclattie, and Dancing Cairns, now produce mostly for the building industry.

In South Scotland there is granite quarrying in Galloway, but on a much smaller scale. There the industry is carried on in two places, Dalbeattie and Creetown. At the former quarrying was commenced about 1820, and more recently manufacturing in all its branches has been well established, though on a comparatively small scale. At the latter, operations are confined to quarrying, but they are carried on in a large way by two companies, the most important being the Scottish Granite Company at Kirkmabreck and Glebe. St. Andrew's House, Edinburgh, is built of granite from these quarries.

In England granite quarrying and manufacturing is centred mainly in Cornwall and Devon, where there are five chief producing centres —Dartmoor, in Devon, and St. Breward, Luxullian, Penryn, and Penzance, in Cornwall. Of these, Penryn is the most important. Though doubtless granite has been used in Cornwall for building and monumental purposes since time immemorial, it is only within the last hundred years that working has been extensive. The pioneer was John Freeman, founder of the present firm of Freeman and McLeod Ltd. About 1837 he made extensive surveys, and finally selected the Penryn district, near Falmouth, as most suitable. Having secured the contract for the Keyham naval dockyard, he was instrumental in opening numerous small quarries in that area. By 1912 the company he founded operated some eighty-six quarries throughout Cornwall, the method of working being to have each quarry under a ganger, who employed his own men and paid them a piece wage. Following an agreement between employers and the men's union, this system was terminated in 1913. Thereafter concentration of production followed, and many small quarries were closed down. This tendency to large-scale production was accompanied by considerable advances in mechanical and technical equipment. To-day all the principal quarries in Cornwall have their electric or steam cranes, compressors, and other mechanical equipment, and claim to be as well equipped as any in the country. Besides the few large quarries there are a number of very small ones, usually ill-equipped, and some still using hand-cranes.

Until quite recently the Cornish industry was almost entirely confined to architectural and constructional work. This remains its chief activity to-day. Its products are found at home and abroad, in bridges like Tower, Waterloo, Kew, and Vauxhall in London; in harbours like Chatham, Portsmouth, Devonport, Bombay; in light-houses like the Bishop Rock and Eddystone; in public buildings like the London County Council Buildings at Westminster, and the new buildings of London University. There is hardly a dockyard in the British Empire which does not contain a very large quantity of

Cornish granite. Even the Singapore dock caisson, sills, and sluice-gates were all constructed of Cornish granite sent out by John Freeman and McLeod of Penryn. Before dispatch the granite blocks were polished to the accuracy of a thousandth of an inch, and on arrival in Singapore were fixed in position without any further labour being necessary to make them watertight.

There is also an extensive roadstone industry in Cornwall, distinct from the granite industry proper. None of the granite quarries which produce blocks produce roadstone, except one, which has two or three veins of elvan running through its rock. Elvan is a very hard stone, chiefly composed of basalt and eminently suitable for road construction. The roadstone industry in Cornwall is very extensive, and is carried on in a big way. Output of the Penlee Quarries, for instance, averages 1,000 tons per day, and there are another four or five which come very near this output. These quarries are mostly situated on the sea-front, and many have bins so constructed that ships can run right in and load up 700 or 800 tons in two or three hours. The other chief centre of the roadstone industry is Leicestershire, where output of igneous rocks (which includes basalt and dolerite as well as granite) was 1,281,085 tons in 1938. Practically all this output goes to road construction.

The manufacture of finished granite products is generally carried on in the neighbourhood of the quarries, the degree of proximity depending on the nature of the product. Street setts, kerbs, crushed granite, and the like are usually produced at the quarry itself, because small stones of good quality are required for street setts, while scrap of all kinds will suffice for crushed granite. It is therefore most economical to have these processes concentrated at the quarries. Monumental work, on the other hand, which requires a good deal of mechanical equipment, like saws, polishing machines of various kinds, as well as a high proportion of skilled labour, tends to settle where labour is available.

North of the Border granite manufacturing has been largely concentrated in Aberdeen. This town has been favourably placed for prosecuting this industry. Its proximity to the quarries from which until the present century it derived almost all its supplies of raw material, its well-established coasting services to the chief ports in the United Kingdom, and its supplies of labour at once gave it an assured position in granite manufacturing. Being first in the field, its workmen were able to establish a tradition of skill and craftsmanship, and this was of immense importance in a trade still so largely a handicraft. Down to the First World War its manufacturers had almost a world monopoly, their products being sold as easily in New Zealand and the United States as in England. In this, as in so many other industries, however, the emergence of foreign competition in recent years, and especially since 1920, has destroyed the privileged position hitherto enjoyed by 'The Granite City'.

Between the production of crushed granite and street setts, on the one hand, and monumental work, on the other, there is the constructional section which produces blocks for bridges, buildings, and large engineering projects generally. Sometimes this is carried on at the quarries themselves and sometimes in large manufacturing yards in Aberdeen. Before the recent war a high proportion of quarry output in Scotland, as well as in Cornwall, was used in constructional work, and this strengthened the tendency to integration, either geographical or financial. But since, as in monumental work, craftsmanship is of considerable moment, the pull of centres of population like Aberdeen, where skill is available, is very strong. The city of Aberdeen is thus the main centre of both the monumental and constructional sections of the granite industry.

At Dalbeattie, in Galloway, all branches of manufacturing—from crushed stones, paving setts, street kerbs, road chippings, and aggregate for cement work to dock copings, bridge material, and building fronts—are found at the largest quarry. In addition, rough blocks for monumental works are sent to 'yards' in various parts of the country. At Creetown, on the other hand, setts and crushed stones are produced on the spot, but granite destined for manufacturing is sent in rough blocks to Aberdeen, Glasgow, and Edinburgh.

In Cornwall, where there is little variety of stone, most of the granite being light grey with a large grain, there are several large firms and many small ones. The former, like Freeman and McLeod. combine quarrying and manufacturing for constructional works, Freeman's yard at Penryn, for instance, is large and well-equipped. An overhead electric travelling gantry with a 50-ton capacity, 420 feet long with a 66-feet span, runs from end to end, while in normal times close on 200 masons are employed on every kind of granite-dressing from massive hollow quoins for dock entrances to the delicate mouldings of a Gothic window. Many of the small firms carry on manufacturing as well as quarrying, but their products are chiefly for the monumental trade.

The relative importance of these various districts is shown in the following table:

SALES OF MANUFACTURED MONUMENTAL AND
ARCHITECTURAL GRANITE

	1928 £	1929 £	1930 £	1931 £
Aberdeen . . .	479,815	510,234	529,082	422,799
Edinburgh and Glasgow	95,055	94,044	81,009	87,902
Cornwall and Devon .	177,938	135,507	167,069	182,625

While the pull of quarries and availability of skill have been dominant factors in determining location of granite manufacturing, there are two factors which tend to decentralization. In the first place, the market for manufactured granite is widely dispersed. Products like polished stones for buildings, bridges, and other public works, street setts, road material, and headstones are in universal demand, especially in urban areas. London and the industrial centres of England, for instance, constitute the largest part of the home market, while the development of manufacturing in Glasgow and Edinburgh, as yet only on a small scale, has doubtless been stimulated by the large market at their doors. More serious for Aberdeen, however, is the expansion of quarrying and manufacturing in countries hitherto supplied by local firms. Canada, the United States, and New Zealand, to mention only three, have built up industries easily able to satisfy their own requirements. As a consequence the overseas trade in Aberdeen-manufactured granite had been gravely reduced before 1939, with very serious effects on some local firms.

A second factor making for dispersion of the manufacturing side of the industry is the importation of raw granite. Since the end of last century increasing supplies of raw granite have come from Sweden and, to a lesser extent, from Finland. Before the recent war Aberdeen obtained no less than 80 per cent of its raw material for monumental work from these sources. This was largely due to the variety of colours produced in the Baltic countries and not obtainable in home quarries, as well as to the quality of the foreign stone. Naturally, there is a conflict of opinion on the latter point. Some maintain that foreign stone is easier to work than the home product; others declare it is softer and does not retain a polish like Scottish granite. However that may be, it is a fact that larger supplies of a given quality and colour of stone can be guaranteed from Sweden than from our own quarries. The changing demand at home, as, for example, in the fashion for polished granite fronts for shops and other buildings, has increased dependence on foreign sources. This has naturally weakened the pull of local quarries, and so has given manufacturers greater freedom in selection of sites for their works. The favoured position of Aberdeen has been undermined in another direction. In the inter-war years foreign granite manufacturers were sending their finished goods into the British market, and so were replacing the products of the Aberdeen yards.

Some Aberdeen manufacturers are not unduly disturbed by the emergence of competition from producers in other parts of Britain. They believe that the reputation of their skilled workmen is sufficient to give them an advantage over all possible competitors at home. There is some justification for this view, for the manufacture of granite, especially on the monumental side, is still a trade requiring a high degree of skill. The availability of labour thus remains a dominant factor in the localization of the industry. Others, however, regard this tendency to dispersion as of major importance and likely to have a detrimental effect on the Aberdeen trade, and especially on the small and ill-equipped firm.

Before the war the extent of competition from home producers beyond Aberdeen was not extensive; nor is it likely to be of major importance in the short period. It is probable, however, that Galloway and Cornwall will play an increasing part in the industry: they have large local sources of stone, economical to work, and they have already established a high reputation for their workmanship in markets at home and abroad. The most formidable competitor of Aberdeen, as well as of Galloway and Cornwall, is the foreign producer who before the war was able to ship his manufactured granite into Britain at a price much below local costs.

EXTENT OF THE INDUSTRY

It is difficult to define the extent of the granite industry, for, at one extreme, there is the clear-cut case of granite used in building and monumental work, in kerbs and street setts, and, at the other, the much larger section concerned with road material. Moreover, official statistics relate to *igneous rocks*, which include basalt and dolerite as well as granite. The proportion occupied by granite, of course, varies from place to place.

The granite industry proper, and the one popularly associated with Aberdeen, is concerned primarily with quarrying and the manufacture of dressed and polished stones for buildings and monuments. Thus defined, Aberdeen is the chief centre of the industry in the United Kingdom. Its reputation for granite rests on the manufacture of these high-quality products, as well as on the fact that practically the whole city is built of granite. Indeed, the city itself is a monument to its craftsmen and a striking advertisement of this important industry. There are, of course, other products like kerbs, street setts, and road material, but in the last-named Aberdeenshire is easily outclassed by Cornwall and Leicestershire.

Judged by material used, the granite industry is but a small part of the larger building industry. According to official statistics issued by the Secretary for Mines (18th Annual Report of the Secretary for Mines, 1940), 'minerals used mainly for building, road-making, lime, cement, concrete, etc.' cover three-fourths of the output and nearly two-thirds of the value of all minerals other than coal produced in the United Kingdom. In 1938 the amount produced was 90½ million tons and the value almost £16½ million. The uses to which these minerals are put fall roughly under three heads: (*a*) building, (*b*) road-making, (*c*) lime, concrete, and plaster manufacture. An approximate apportionment for 1938 is as follows:

	Quantity Tons	Net Selling Values £
(*a*)	44,575,000	7,217,000
(*b*)	24,680,000	6,257,000
(*c*)	21,263,000	2,971,000

Of this quantity, igneous rocks represented 11,435,000 tons valued at £3,671,000 (net selling value at quarry), and the principal uses to which they were put were as follows:

	Tons	Percentage of Total
Building stone (including monumental stone)	122,000	1·1
Artificial stone	678,000	5·9
Concreting	578,000	5·1
Road-making and ballasting . .	9,850,000	86·1
Kerbs and setts	165,000	1·4
Other uses and mineral not classified .	42,000	0·4
All Purposes	11,435,000	100·0

It will be observed that 86 per cent of igneous rocks quarried goes to road-making and ballasting, but probably a large proportion of this consists not of granite, but of basalt and dolerite; 11 per cent goes to artificial stone and concreting and only 2·5 per cent to building (including monumental), street kerbs, and setts. The last-named category is probably entirely granite. Viewed against this statistical background, expressed, it should be noted, in quantities of material used, it is seen that the architectural and monumental sections of the granite industry constitute a very small part of the building industry. A different picture would be obtained, however, if values of finished articles were taken. Output of the architectural and monumental sections consists of public buildings, frontages to shops, offices, etc., bridges and monuments, and all these involve expenditure of much labour and capital after the stone leaves the quarry. The increasing use of artificial stone in construction and the practice of using veneers of granite in place of blocks for frontages naturally reduces the proportion of quarry output going to 'building stone'.

In estimating the geographical distribution of the industry the same difficulty, arising from official statistics, confronts us. In 1938 the total quantity of igneous rocks produced in England amounted to 5,461,098 tons, in Scotland 4,312,781 tons, and in Wales 1,585,022 tons. Within England the largest quantity was raised in Leicester-shire (1,281,085 tons), but possibly only one-quarter was granite. In the case of Cornwall (1,076,929 tons) and Devon (375,438 tons), on the other hand, a very high proportion was granite. Cornwall was clearly the chief centre of granite quarrying and granite manufactur-ing in England. In Scotland, the counties of Aberdeen (435,814 tons), Kirkcudbright (138,717 tons), and Dumfries (46,031 tons) were the main producers of granite as well as the principal centres of granite manufacturing. Caernarvon, with a production of 1,051,258 tons of igneous rocks, of which possibly one-half was granite, headed the list for Wales.

THE ORGANIZATION OF PRODUCTION

The first step in production is, of course, quarrying. In a paper read before the British Association at Aberdeen in 1934, Mr. F. S. Anderson, a prominent local granite manufacturer, explained the principles governing quarrying in Aberdeenshire. 'The best-quality rock,' he said, 'is found in "posts" or masses separated from each other by bars of inferior and sometimes worthless rock. There are no natural working beds and the joints are highly irregular, running in all directions. These features are characteristic of Aberdeenshire quarries and make quarrying a very difficult matter. On the ground surface, overlying the granite, is a more or less thick covering of exceedingly hard boulder clay, and for some distance down the surface rock is usually of inferior quality. This overburden is costly to remove and the quarrying of the top rock unremunerative. Under these circumstances, the main principle underlying the development of Aberdeenshire quarries is to work downwards. As a rule, the quality of rock improves with the depth.' Thus, Rubislaw Quarry, which has been worked almost continuously for 168 years, is conical in shape, being approximately 900 feet long, 750 feet wide, and 370 feet deep—this being 70 feet below sea-level.

The first operation is blasting. After a charge has been exploded the loosened rock is examined and the stones classified according to suitability for particular classes of work. The larger blocks are reserved for monumental and engineering work, while smaller or poorer quality stones are manufactured on the spot into street setts and crushed granite for road surfaces. The great depth of Rubislaw Quarry involves heavy expense in raising the stones to the surface. Until the quarry was 200 feet deep horse-drawn carts were used on a winding roadway for this purpose. The first suspension cableway with a travelling carrier to be employed in granite quarrying was designed and erected by John Fyfe at his quarry at Kemnay in 1873. This was called a 'blondin', after the tight-rope walker of that name, then at the height of his fame. To-day there are four blondins at

Rubislaw. Two with a capacity of 3 tons each are used mainly for lifting rubbish and small stones suitable for setts from the quarry floor. A third, of 10 tons capacity, carries material to the crushing plant on the surface, while the fourth, capable of handling 20 tons, lifts all the larger stones required for monumental and engineering purposes. The last-named blondin is reputed to be the largest in the world. Before its erection in 1928 three cranes were required in the bottom of the quarry and one 20-ton crane on the top, and it took 1 hour 15 minutes to remove a large-sized block from the south-west end of the quarry floor to the top at the north-east end—a distance of 1,200 feet. To-day the 20-ton blondin, driven by an electric motor of 160 b.h.p., can do the same operation in about five minutes, including the return journey for the next load.

On reaching the top the blocks are again inspected and classified according to size and quality. Best-quality blocks, destined for monumental and decorative work, are cut to special sizes as required, squared and hammered to a straight-edge face, and then dispatched to granite manufacturers, who produce monuments, shop-fronts, and the like. Blocks for building purposes are also cut into suitable sizes, according to requirements, on the quarry bank, the cutting being done by pneumatic plug drills, capable of boring holes 3 inches deep by $\frac{7}{8}$ inch diameter at the rate of one per minute. Material for sett-making is generally prepared on the quarry floor into pieces about 18 inches long by 12 broad and 8 thick. These are carried in boxes by a light cableway to the sett-makers' bank, where they are cut into various sizes suitable for causeway.

The crushing and screening plant at Rubislaw is the most modern of the mechanical equipment at the quarry. Material for this plant is prepared on the quarry floor into pieces of 12 cwt. or less. Loaded into a steel box of about 8 tons capacity, it is conveyed to the surface by the 10-ton blondin, where it is tipped into a hopper leading to the crushing plant. It is then passed through various crushers until it is finally reduced in size to $\frac{1}{16}$ inch, $\frac{1}{4}$ inch, $\frac{1}{2}$ inch, and $\frac{3}{4}$ inch, each size being ejected into separate bins so situated that lorries can be run underneath and loaded quickly. The material is never handled by labour after being loaded into boxes on the quarry floor, and only three men are required to supervise the working of the entire plant, which is capable of crushing and screening 500 tons of granite in eight hours. Crushed granite is used mainly for road-surfacing, and as the basic ingredient in mass concrete, reinforced concrete, grano-lithic, etc., as well as for garden paths and numerous other purposes.

From the foregoing it is clear that a large quarry requires con-siderable equipment involving a high capital outlay; Rubislaw Quarry Company, for instance, has a capital of £36,000, invested in its single quarry. The other leading company in this area—John Fyfe Ltd.—

has a capital of about £80,000, but it owns a number of quarries in addition to Kemnay. Before the war some of the smaller units had been closed down as a result of foreign competition and high costs of transport, while others continued to produce road material. In Cornwall the largest quarries, mostly concerned with roadstone, produce as much as 1,000 tons a day. But there are many small quarries, working independently and specializing in street setts, and road and building material.

Quarry-owners generally deal directly with manufacturers, a notable exception being Rubislaw Quarry, which acts through an intermediary—the Aberdeen Granite Supply Association, to which reference will be made presently. Manufacturing yards, however, do not absorb all the output of quarries, and so most of the large quarries combine manufacturing and quarrying. At Kemnay, Dalbeattie, and Penryn, for instance, architectural stone for large works, like bridges and public buildings, as well as kerbs, street setts, and road material, are produced. They also supply rough stones to manufacturers whose main activities centre on constructional and architectural work, as well as to the host of monumental manufacturers who engage in cutting and polishing monuments, gravestones, and the smaller classes of polished stones for shop-fronts and other buildings.

Generally speaking, however, granite manufacturing is carried on by firms who have no connexion with the quarrying side of the industry. In 1939 there were forty-five such firms in Aberdeen, varying in size from the small firm with a capital of £3,750 and a labour supply of about twelve to the largest with a capital of £20,000 and a labour force of about 120. The number of firms and the number of establishments is practically identical. The following table shows the range of employment at August 26th, 1939:

Below 10 employees	2 firms	
11– 24	,,	13 ,,
25– 49	,,	21 ,,
50– 99	,,	5 ,,
100–199	,,	2 ,, (113 maximum)

At the same date the total employment was as follows:

Workmen of all Classes	Office Staff	Management	TOTAL	Men	Women
1,421	73	101	1,595	1,545	50

Down to the First World War it was a common practice for working masons to emigrate to America and, having saved a few hundred pounds, to come home and set up as granite manufacturers. American agents visited Aberdeen and financed these small people by giving them three months' bills against orders for the United States. The export of tombstones to America thus became a staple part of the Aberdeen industry. In those days it was easy to start a 'yard' because little capital was required and the profits offered by the American market were large. Since 1914, however, there has been a steady fall in the number of establishments as the following table shows:

NUMBER OF GRANITE MANUFACTURERS IN ABERDEEN

1914	.	.	71	1930	.	.	51
1920	.	.	60	1935	.	.	51
1925	.	.	57	1940	.	.	46

Two reasons may be advanced to explain this reduction. In the first place, over the last couple of generations there has been a considerable increase in the amount of capital required to finance a yard. The machine age in granite manufacture commenced about the close of last century and since then mechanization has proceeded rapidly. Before 1900 steam power was used to lift and move granite blocks, but most cutting and polishing was done by hand. The introduction of pneumatic drills, imported from the United States and first demonstrated in Aberdeen in 1895, the use of sand blast and the electric polishing machine, and most recent the carborundum saw, which speeded up production and made possible the cutting of deeper grooves and the execution of more artistic designs, have all contributed to greater capital outlay. In 1939 the establishment of a medium-sized yard involved a capital of about £8,000; even a small yard cannot get along with less than about £4,000, a sum quite beyond the capacity of the working mason. And so there is no steady inflow into the industry as was the case in Victorian days. Moreover, it should be noted, though there is a good deal of mechanization in most yards, granite-working is still mainly a handicraft industry, and unless a man has practical experience of the trade he is ill-qualified to commence manufacturing on his own.

In the second place, the death of an employer has often been followed by the closing of the yard he himself had founded. Perhaps there was no son to take his place, or, if there were, he might lack industry and practical skill, or wish to enter some other trade or profession. Thus the yard would be sold and, having been dismantled, would be closed down.

It is significant that for many years no new granite yard has been established in Aberdeen. It is urged that since 1918 conditions in the industry have been too precarious to invite new investment, yet when an establishment is closed the plant is immediately bought up, usually by firms from the south. Competition is very keen among granite manufacturers in Aberdeen, and doubtless the closing of a

7

yard is hailed with relief by the remaining firms, for the general opinion is that there are too many manufacturers. This may explain why there is no rush to buy yards as going concerns.

The combination of mechanization and handicraft, so typical of this industry, can readily be appreciated when one considers the processes involved in manufacture. The raw material of the granite manufacturer is the rough stone as it is received from the quarry. First the stone is faced by hand, the masons working with chisels and hammers, or with a machine called a dunter or surfacer operated by compressed air and whose action is comparable to a steam hammer. A special tool repeatedly hits the stone, knocking off the rough bumps and leaving a relatively smooth surface. If the stone has to be cut to a given thickness, as in the case of veneering for shop-fronts, it is next passed to the sawing machines. This is naturally a very slow process, the actual cutting being done by metal grit agitated by a horizontal moving steel saw. The third process is polishing, and usually there are three distinct steps. Firstly, the block is treated by sanding with cast steel rings and iron grit in order to make the face dead level. Secondly, and on the same machine, the stone is polished by a revolving cast-iron ring with carborundum or emery until a glazed surface is obtained. This gives a dull polish. Thirdly, wooden blocks faced with felt and putty powder (oxide of tin) are used until a bright polish is secured.

The polished stone is then passed to the stone-cutting shed, where it is dressed by hand, the masons using chisel and hammer or pneumatic tools. It is here that skill still plays a predominant part. If the product is a tombstone or monument the ends and mouldings have generally to be cut and polished entirely by hand.

The position may be made clearer by considering a particular works. In a medium-sized establishment with a capital of about £8,000 and an employment roll of about forty in 1939, the distribution of machinery and labour was as follows:

1 dunter machine for surfacing (1 man, sometimes 2)		1
5 saw machines		
3 polishing machines (large)		
4 vertical polishing machines for small stones . . .	1 man	
2 electric polishing machines for small stones that cannot be done by vertical machine	each	14
Stone-cutting by hand—18 skilled stone-cutters . .		18
		33
Bed-setter, sawman, craneman, labourer, foreman, manager, and 2 office staff		8
		41

The same types of machine are used in all establishments, and so the chief difference between small and large units is in numbers employed. The large concern covering a greater acreage can have overhead cranes and other mechanical equipment for transporting material, but, it is to be noted, the small yard properly laid out can be a quite efficient unit. The great weight of material to be handled makes good layout an important consideration. The small yard arranged in a square, with sawing machines on one side, polishing mill on another, and stone-cutters and polishers on another can employ a derrick placed in the middle for moving material from one process to another. It is not easy to add to the size of an establishment without unduly increasing costs. Additional machinery or an extra stone-cutters' shed beyond the radius of the derrick results in extra handling. This is perhaps a reason why so many yards have changed but little in size. Good layout is a matter of prime importance to the large as to the small yard, and unless great foresight is shown additional costs are incurred in moving material.

Mechanization implies power production. As we have seen, steam power was used in most yards last century. In the present century electricity and the internal combustion engine have proved a great boon to all manufacturers. Electricity especially has led to economies, for by a judicious arrangement of motors power can be readily obtained and cut off when not required. This has been of great benefit to all manufacturers, small and large. Moreover, machines are standardized, and so are of the same capacity irrespective of the size of the firm. Thus, costs of production do not vary to any material extent between large and small yards. In short, the economies of large-scale production are not evident in granite manufacture. Over the last generation, however, there has been little advance in mechanization, the only important innovation being the circular carborundum saw which cuts more quickly and more evenly than the heavy type of saw already mentioned. The carborundum saw, however, is only suitable for small jobs.

Integration of the two main stages of the industry—quarrying and manufacturing—is uncommon. One or two quarry-owners, as we have seen, have their own yards, but for obvious reasons complete integration is impossible. The output of a large quarry is far too great for the needs of a single yard. Furthermore, a variety of products come from the quarry—blocks for architectural or monumental work, stones for street setts, kerbs, and a great deal of road material. Hence, granite manufacturers confine themselves to fashioning the rough stone into finished products and leave the quarrying to the quarriers. Though one or two of the larger manufacturers have an interest in quarrying, this is quite exceptional.

All the manufacturers of Aberdeen and district are members of the

8

Aberdeen Granite Manufacturers' Association. The Association is consequently a powerful body and directly or indirectly can exercise considerable influence over the industry. Its high entry fee is likely to discourage new enterprises, and unless a new manufacturer joins the Association he would find himself without labour, for the Association has an agreement with the local trade union that members will employ union labour only, while the trade union, on its part, agrees to work only for members of the Association. Efforts have been made by the Association to limit competition and agree on prices, but, it is said, with little success. A price list was issued which served as a guide to manufacturers, but this is the extent of their efforts to influence prices. Competition remains extraordinarily keen, due largely to the strong individualism of the trade. Establishment of a central selling agency has been mooted, but the proposal is regarded as quite impracticable where so many small employers are involved. The only matter on which there is general agreement is on the exclusion of foreign manufactured granite. Recently the Aberdeen Granite Manufacturers in association with producers of stone in Bath, Portland, Cornwall, Forest of Dean, and Wales took steps to form a British Stone Federation. At a meeting held in Birmingham in September 1941 the general plan was discussed and approved.

LABOUR

The Aberdeen granite operatives are organized in the Building and Monumental Workers' Association of Scotland, which recently was absorbed by the Amalgamated Union of Building Trade Workers. The union has two sections, one covering workers in the granite yards and the other building masons. It is 100 per cent strong in Aberdeen, for, as already mentioned, the union has an agreement with the Employers' Association that only union men will be employed and, conversely, they agree to work only for members of the Aberdeen Granite Manufacturers' Association. The following table shows the number of men employed in the trade over a number of years:

Date	Skilled Workers	Apprentices	Total
June 1914 . .	1,606	275	1,881
1920 . .	1,110	108	1,218
1925 . .	1,118	120	1,238
1 August 1930 . .	1,126	230	1,356
31 December 1938 .	1,116	119	1,235

It will be noticed that there has been a considerable drop since 1914, but numbers have remained fairly constant since 1920. There are two main grades of skill—granite-cutters and stone-polishers. The former often includes men of considerable skill—almost approaching the rank of sculptor. Many of the finest monuments in this area have been cut by Aberdeen workers to the design of the artist—the best-known example is that of the statue of Edward VII in Union Street.

Apprentices are medically examined before being indentured, and serve a period of five years. Special evening classes are provided for them in Gray's School of Art, extending over three sessions and including Drawing of Ornament and Lettering, Modelling and Carving, Workshop Drawing and Architectural Drawing.

RAW MATERIALS

The raw material of the granite industry is derived from both home and foreign quarries. We have already noted the geographical distribution of the former and how each district tends to supply its own area. The Aberdeen manufacturers, for instance, obtain the bulk of their home supplies from local quarries, like Rubislaw and Kemnay, but a certain amount is brought from Galloway, which also supplies Glasgow, Edinburgh, Carlisle, and various other places. Cornwall, on the other hand, manufactures most of its produce locally.

Before the recent war large quantities of raw granite in blocks were imported. In 1934 they amounted to 17,305 tons, and in 1938 to 19,184 tons. Most of this was for monumental work in Aberdeen, and represented about 80 per cent of the granite so employed. Sweden and, to a lesser extent Finland, were the main sources.

Swedish granite has been worked since the 1880's when A. K. Fernström of Karlshamn commenced extensive operations. The success of this company was accompanied by absorption of many smaller concerns until just before the recent war its quarries and installations covered 40,000 acres and employed 3,000 workers. The company owns its own ships, has an elaborate world-wide sales organization, and in normal times handles upwards of 200,000 tons of granite per annum. Its success is partly due to low costs of production. Granite is blasted out of the hillside, unlike the practice in Aberdeenshire, where quarries are worked from the top downwards. Moreover, the stone can be loaded direct on to ships at the company's wharfs, whereas in Aberdeenshire it has to be hauled some 400 feet from the bottom of the quarry and then transported by road or rail to its destination. Another important reason for success is the variety of colours available in Swedish quarries. Fernström granite, or AKF, as it is known in the trade, comprises black, blueberg, green, red, and grey granites, the most common being black, which is said to harmonize well with stainless steel, iron, and other metals used in modern buildings.

8*

In the early days of granite imports to Aberdeen, all sorts of merchants engaged in the trade, but most prominent were coal merchants. About fifty years ago, however, the Aberdeen manufacturers, anxious to handle this trade for themselves, founded the Aberdeen Granite Supply Association. This was originally a sort of co-operative concern in which manufacturers held shares and through which they obtained foreign supplies of raw material. It was able to effect many economies, especially in transport charges and in commercial organization. So long as the Association was representative of the trade and was not dominated by any group of manufacturers it served a most useful purpose and was of great benefit to all concerned. In recent years, however, the tendency has been for its control to become highly concentrated so that it has become, in effect, a monopolistic body controlling the supply of foreign granite (and Rubislaw granite) to the Aberdeen manufacturers. Its continued success, however, is due to the fact that it can make bulk purchases and can keep large stocks of every variety of granite at its depot in Aberdeen. This last point is of great importance to local manufacturers who may want a special quality or colour of stone at short notice. In normal times the Association carried a stock of between £20,000 and £30,000. It checks independent imports by refusing to supply firms which do not buy all their foreign granite through its channels. It is thus in a strong position when selling in the home market. The Association also supplies timber, putty powder, and other materials required in manufacture. The following table shows the quantities of raw material imported in to Aberdeen in each of the ten pre-war years:

Year ending 30 September		
1930	.	18,238 tons
1931	.	11,574 ,,
1932	.	14,434 ,,
1933	.	15,489 ,,
1934	.	14,458 ,,
1935	.	14,348 ,,
1936	.	12,333 ,,
1937	.	16,381 ,,
1938	.	16,392 ,,
1939	.	9,497 ,,

NATURE OF DEMAND AND MARKETING

Granite varies a good deal in quality, in colour, and in general texture. These factors determine to a great extent the market for the produce of a quarry. There is, however, another important factor to be taken into account. Unless a quarry can produce considerable quantities of stone of a given colour and quality and in largish blocks, it is of little use to the constructional side of the industry which goes in for large undertakings, like bridges and public buildings, where uniformity in material is essential. At the other extreme are quarries, like several small ones close to Aberdeen, where quality and colour are not in the first rank, but whose stone is satisfactory for ordinary house-building. Their market is therefore a local one. Between these two extremes there are quarries producing good-quality granite, but in small blocks. They concentrate on the production of street setts and road material.

The uses to which the output of a granite quarry are put, therefore, depend on the nature of the product. But, of course, quarries producing the best stones for architectural and monumental work also have much small material as well as considerable quantities of scrap. And so, as we have seen, the produce of a large quarry like Rubislaw or Kemnay or Creetown is used not only for architectural and monumental work, but for kerbs, setts, and road material. Granite dust is a by-product of most large quarries. At Kemnay this is manufactured into granite bricks. For this purpose an elaborate plant was installed for conveying the material to the machine which mixes, presses, and finally ejects the completed bricks. Removing the finished bricks from a revolving table is the only operation performed by hand. These bricks are said to have great advantages over ordinary bricks; they have a fine finish, and so have no openings where water and frost may do damage. Some large quarries, like those in Cornwall, produce only roadstone, for their stone breaks readily and is therefore of little use for building purposes, though excellent in quality for road construction.

The chief product of the Aberdeenshire industry is dressed stones for constructional and engineering purposes, and this is the business of the largest and best-equipped firms. These may simply be dressed granite blocks for large public buildings, bridges, etc., or they may consist of polished slabs of 1½ to 2 inches thickness for frontages to shops, picture-houses, banks, and similar buildings. Down to the 1914–18 war solid granite blocks with one side polished were used for such purposes, but now with steel construction and reinforced concrete only a veneer of granite is necessary. Thus, a block of granite can go much further, since it can be sawn up into a number of slabs. The production of these polished veneers of granite is naturally a slow business. The actual sawing, for instance, is carried out at the rate of about 1 inch per hour, though this varies according to the nature of the stone. The hardness of granite makes working difficult and speedy production impossible. This is also noticeable in house-building. Though there is little difference in cost of materials between a granite- and a brick-built house in North-east Scotland, the former takes longer to construct. But if production is slow the finished article is lasting, and it would be a short-sighted policy to sacrifice granite for other building material which can be more cheaply produced, but which is not so enduring or so handsome.

Because of the time element in production, large contracts for architectural stones are sometimes sub-contracted. It used to be the practice for agents from the south to split up their contracts amongst a number of firms in Aberdeen, so that one might get a few hundred pounds of work, another a few thousand, according to producing capacity. Nowadays, however, the large firms refuse to handle a contract except in its entirety, and then, if circumstances demand, they sub-contract with smaller firms. This applies only in the case of slab work for shop-fronts and similar products. Since granite of only 1½ to 2 inches thickness is desired for this purpose, the problem of handling a large contract is not now so difficult. The work is more easily standardized. Some firms which specialize in this product attempt to carry a stock of polished slabs, drawing on it as required and replenishing in slack times. To be effective, however, such a policy involves colossal stocks and a great variety of colours, and so does not offer significant economies, though it helps to retain skilled men who otherwise would drift away. About 60 per cent in value of the Aberdeen output consists of polished and dressed stones for architectural and constructional works.

The other chief product of the Aberdeen granite industry is tombstones, and this is mainly the business of the small firms, though some of the larger firms also engage in its production, when times are slack, as, for instance, during war-time. The latter, nevertheless, prefer to devote all their time and energies to architectural work, which they regard as a higher and more constructive form of industrial activity. The custom of marking burial-places by monuments is, of course, an ancient one, and it dies hard, but the practice of cremation is likely in the long run to have a detrimental effect on this branch of the trade. At the present time the amount of granite consumed in monuments is considerable and, since solid blocks of stone are used, possibly exceeds that used in architectural and constructional work.

The market for tombstones is not determined solely by ordinary economic forces. Sentiment is an important factor, and for this reason the merchant or manufacturer, if he deals directly with consumers, is in a very strong economic position. The retail buyer of a headstone is generally not prepared to haggle about price. To allow free play to economic considerations seems sordid and unworthy of one whose sole desire is to perpetuate the memory of some loved one. Where the manufacturer makes direct contact with the consumer, as a few do in the local market, he is able to cash in on this sentimental element in price. In wider markets, however, the usual practice is for the manufacturer to deal through agents on a commission basis or to sell outright to merchants who thus stand to gain from the peculiar nature of the demand. In the latter case obvious economies are made. The large merchant, through his designs department, can produce working drawings which are made available to manufacturers, while his wide connexions enable him to buy in quantity and so enable the manufacturer to make full use of his material and machinery.

FOREIGN TRADE

(a) *Exports.* Aberdeen early established an international reputation for its granite products. It was in Aberdeen that the art of polishing granite was first established in modern times, and this at once placed her manufacturers and craftsmen in an unrivalled position in world markets. Before the First World War, however, this position was being challenged, especially by the United States and several European countries. In the inter-war period the fall in exports was most rapid. At one time, for instance, Aberdeen had a large trade with the United States. In 1909, it amounted to 4,013 tons valued at £40,767. In 1921 it was not more than 569 tons valued at £20,280; in 1930 the exports were nil. The decline in exports has not been confined to the United States. A similar tendency though not so marked is seen in the figures of trade with Canada, Australia, and New Zealand. Granite exports to the Empire fell from 6,013 tons, valued at £51,440, in 1909; to 1,410 tons, valued at £41,295, in 1930; and to 224 tons, valued at £8,665, in 1938.

Two reasons may be advanced for this fall in exports. First and most important is the development of granite manufacture abroad, especially in the United States, in which Aberdeen craftsmen played a notable part, as well as in Czechoslovakia and Germany. A second reason is found in tariff barriers. By 1930 granite imports into the United States were subject to a duty of 60 per cent; in the case of Canada, 35 per cent; and in the case of Australia and New Zealand, 40 per cent. It is significant, however, that the decline in exports set in before high protection was widely established. From the following table it will be seen that the value of exports to foreign countries fell from £51,965 in 1909 to £4,325 in 1930, and to £1,444 in 1938; and exports to the British Empire from £51,440 in 1909 to £41,295 in 1930 and to £8,665 in 1938.

(b) *Imports.* Imports of granite in all forms from raw blocks to finished monuments rose steeply in the inter-war period until checked by the high import duties of 1936. Within the industry there is, of course, no unanimity on policy in this matter. Quarry-owners naturally dislike imports of raw granite, while manufacturers welcome them. The latter, however, urge exclusion of manufactured products, and the former, realizing the benefits likely to accrue to home quarries

EXPORTS FROM THE UNITED KINGDOM OF GRANITE, WHOLLY OR MAINLY MANUFACTURED

	1909		1913		1921		1925		1930		1935		1938	
	Quantity tons	Value £	Quantity tons	Value £	Quantity tons	Value £	Quantity tons	Value £	Quantity tons	Value £	Quantity tons	Value £	Quantity tons	Value £
Foreign Countries	4,931	51,965	3,374	39,223	763	38,081	831	21,688	133	4,325	55	1,292	45	1,444
British Empire	6,013	51,440	4,711	56,157	677	29,708	2,198	57,006	1,410	41,295	384	7,577	224	8,665
Total	10,944	103,405	8,085	95,380	1,440	67,789	3,029	78,694	1,543	45,620	439	8,869	269	10,109

through expansion of manufacture, generally support them. Merchants engaged in the import trade, of course, oppose such restrictions, maintaining that home production is inadequate both in quantity and quality.

Quarry-owners, have to face further foreign competition. In addition to the considerable importation of raw granite, amounting, as we have seen, to 19,184 tons in 1938, there was also a large import of 'crushed Macadam and chippings of granite' amounting to 308,093 tons, valued at £174,224, as well as of kerb-stones and setts. Since these articles are produced mainly at the quarries, quarry-owners suffer most from their importation. Sweden and Norway were the chief sources, but before the recent war India had entered the market. Street kerbs made by native labour, railed 100 miles to the seaboard and shipped to the Thames, came into competition with the products of the British quarries. Being classed as 'Empire products', they were given preferential treatment. In 1938, 40,976 tons of granite pavement kerbs and setts, valued at £118,582, were imported into the United Kingdom.

Prior to 1921 there were no imports into the United Kingdom of manufactured monumental or architectural granite. The very extensive domestic market was supplied entirely by home manufacturers. In that year, however, imports amounted to 989 tons, valued at £23,522. This was the beginning. By 1930 they had increased to 6,550 tons, valued at £208,181, almost three-fourths of this coming from Germany and most of the remainder from Czechoslovakia. By 1938 imports had risen to 12,559 tons, valued at £348,294. Finland, Germany, and Czechoslovakia were the chief sources.

The table on page 204 shows the steady rise in imports from 1921 to 1938.

According to employers the main reason for these large importations of manufactured granite is the inferior conditions of employment in foreign countries. Before the recent war standard rates of wages in Aberdeen, fixed by negotiation between the Employers' Association and the Trade Union, were 1s. 6d. per hour for granite-dressers and 1s. 5d. per hour for polishers. These were regarded as minima, and on an average the rates were 1d. per hour higher. Some workers earned a good deal more, for a skilful granite-worker is an artist and is worth a great deal to his employer. Edinburgh rates were similar, in Glasgow slightly higher, and in Dalbeattie and Dumfries slightly lower. It is difficult to determine what wages were paid abroad, but, according to a statement of the Aberdeen employers, skilled workmen in Germany, Czechoslovakia, and Finland received 8d. per hour for a 48-hour week. Wages in the United Kingdom were thus roughly 125 per cent higher, and hours often shorter, than in the competing

IMPORTS OF GRANITE—MONUMENTAL AND ARCHITECTURAL—WHOLLY OR MAINLY MANUFACTURED
1921-38

	1921		1925		1930		1935		1938	
	Quantity tons	Value £	Quantity tons	Value £	Quantity tons	Value £	Quantity tons	Value £	Quantity tons	Value £
Finland	—	—	221	5,783	556	14,822	54,313	111,852	5,008	122,351
Sweden	76	1,106	231	8,126	208	1,753	256	7,129	523	7,533
Norway	347	6,353	291	2,364	79	2,046	—	—	—	—
Germany	420	11,392	2,163	65,867	4,162	143,423	2,288	93,274	2,235	95,957
Czechoslovakia	—	—	600	18,586	1,302	42,528	1,278	41,562	3,090	104,350
Other Foreign Countries	144	4,606	145	3,496	165	2,540	430	3,347	1,262	12,910
Total from Foreign Countries	987	23,457	3,651	99,222	6,472	207,112	9,685	256,664	12,118	343,101
Total from British Empire	2	65	33	762	78	1,069	55	903	441	5,193
Grand total	989	23,522	3,684	99,984	6,550	208,181	9,740	257,567	12,559	348,294

continental countries. This is the main argument of the manufacturers and a comparison of prices quoted for different classes of manufactured granite show that there is substance in their contention. The merchants, on the other hand, maintain that difference in wage-rates is not such an important factor as the manufacturers suggest, and that the real advantages of the foreigner are found in subsidies granted by their governments and occasionally in superior technique. In 'all polished' memorials, they say, skill and capital equipment probably give the Aberdeen manufacturer an advantage over the foreign, but in 'part polished' monuments, advantage lies with the foreign producer.

Imports from Germany, Czechoslovakia, and Finland commenced in a period of currency depreciation after 1920, and the hold thus secured by foreign manufacturers in the United Kingdom was easily maintained and extended. In 1927 the Aberdeen Granite Manufacturers' Association, with the support of the Cornish Association and the Glasgow and Dundee Associations, made application under the Safeguarding of Industries Act for the imposition of a duty of 35 per cent for a period of five years on imported monumental and architectural granite wholly or mainly manufactured. On reference to a committee, the application was refused on the ground that the industry was not of substantial importance by reason of the volume of employment. A later appeal resulted in the application of the Merchandise Marks Act to imported manufactured granite. This concession, however, was never regarded as of much importance, since the marks of origin were merely pencilled on the imported granite monuments and so were easily erased. Moreover, according to the manufacturers themselves the order was honoured more in the breach than in the observance. Prosecutions had to be undertaken by the Manufacturers' Association, and this generally proved a costly business. They claimed that foreign manufactured granite was frequently sold as British, and this was very difficult to detect, for it requires an expert to distinguish between, say, Kemnay granite and Swedish greys. This confusion was increased by a practice adopted by the Aberdeen Granite Supply Association of giving Scottish names to foreign granites. Finnish granites, for instance, were called Birkhall, Balmoral, Abergeldie, Glencoe, Braemar, etc., and the famous Swedish black granite was called Bon Accord Black.

The Import Duties Act of 1932 imposed an 'ad valorem duty' of 10 per cent of the value of all imported goods with a few exceptions. Aberdeen manufacturers, believing this duty inadequate for manufactured products, made application to the Import Duties Advisory Committee for an additional duty. This resulted in a further 10 per cent, making a total duty of 20 per cent on imported manufactured granite. Despite this considerable degree of protection, which, of course, was strenuously opposed by the merchants, imports of granite continued to increase. In December 1934 an application was made for a further duty, and this was granted in September 1936, when the rate of duty was raised to 30 per cent, the duty on rough and unmanufactured granite remaining at 10 per cent.

On these occasions local manufacturers were supported by all associations of firms in the United Kingdom interested in the manufacture or sale of monumental and architectural granite, viz. the Cornish Granite Merchants' and Quarry Masters' Association; the National Association of Master Monumental Masons; the Scottish Master Monumental Sculptors' Association; the Edinburgh and District Master Monumental Sculptors' Association; and the Dundee and District Master Monumental Sculptors' Association. Of these associations the Cornish Granite Merchants' and Quarry Masters' Association consists of manufacturers and quarry-masters; the Scottish Master Monumental Sculptors' Association and the Edinburgh and District Master Monumental Sculptors' Association have a few manufacturing members, the others being retail merchants interested only in the sale of finished products. The members of the other associations consist solely of retail merchants.

The import duties applied both to raw granite and manufactured granite, the former being subject to 10 per cent and the latter to 30 per cent. Scottish quarry-owners urged that they too should be given greater protection, for though a considerable part of the imports of raw granite might be justified on the ground that the colours secured were unobtainable in home quarries, a large part consisted of grey granite of the same general colour and quality as that produced at Kemnay and Rubislaw in Aberdeenshire. The following table illustrates this point:

QUANTITIES IN CUBIC FEET OF IMPORTED GRANITES SOLD TO GRANITE MANUFACTURERS IN ABERDEEN FOR MONUMENTAL AND ARCHITECTURAL PURPOSES (1928–1931)

	1928	1929	1930	1931
Blacks . .	29,236–6	30,635–3	32,291–0	26,025–9
Pearls . .	17,464–0	15,226–10	22,473–10	15,398–11
Reds . .	17,459–3	21,977–5	16,099–9	11,816–6
Greys . .	26,812–9	32,813–0	27,190–3	28,598–1
White . .	3,233–5	2,358–8	3,320–2	3,303–10
Various .	2,581–8	2,706–2	2,339–3	2,669–11
	96,787–7	105,717–4	103,714–3	87,813–0

The protection afforded to the granite industry did not check importation. On the contrary, as we have already shown, imports of raw and manufactured granite steadily increased. English merchants, who are the main importers, strenuously opposed the imposition of tariffs and disputed the manufacturers' claim that foreign costs are so much lower than theirs.

A preliminary investigation of the granite industry cannot fail to reveal certain facts relevant to this problem of costs and imports. In the first place, there is the comparatively large number of firms, most of which are quite small both in capital equipment and in labour employed. As we have seen, skill is of first importance, and the economies of large-scale production are not easily secured, yet it would be rash to say that larger production units and a higher degree of specialization might not contribute to lower costs. It is surprising that the organization of the industry should have remained substantially the same over a long period of years, and that, with the exception of the carborundum saw, no important change in mechanization has been introduced during the last generation. Some Aberdeen manufacturers admit that the Germans have advanced the art of polishing granite, so that low labour costs are possibly not the only cause of the large imports of manufactured granite. Moreover, nearly all continental producers make fuller use of sand-blasting than the home manufacturers. As in production, so in marketing there has been no appreciable change. Local manufacturers, as we have seen, took steps to import granite on a co-operative basis through the Granite Supply Association, but on the selling side no comparable steps have been taken. It is true that the Aberdeen Granite Manufacturers' Association issued a price list, but this did not result in any economies. Before the war the Association also carried on a publicity campaign, and a company known as Aberdeen Designs Limited, founded in 1936 by the manufacturers themselves, attempted to give the trade the benefit of expert advice on design. Beyond this no concerted effort has been made to expand sales and examine the possibilities of the market. The fact seems to be that manufacturers have so long enjoyed a virtual monopoly of the granite trade in this country that they find it difficult to see anything wrong with their organization and are reluctant to face up to a situation radically different from that of a generation ago.

THE EFFECTS OF THE WAR

The chief effects of the recent war on the granite industry may be grouped under three heads. In the first place, there was a complete stoppage of imports of raw material. Since the industry drew 80 per cent of its raw material for monumental work from abroad, the new situation naturally created boom conditions for home quarries. Many small quarries which had been closed down in pre-war days were reopened for the production of street setts, kerbs, and especially crushed granite, while the larger quarries in Aberdeenshire, Galloway, and Cornwall were worked to full capacity, the only limiting factor being labour. For the manufacturers, the effect of cessation of imports was of a different kind, for the range of colour and quality of stones was drastically limited.

Almost all granite produced in Scotland, at least in any considerable quantity, is grey, and so manufacturers had to content themselves with this single colour, whereas before the war they had a wide variety from Sweden. This limitation may have a salutary influence on the market which before the war had been greatly influenced by fashions in colour, like the vogue in black granite for shop-fronts and, to a more limited extent, for headstones. The supply of granite for manufacturing purposes was further limited by Government requirements, a considerable proportion of output being used in aerodrome construction and other defence works.

A second effect of the war on the industry was loss of markets. Foreign markets, already considerably restricted before the outbreak of hostilities, were now completely cut off, while the cessation of building operations at home seriously affected the larger and most important manufacturing establishments which specialized in architectural work. In order to keep some of their plant going they manufactured tombstones, but this was but a small and temporary activity of such firms. The smaller yards, however, continued to manufacture what had always been their main product—tombstones—though with an attenuated labour force.

A third and obvious effect of the war was a shortage of labour. About 60 per cent of the employees in the Aberdeen industry enlisted in the armed forces. The largest reduction in labour supply took place in the early part of the war; thus at the end of 1941 there were 547 skilled workers and 13 apprentices as against 1,116 skilled workers and 119 apprentices in 1938. Before the end of hostilities numbers were further reduced. While it is probable that skilled men will return to the industry, the most serious aspect of the situation relates to apprenticeship. Since skill plays such a vital part in the industry, the training of new recruits is a matter of considerable importance.

Future prospects of the industry are thus bound up with the re-establishment of an adequate supply of highly skilled labour. But this, of course, is not the only consideration. Readiness to explore the possibilities of further mechanization and technical improvements, as well as of the possibilities of economies in production and marketing are matters of the first importance. For a time the industry will doubtless experience boom conditions due to the expansion of building, but this will simply postpone but not render unnecessary consideration of the fundamental problems of technique, of organization, and of marketing.

CHAPTER IV

THE BREWING INDUSTRY OF EDINBURGH

By Dr. MARY RANKIN

INTRODUCTION

BREWING is one of Edinburgh's oldest, most characteristic, and most firmly established industries and is closely woven into the general commercial fabric of the city. How old exactly the industry is it is naturally impossible to say, but it is known that the monks of the Abbey of Holyrood in the twelfth century made a much appreciated ale. The main breweries of Edinburgh are still clustered round the Abbey locality, where a plentiful supply of suitable brewing water from wells sunk in the old red sandstone is to be found to this day. About seventy years ago the discovery of suitable wells or an underground lake farther round Arthur's Seat to the south at Craigmillar led to a new cluster of breweries there, some of which were originally located in the old Holyrood area. The reason for the shift in location of these breweries seems to have been twofold, namely, a possible falling off in the water from the old wells and a desire of the railway company to acquire the brewery site for the purposes of the Waverley Station. The railway company's offer to build a new brewery at Craigmillar was accepted.

Edinburgh is the centre of the brewing industry in Scotland. Of the thirty-seven firms in the country, twenty-one are situated in Midlothian (twenty in the city itself and one on its outskirts at Dalkeith). Alloa, with seven breweries, comes next in importance. Glasgow, Dumbarton, Dundee, Laurencekirk, Montrose, Coldstream, and Perth account for the remainder.

The Edinburgh industry produces 80 per cent of the total Scottish output. This output in 1941 is given in the *Brewers' Almanack, 1941*, as 1,654,392 standard barrels. On this basis the output of the Edinburgh industry would be in the region of 1,300,000 standard barrels, a standard barrel being 36 gallons of specific gravity 105·5 degrees.

RAW MATERIALS

The main raw materials required for brewing itself in normal times are barley, hops, sugar, yeast, and water of a certain peculiar hardness. It is no doubt to the natural supply of such water afforded by the old sandstone wells that the success of the Edinburgh industry is mainly due.

Barley. Part of the barley used is home-grown and supplied by the Lothian farms, but for the last fifty years or so imported Californian barley has come greatly into favour on account of the sunnier and drier climate in which it is grown. Barley is also imported from North Africa, Australia, Chile, and India. Technically, for brewing purposes the dry imported barley is superior and produces a higher quality of beer. Home-grown barley, especially in a wet season, requires special drying machinery, delaying the process of production as well as adding directly to production costs. Brewers generally are anxious to help home agriculture and to use as much home-grown barley as they can having regard to the varying quality resulting from weather conditions, and the normal practice before the war was to use a certain proportion only of the imported grain. In 1933 the Brewers' Society gave an undertaking to the Chancellor of the Exchequer, when he reduced the duty on beer by a penny per pint, that in order to give the maximum assistance to British agriculture the Society would recommend all brewers to increase as far as possible the proportion of home-grown barley in the brewing of all classes of beer. There then took place a gradual increase in brewers' purchases of home-grown barley and malt from 5,619,612 cwt. in 1933 to 9,526,604 cwt. in 1938. These figures refer to the Brewing Industry of Great Britain as a whole and are given in the *Brewers' Almanack, 1941*. In 1938 a conference was called by the Minister of Agriculture in order to evolve a scheme for the more permanent benefit of growers. The scheme favoured by the Brewers' Society was based upon a minimum average price coupled with a minimum quantity of home-grown barley to be purchased for brewing purposes. The Ministry decided there was not time to get such a scheme into operation for the 1939 crop, and a temporary scheme for that year only was agreed upon. It consisted eventually in a levy of 1s. per standard barrel of beer with a corresponding levy on distillers in order to provide a subsidy of 30s. per acre if the average price was 8s. 1d. per cwt. If the average price of barley rose above 8s. 1d. the levy and the subsidy would correspondingly diminish and at a price of 9s. 11d. per cwt. neither would be payable. At the outbreak of war it became obvious that the average price of home-grown barley would rise above 9s. 11d. per cwt., or 40s. per quarter. The scheme was therefore withdrawn and amounts collected by way of levy were returned. It is, however, quite evident that this question of preferences to home-grown barley will, in due course, again have to be faced.

Hops. Hops represent a relatively small percentage of the raw materials required. It is estimated that 2 cwt. of hops are required for every 260 standard barrels of beer. Hops are obtained partly from Kent and other English counties and partly from Central Europe, the Dominions, and America. The English hops have the pleasanter flavour, but the imported product is used on account of its greater preservative qualities, and on the whole the drawback as regards flavour is less important. Much of the unpleasant flavour evaporates in the steam during the brewing process. According to Agreements under the Hop Marketing Scheme and reaffirmed in 1939, the quantity of imported hops may not exceed $17\frac{1}{2}$ per cent of the total market demand for all hops. No attempt has yet been made in this country to grow the overseas variety, though at research stations experiments in this direction are being made.

Sugar. The quantity of sugar or sweetening material used in normal times averages about one-fifth of the quantity of grain. Whereas in 1938 the weight of the malt and grain used in brewing in the United Kingdom was over 10,000,000 cwt., that of sugar was less than 2,000,000 (*Brewers' Almanack, 1941*). The figures for Scotland are not separately stated, but the output of beer in Scotland in the year 1941 was a little more than one-eleventh of the total output of the United Kingdom (United Kingdom and Northern Ireland, 19,158,219 standard barrels; Scotland, 1,654,392). If we may assume the raw materials used to be in somewhat like proportion the Scottish industry would seem to use about 1,000,000 cwt. of grain and 200,000 cwt. of sugar. Again, on the same assumption, 80 per cent of these quantities may be credited to the Edinburgh breweries, viz. 800,000 cwt. of grain and 160,000 cwt. of sugar. On the general basis of 2 cwt. of hops to 260 standard barrels of beer, Scotland uses roughly 12,700 cwt. of hops, 10,200 cwt. of which is accounted for by the Edinburgh industry.

PROCESSES AND LABOUR EMPLOYED

Methods of brewing in Scotland differ from those in England in various ways. On the production side one main difference is that Scottish brewers are also maltsters, whereas in England it is usual for malting to be carried on by separate firms. The processes involved are briefly: (1) The barley is turned into malt by a process of germination which may take from seven to fourteen days, after which the malt is dried and after storage is passed on to the brewer. (2) The malt is then ground by rolling mills and mixed or mashed with brewing water of a certain temperature, thus producing the wort. (3) Liquid wort is then drained off from the mash tun into copper vessels. The sediment or mash which remains is the by-product or draff available for feeding of cattle, and normally amounts in Edinburgh to about 50,000 tons per annum. (4) The hops are then added to the wort and boiled with it to impart the flavour and preservative qualities and the sugar or sweetening material is also now added. The boiled wort is next separated from the spent hops, which form another by-product which is used as a fertilizer. The liquid is then cooled down by means of refrigerators and passed to the fermenting tuns. At this stage its strength and quantity are checked by Excise officials for purposes of duty. Yeast for fermentation is then added, about 1 lb. of pressed yeast to each barrel of wort—a barrel is 86 gallons. In the process of fermentation the yeast multiplies itself, and when withdrawn to stop the fermenting process the original 1 lb. of yeast has increased to 5 lb. This gives the brewer an excess of yeast over what he requires for subsequent fermentation, and so forms another by-product, part of which is supplied to distilleries. while the remainder in Edinburgh is now dried and converted into a valuable food substance on account of its richness in vitamin B. The process of fermentation lasts from four to five days, after which the beer is passed from the fermenting tuns to settling vessels. After certain minor processes, which differ in different firms and are designed to add clarity and sparkle to the beer, it is put into casks ready for delivery to customers. If the beer is to be bottled the bottling is done on the premises.

LABOUR

The labour involved in the above processes in a modern brewery may be divided into three main classes: (1) the trained chemists in the laboratory, (2) the skilled workers, the maltsters and brewers and coopers, and (3) the unskilled workers.

(1) *Trained Chemists.* It must be emphasized that brewing is still an art and not a science, a great deal still depending on the skill and experience of the maltster and brewer; but the trained chemist in the laboratory has eliminated and is eliminating much of the element of trial and error. There is, in this way, a much better understanding of the reasons for the processes involved, and a greater certainty of results, though the processes themselves have not changed. The successful use of the different substitutes for barley (oats, flaked barley, and, for a short period, rice) and for sugar, which the war necessitated, would have been impossible without the scientist's aid. All breweries in Edinburgh have a trained chemist and a laboratory on the premises. In the case of the largest firms the laboratories are elaborately equipped, and in normal times have a considerable scientific staff.

(2) *Maltsters and Brewers.* Apprenticeship applies only to the brewers and maltsters, brewery workers as such, and is regulated by the Institute of Brewing. The Institute insists on the Higher School-Leaving Certificate or its equivalent as a preliminary qualification for its examinations. The period of apprenticeship is two years, and is combined with instruction at a Technical College, like the Heriot-Watt College in Edinburgh. Birmingham, Edinburgh, and London took the lead in facilitating this scheme and providing the instruction

required. The certificate of a college like the Heriot-Watt, granted at the end of a three years' course, secures exemption from the Institute's Intermediate Examination for its Diploma. Apprentices are recruited chiefly from those families connected with the industry, and many of them are sons of brewers. This recruitment of young workers from the labour within the industry seems to be a general feature in all sections of the workers employed. An apprentice brewer pays a premium of £100 and during his apprenticeship receives no salary. At the completion of apprenticeship he becomes an 'improver' and receives a small salary. On attaining the Diploma of the Institute he is qualified to become a managing brewer. The large breweries do not as a rule accept apprentices, so that the training-ground for future brewers is provided by the smaller firms. Without the practical training it is not possible to enter for the Institute's examinations. A brewer is also a maltster, the training covering both processes. A maltman who assists the maltster is one of the unskilled workers. Brewers and maltsters are salaried workers and represent about 2 per cent of those employed. It is still possible for a brewery worker to become a brewer without the qualifications laid down by the Institute, but in practice this is now rare. It is customary in Edinburgh for members of the firm to take an active part on the production side. This is not only to be explained by the strong family element in these firms, but also by the importance of maintaining the characteristic flavour of the firm's products. The differences in beer are those of taste or flavour rather than quality—an element of imperfect competition which greatly protects the staying power of a small conservative firm: in fact, makes of its conservatism a virtue and not a defect.

Coopers. The casks required by the Edinburgh brewers are obtained from firms of coopers, but all breweries employ a certain number of coopers on the premises for general maintenance and repair. Coopers are highly skilled workers with an apprenticeship period of five years, and are organized in their own trade union. They are perhaps the most highly paid wage-earners in the trade, their wage in pre-war days being 74s. 5d. per week of 47 hours (1s. 7d. per hour) at the end of the war it stood at 101s. 10d. (2s. 2d. per hour). Wage negotiations are conducted to the general satisfaction by the Joint Industrial Council set up in 1920.

(3) *Unskilled Workers.* The unskilled workers sometimes represent over 90 per cent of those employed. Their work consists in cleaning the vessels, bottling, fetching and carrying materials, etc., and in carting. These workers are only partially organized, some of them only belonging to the Brewing Section of the Transport and General Workers' Union. The number of unionists has, however, increased during the war. Agreements entered into between the organized

element and eight or nine leading brewers are observed by all other firms, and apply to all their workers. The wages varied before the war from 56s. to 62s. for a 47-hours' week, plus 6s. for Sunday work. At the end of the war the rates prevailing were from 83s. upwards with double pay for any Sunday work. Women are employed, if at all, in the bottling section, and to some extent also in clerical work. Much of the clerical work is, however, done by men, who combine it with duties of inspection in the yards.

The brewing industry in Edinburgh before the war employed over 3,000 workers and, being considered a necessary industry, this number has not in the war period appreciably diminished. One-third of the total is accounted for by the two largest firms, McEwan and Younger, which employ at present about 650 and 450 respectively. Four other firms employ from 100 to 170 workers each, while the majority of the remaining fourteen firms must employ somewhere about 90 workers each. The two smallest firms employ about 30 workers each. The number of workers employed in brewing is small in proportion to the capital. It was estimated in the Census of Production that wages represented only 16·3 per cent of the gross output. The smaller Edinburgh firms (ten firms) employing less than 100 workers are, therefore, not 'small' in the sense that the capital and output are negligible or not of considerable value.

It is sometimes counted a disadvantage of the brewing industry that the employment it itself affords is small in relation both to other industries and to the capital employed. But experience even in the 'twenties and 'thirties suggested that there is another angle; an industry which is so dependent on the general prosperity of other industries, particularly of the heavy industries, may count it as a virtue that in slack times and times of unemployment its surplus of workers is relatively small. In any case, the days are passing when lavish employment of labour was a mark of merit.

CAPITAL AND ORGANIZATION

Brewing firms in Edinburgh are either private or public limited companies—chiefly private, thanks to the strong family element. Most firms have been in the family for generations. Two have disappeared since the First World War, and a third has been taken over by another: otherwise, all the firms and their location are the same as they have been for fifty years and, in most cases, much longer. Even in the case of the public companies it is only the debenture and preference shares that are offered to the public. The ordinary shares do not appear on the Stock Exchange, but are retained in the family's hands. The total amount of capital represented by the Edinburgh firms was estimated before the war to be between five and six million pounds.

A large initial amount of capital is required for three purposes—

(1) *To meet the cost of buildings and expensive and elaborate machinery.* Of recent years the cost of machinery has greatly increased through the extension of bottling and improvements of bottling machinery. It would seem that this machinery is very expensive, is being constantly improved upon, and requiring to be renewed and kept up to date.

(2) *To meet the cost of raw materials and materials in process, together with taxation.* The brewing industry would seem to be in process of becoming the milch cow of the farmer as well as of the Exchequer.

(3) *For purposes of advertising.*

With regard to (1), the initial capital required in Scotland, where the brewer does his own malting, is greater than in England, where more usually the malting is done elsewhere. Malting involves considerable cost in buildings and building-space, in addition to the requisite machinery.

(2) The amount of capital involved here depends on technical fiscal arrangements and again on a difference in practice between Scotland and England as regards retail selling, as well as on the time involved in the production process.

In England brewers do their own retail selling through their own public-houses. In Scotland they do not. The Scottish brewer gives considerable credit to those public-houses whose customers demand his beer on draught. Such public-houses are, therefore, to some extent tied to certain brewers, but if they paid off their loans they could go elsewhere. This demand for draught beer of a certain taste or flavour stands, it may be noted, in the way of amalgamation of brewing firms for production purposes, involving as it would considerable risk in its effect on sales.

The credit thus given to public-houses, together with the beer duty, involves very large working capital; for example, in the case of one of the large Edinburgh firms more than £1,000,000 a month was mentioned as required. The duty is levied on the quantity of standard beer brewed during the month, and has to be paid on the 25th of the month following. Meantime the beer may not be sold until the month following this, and the brewer's customers require credit. The brewer, therefore, not only advances the tax to the Government, but provides credit facilities for his customers. A further cost involved in Scotland is that the beer is sent to public-houses and other outlets in casks, and often for considerable distances. The chief markets are, in fact, the centres of heavy industry in the West of Scotland and the North of England, together with the London area. The casks are very expensive in themselves, and beer requires careful handling in transit. In England, on the other hand, in large industrial centres the beer is simply carted from the brewery in tanks to the brewer's public-houses in the district around. Comparisons between costs of production in English and Scottish firms which are not based on a realization of such differences are, of course, quite misleading. The same is true of comparisons of profits which in England frequently include profits made on the sale of spirits and wines.

(3) *Advertising.* Advertising has become a heavy item with the increase in the quantities bottled for sale. The publican in Scotland who receives a loan from a brewer undertakes to sell only this brewer's beer on draught, but he may sell different makes of bottled beer, and the demand for this bottled beer depends on advertising. The necessity for advertising has increased since the extension of beer-drinking among women. Women are said to prefer beer from the bottle: it froths more, sparkles more, and seems generally more attractive to them. It is also easier to handle and serve than draught beer, but the brewers themselves seem convinced that while all beer is good, draught beer is best! The demand for bottled beer does extend the more distant market for the individual brewer, but it may contract his market for draught beer nearer home. He is thus more or less forced to advertise and make his product known so that he may, so to speak, gain on the bottle what he loses on the draught. It does seem, however, that this situation constitutes the most disruptive element particularly from the point of view of the future of the smaller firms. A local demand for draught beer is their strongest asset, and that is increasingly threatened, while advertising and bottling pay best on the large scale. This explains the preoccupation with bottling machinery and processes clearly observable in the large and the smaller firm alike. It is not merely the general adoption of this expensive machinery that is significant, but the constant improvements in it which are going on, and the evident determination to procure successive improvements as they become available, high as the cost may be.

AMALGAMATION OF BREWING FIRMS

Edinburgh firms do co-operate for certain limited special purposes, such as the collection and marketing of waste products—for example the draff—but not on the production side. In spite of the fact that fifteen out of the twenty-one firms, if the Dalkeith firm be included, are relatively small firms and much smaller than the two largest firms, any likelihood of amalgamation is said to be slight. During the depression in the inter-war period some firms in other places did amalgamate, and one firm in Edinburgh was taken over by another, but the reasons for this solitary amalgamation were of a particular and fortuitous character. As will be explained later, the two largest firms of recent years combined on the financial side to some extent. Other amalgamations during the trade depression were in order to close down the unused productive capacity, but firms which did so are said to have regretted it when, as in the war, business rapidly improved and new structural extensions became unprocurable. It is stated that in some respects the production costs of the smaller firms are lower than those of the larger firms. Many of the small firms have wells of the right water on the premises, whereas the largest firms have now to bring the water required from some distance in pipes. The premises of the smaller firms are more compact. The large firms' cartage and handling costs to and from the different yards are considerable. Another important factor would seem to be that once a brewery is established the elements of obsolescence and depreciation in the fixed capital are not large— apart, that is, from the bottling machinery. The necessity for close inspection in the yards, for both production and fiscal reasons, en- sures careful handling of the auxiliary capital—various vessels in use and the casks in transit—and avoids unnecessary wear and tear.

The smaller firms' product might, it is thought, in some cases, be slightly inferior for certain purposes (for example, prolonged keeping) owing to their less adequate technique, but the element of monopoly or imperfect competition—the demand for their particular product— overcomes any such disadvantages. Apart from the internal econo- mies there are also, of course, certain external economies which the smaller firms share with the larger firms in an industry long estab- lished and highly localized; for example, suitable transport, proximity to raw materials and markets, and labour supply, etc.

COMBINATION OF TWO LARGE FIRMS

Combination among brewers in Edinburgh has not been in order to reduce production costs but to keep the trade from getting into the hands of outsiders. An attempt in this direction was made in the inter-war period, but was successfully countered. From this point of view the combination of Edinburgh's two largest firms is of con- siderable interest. This combination took place largely for domestic reasons, and on the production side the two companies go on as before, in separate breweries, each producing its own special product for its special customers. Doubtless even this degree of combination will in time pave the way for certain economies, particularly as the Scottish export trade, apart from lager beer, is almost entirely in the hands of these two firms. The fact remains, however, that any such economies were not the reasons for the combination. The chief motive was to keep the control of the firms within the families, and to stop any powerful extraneous influence from entering the Edinburgh trade.

Apart altogether from such family and local influences and interests tending to protect and maintain the existing position, it is regarded as in the interests of the brewing industry in the United Kingdom as a whole that the smaller firms should remain and flourish, in view of the threat of nationalization. There is no desire to make the path of nationalization easier and smoother through the formation of large units. The grip the State already has on knowledge and organization of the industry is very considerable. The attitude of firms within the industry towards one another is friendly and helpful and no attempt is made to squeeze out the smaller concerns.

COMBINATION AND CO-OPERATION FOR GENERAL PURPOSES

Brewers in the United Kingdom are combined in the Brewers' Society and its large number of subsidiary organizations for guidance and information on all points of general interest affecting the industry, such as fiscal demands or criticism of the trade on moral grounds, as well as on all the technical matters involved in trade processes and materials. The Society also undertakes the advertising of beer in general in order to keep the product before the community and make known the extent to which the Exchequer benefits from its taxation—hence the injunction, 'Drink more Beer', and such flashes of alliterative insight as 'Beer is Best'.

Education and research are under the guidance of the Institute of Brewing. The accepted aim of British brewing firms is to have all brewers and maltsters certificated students of the Institute and increasing importance is being attached to research. The Institute's Research Laboratories are stationed at Birmingham University, where there is a Chair of Brewing, and the College of Technology, Manchester. There are also experimental hop kilns at Beltring, Kent. Most brewing firms have laboratories of their own, and these keep in touch with the Central Laboratories, while the Central Laboratories keep in touch with reasearch organizations abroad.

The brewers of Edinburgh have for long been associated for similar general purposes. The original association was the Edinburgh Brewers' Association, which was dissolved in 1906 and converted into the Brewers' Association of Scotland. This association is affiliated to the Brewers' Society, and Edinburgh brewers in particular are keen supporters of the educational aims of the Institute of Brewing.

At the Heriot-Watt College the necessary apparatus and equipment are provided for the study of Biochemistry (Fermentation Industries), and complete courses of instruction have been arranged for students engaged in these industries, brewing, distilling, etc. The course for the College Diploma extends over three years, and is recognized by the Institute of Brewing as qualifying for associate membership and for exemption from the intermediate examination for the Institute's Diploma.

COMBINATION FOR PARTICULAR LIMITED PURPOSES

Edinburgh brewers are combined in the Brewers' Food Supply Company for the purpose of disposing of brewing waste products—the bulky draff for cattle food, the spent hops for fertilizers, and the super-abundant yeast not taken up by the distilleries for vitamin B food products.

So far as public-house goodwill is concerned, there is a tendency towards sharing out the market by not outbidding each other in the market for draught beer—another indication that the real competitive element lies in the bottled product. It is also a step towards protecting the smaller firms from being squeezed out of their local market, and is thus in line with general trade policy.

CHANGES INTRODUCED BY THE WAR

These changes have been chiefly in the supplies of raw materials barley, hops, and sugar. The two latter have been severely rationed and foreign barley has been superseded by home barley. Immediately on the outbreak of war in 1939 import of barley for brewing purposes was stopped and home-grown barley was gradually and increasingly turned to other uses. Rice, maize, and other similar substitutes have been used, and potatoes were attempted, but without success. Fortunately, water is still unrationed and has admittedly played an increasing part in production! A compulsory reduction of 15 per cent in brewing strength was imposed by the Excise authorities.

There have also been changes in the wood required for the casks. Prior to 1939 the wood used for this purpose was Russian oak, a beautiful flawless wood for coopering purposes, and one which preserved intact the flavour of the beer. Since the war this wood has been unobtainable and Californian oak has taken its place. The Californian oak has a resin which ruins the flavour of the beer. The casks have, therefore, to be enamelled inside, the smallest flaw or crack in the enamel being sufficient to make the beer deteriorate. This enamelling process is very costly, and very high prices have also had to be paid for the oak itself. In addition, extra large supplies of these casks have had to be obtained on account of railway hold-ups. A return to the Russian oak may take place if it should again become available, but how long this will take remains to be seen.

At the present moment the demand for beer is putting a strain on the productive capacity of many firms, particularly as regards malting. Malt, contrary to usual practice, is being purchased from outside. With some abatement in the post-war demand this position, it is thought, will right itself and extensions to the existing malting capacity do not seem to be contemplated.

PROBABLE POSITION IN THE POST-WAR PERIOD

The prosperity of the brewing industry depends on the prosperity of industry in general and particularly of the heavy industries. If the Clyde and the North-east Coast are busy, and there is no depression in the local Edinburgh market or in London, Edinburgh brewing is likely to flourish. Owing to the extent to which the demand for beer generally fluctuates with prosperity and its reverse, it is difficult to estimate whether the long-period tendency is for the demand to increase or diminish. Some brewers seem to think that on the whole the demand in the future, other things being equal, will tend to diminish. People are more temperate, and cinemas and other social activities are strong counter-attractions to the public-house. On the other hand, it is pointed out that although the tendency is towards greater temperance, the number of people who drink beer is on the increase, particularly as regards women and girls. The lack of whisky due to the practical cessation of distilling during the war should also help to maintain beer sales for a few years to come. On balance there is little reason to fear any serious setback to the Edinburgh brewing industry in the near future.

Barley. The most difficult problem to forecast is in connexion with barley. At the outbreak of war the price of home-grown barley was at first left uncontrolled, and rose from what was previously considered a satisfactory price—40s. a quarter—to £15, £17 and even, in isolated cases, £20. In due course the acreage under barley increased to more than double the pre-war figure, and prices fell again; but they remained, and seem likely to remain for the future, far above the level of 1936-8. The very steep rise in farm wages suggests that barley prices, like farm prices in general, may prove to have risen not only absolutely but also in relation to British prices as a whole. It is more than probable, however, that brewers will be expected to use home-grown barley whatever the price, and endeavours may be made to keep out the imported product. The imported product, as explained before, is technically superior, an important consideration for the export trade, where only the highest quality of beer stands the test of exportation or keeps for any length of time. There are, moreover, great risks at any time in relying entirely on home-grown barley, where, as perhaps in a wet season, only 10 per cent of the crop may be harvested in a usable condition.

Reconditioning of Machinery. A great deal of re-tooling will be required as the machinery has been working full strength and has had to be neglected in the war period. For the reconstruction period a good deal of new machinery will be necessary, chiefly in connexion with bottling. As previously explained, this aspect of the trade is becoming of ever-increasing importance. Orders for this machinery have been placed by most firms.

Future Changes in Location of Firms. Any changes in the location of existing firms in the near future is regarded as unlikely. The overwhelming consideration in location is proximity to a suitable water-supply. If any of the wells in use did become exhausted a firm might shift, as it is thought improbable that permission to bring water long distances in pipes would now be granted by the local authority, although it had been granted previously to one of the largest firms. This firm brings its water from a well a considerable distance to the south-west of the Holyrood Brewery site. It is admitted that chemical science might in the future be able to supply the deficiencies in any water-supply and thus make it suitable for brewing, but the time for this is not yet. There seemed to be no desire whatsoever to launch out on any such experiment.

Transport Facilities. Transport facilities are regarded as satisfactory. Railway hold-ups at Carlisle or Newcastle are by no means negligible, but otherwise there seems to be no particular criticism. The Port of Leith is used for bringing in the imported raw materials and the wood for the casks, and for the coasting trade with Newcastle, Aberdeen, Orkney, and Shetland.

EXPORT OF BEER

British beer is produced for home consumption. The total quantity of beer brewed in the United Kingdom in 1938 was 18,055,339 standard barrels, and of this only 271,114 barrels were exported, or slightly less than one and a half per cent. The export of beer is, in fact, confined to comparatively few firms. Imports of beer in 1938 amounted to 1,112,737 standard barrels, 95 per cent of which came from Eire. So far as Scotland is concerned the bulk of the exports is in the hands of the two largest Edinburgh firms, though a third firm, also in Edinburgh, does the main export trade in lager beer. The amount of Scottish beer exported is much larger in proportion to the total output than in England, since its high quality enables it to stand up well to being transported, and to keep better than Southern beers in hot climates. The bulk of the Scottish export has always been for the use of British troops abroad, and for the Dominion and Colonial market.

The probable future of the Edinburgh industry's exports can be judged from a brief survey of the prospects in the more important markets. The export of beer may be divided into three sections:

1. True exports for consumption by the inhabitants of the importing countries.

2. Beer exported for the use of our armed forces, either abroad or in transports, and also as ships' stores in ordinary ocean-going vessels.
3. Lager beer.

For Section 1—export beers—the prospects in almost all markets are distinctly poor. South Africa and Australia have ceased importing beer for some considerable time owing to high import duties and the establishing of good local breweries. Of the potential American markets, Canada will probably continue to import a small quantity of Scottish beers, but the rest of America has never really been interested in these products. The West Indian market was principally for stout, and the sale of this was always dependent on the prosperity of each island. It seems doubtful whether there will be any encouragement to export much to these Colonies. The continent of Europe, generally speaking, has not imported Scottish beers, and there seems no reason why in the future this should be changed. The exception to this is Belgium, which imported a large quantity of strong ales before 1939, but as these were expensive it is very doubtful if this will continue in the future—certainly not for some time.

Among Eastern and Mediterranean markets, the Straits Settlements and Hong Kong have in the past been large buyers of both ale and stout, although two local breweries were established in recent years. It is impossible to forecast how this trade will progress in future, as sales depend almost entirely on local economic conditions and native income levels—particularly, in the case of Malaya, on the state of the rubber industry. Burma at one time was a very large market, but of recent years there has been considerable competition from Japan. Here again, a main factor is native prosperity or depression. In India a large quantity of beer used to be imported, but, in view of the express views of the Congress Party, it seems doubtful if this will continue, especially as there are several large Indian breweries. A certain trade used to be done with Egypt and Palestine in beer for the civil population, but in recent years local breweries have been established in both places. The future here, therefore, is also doubtful. In the case of Malta and Gibraltar, finally, exports are of course chiefly for the use of the armed forces; but there has always been a certain amount of civilian trade, for which the prospects are perhaps not quite so gloomy as elsewhere. Malta has already two small breweries which are prosperous, but Gibraltar is dependent on imported beer. These markets should continue more or less on the same lines as before the war.

In the case of exports for the Forces and ships' stores, it seems probable that trade will continue at a higher level than before the war for at any rate some years, since, whatever may happen to ships' stores, there seems no doubt that the strength of the British Forces throughout the world will remain greater than before 1939.

In the third group of exports—lager beer—the position is similar to that of other export beers, except that the competition to be faced from brewers in other countries is even greater. Much is said to depend on Government policy. Lager beer is shipped to some sixty-five markets—the principal trade being, however, with the Crown Colonies and India. Since the 1914–18 War the opportunities for business have been greatly curtailed by the setting up of new breweries in the Crown Colonies—Jamaica, Gold Coast, Kenya, Malaya, etc.—all of which are protected by high rates of duty on imported beers, which in most cases stand at prohibitive levels. The trade's own view of the matter is suggested by a comment from the exporting firm—a comment, incidentally, which is as illuminating on the trade's general background of ideas as on this particular issue:

'All that we ask of the Government is that they confine themselves to their legitimate job of ensuring fair play in the matter of tariffs and otherwise leave the industry alone. If they intend to interfere as they are doing now, and we believe that they do, it would be a hopeless task attempting to compete in the world's markets. For some years previous to the war the Government's policy of appeasement and the making of trade treaties under all of which Britain was the loser had a detrimental effect on our business, and we hope that the process will not be repeated.'

So far, then, as market prospects are concerned it would seem that, apart from sales to the Forces and for ships' stores, the export of beer will in all probability be a diminishing quantity in the future. Another limiting factor concerns the extent to which the export of cereals in the form of beer will be permitted. The future also depends on whether competitors on the Continent and in Japan will be allowed to manufacture for export.

INDEX

Aberdeen, 8, 9, 14, 101, 104, 108–29, 138, 147, 154, 157, 162, 181–3, 185–8, 190, 192, 197, 198, 201, 203
Aberdeen Fish Trade Association, 123
Aberdeen Granite Manufacturers' Association, 196, 205–6
Aberdeen Granite Supply Association, 192, 198, 205–6
Aberdeen Steam Fishing Vessels Association, 114
Aberdeen Steam Trawling and Fishing Company, 113
Aberdeen Trawl Owners' Fish Curing Company, 122
Advertising, 82, 216
Ages of Trawlers, Table, 173
Amalgamated Union of Building Trade Workers, 196
Amalgamation of brewing firms, 216–18
Argentina, 65, 72–4, 84, 87, 89
Associated Fisheries Ltd., 136
Associated London Flour Millers, 44, 81
Associations of granite manufacturers, 206
Australia, 72–4, 84–5, 87, 201
Average Annual Imports of Wheat, Table, 38
Average Value of British taken fish, Table, 180
Avonmouth, 45, 46

'Bakers', 31
Baking Trade, 58–61, 78–9, 81, 93
Barents Sea, 8, 135, 148, 151
Barley, 209–10
Bear Island, 8, 117, 127, 135, 151
Beeching and Kelsall, 158
Beer, bottled, 216, 219
  draught, 216, 219
  output, 209
Belfast, 45, 91
Billingsgate, 124, 125
Birmingham, 45, 125, 166
Biscuit flours, 32–3, 35, 86
Boston Deep Sea Fishing and Ice Company Ltd., 162
Bottled beer, 216, 219
Blending of flours, 30–1, 35, 65–6
Bran, 25, 27 89
Bread Advertising Campaign, 78
Bread-making flours, 30–2, 35–6, 39, 66, 82, 91
Brewers' Association of Scotland, 218
Brewers' Food Supply Company, 219

Brewers' Society, 210, 218
Brewing industry, 13–14, 16, 209–23
  methods, 211–12
Bristol, 38, 45, 47, 83, 89, 91
British Millers' Mutual Pool, 91
British Stone Federation, 196
British Trawlers' Federation, 145, 168
British Trawler Owners' Federation, 114, 139
Brown, Chas., 46
Building and Monumental Workers' Association of Scotland, 196

Cake flours, 32–3, 35, 86
Canada, 65, 72–4, 84, 87, 95, 187, 201
Canadian Wheat Board, 95
Canadian Wheat Pool, 68, 84
Canning of fish, 141
Capacity of flour mills, 42, 50
Capital, 41, 109–10, 115, 138, 145, 154–5, 161, 191–3, 214–16
Cardiff, 38, 45
Cereals Advisory (Defence) Committee, 90
Cereals Control Board, 81, 90
Cereals Import Committee, 91
Cereals Import Division, 93
Chemical Agents, 26–7, 75, 77–8, 96
Chief Suppliers of Wheat to the United Kingdom, Table, 75
C.I.F. Prices of Imported Flour, Table, 87
Coal, 103, 105, 120–1, 134, 147, 154
Cod, 102, 110, 135, 148, 149
Cold Storage, 117, 125, 135, 163
Colony Wheats, 30
Consolidated Fisheries Ltd., 137
Consumption of bread and flour, 76–9, 97
  of fish, 102, 156, 167
Co-operation, 13, 153–4, 169, 218–9
Co-operative Wholesale Society, 4, 12, 45–6, 57, 81
Cornwall, 181, 184–5, 186, 188, 190, 192, 197
Costs of fishing, 103–4
Country mills, 22, 34–7, 39, 40, 86, 98
Curing of fish, 110, 126, 135, 141, 149, 164
Czechoslovakia, 201, 203, 205

Dalbeattie, 186, 192, 203
Departmental Committee on the Treatment of Flour with Chemical Substances, 27

Department of Scientific and Industrial Research, 117
Devon, 184, 190
Distribution of fish, 122, 128, 138–9, 140, 148, 165
    of flour, 79–82
    of flour mills, 38–9
    of machinery and labour, 194
Dogger Bank, 135 147–8
Draught Beer, 216, 219
Drying facilities (flour), 94, 98

Edinburgh, 38, 45, 47, 197, 203, 209, 214, 221
Edinburgh Brewers' Association, 218
Empire flour, 73, 84, 87
    granite, 201
Estimated production of home-grown wheat, Table, 70
    Quantities of home wheat taken up by flour mills, 71
European flour, 85
    wheat, 65, 72, 74, 99
Expenses and profits of fishing vessels, 175, 176
Exports of beer, 221–3
    of fish, 110, 126–7, 135, 150, 164
    of flour, 34, 88–90
    of granite, 187 193, 201, 202 (Table)
    of wheatmeal, and flour, Table, 88
Extraction of flour, rate of, 27–8, 31–2, 39, 95–6, 99

Factors, 48, 79, 80
Faroe Islands, 116, 117, 135, 147
Fernström, A. K., 197
'Filler' wheats, 30, 65
Filleting, 103, 135, 141, 149, 163
Finland, 197, 203, 205
Fish and chip shops, 102, 106, 141
    canning, 141
    consumption, 102, 156, 167
    curing, 110, 126, 135, 141, 149, 164
    docks, 133–4, 151, 157, 165
    friers, 103, 104, 149
Fishing-grounds, 8, 116–17, 127, 131, 134, 135, 147–8, 151, 157
Fish manure, 103, 134, 153, 164
    meal, 141–2, 150, 164
    merchants, 123–4, 126, 135, 140, 162–3
Fishmongers, 104, 106
Fish products, 13, 141–2, 150, 152, 160, 164–5
    types of, 101–2, 110, 116, 122, 126, 133, 135, 148–9, 151, 157, 158–9, 164, 166
Fleetwood, 8, 9, 101, 104, 107, 110, 153, 157–67
Fleetwood Fishing Vessel Owners' Association, 162

Flour blending, 20–1, 35, 65–6
    composition of, 25
    contracts, 59
    exports of, 34, 88–90
    imports of, 83, 87, 89–90
    milling, 4, 21–100
Flour Milling Employers' Federation, 46, 48–9
Flour-milling process, 23–7
Flour Mills Control, 80
    Control Committee, 91
    location of, 22, 33–9, 45, 46
    number of, 39–41
    size of, 39, 42–3
    types of, 21, 63, 91–3
Flour, output, 28, 39, 40, 42
    prices, 29, 86, 87
    types of, 25, 30–3, 35, 36, 39, 66, 82, 86, 91
    utilization, 78–9
Food and Drugs Act, 27
Food (Defence Plans) Department of the Board of Trade, 90
Foreign trade, 22, 34, 82–90, 94, 116, 126–7, 150–1, 164, 187, 193, 197, 201–7, 221–3
    wheat, 65–9, 72–5, 83–4, 87
France, 84, 87
Freeman & McLeod Ltd., 184, 186
Fresh fish, 125, 128, 141–3, 170
Futures, 67, 73, 94
Fyfe, John, Ltd., 191
Fylde Ice & Cold Storage Company, 158
Fyvie, 46

Galloway, 184, 188, 190
Germany, 84, 87, 88, 201, 203, 205
Glasgow, 38, 45–6, 83, 89, 91, 104, 186, 197, 203
Grading of fish, 131, 170
    of wheat products, 24–5, 27, 30–1, 50, 65, 98
Grain-drying plant, 94, 98
    ports, 38, 91
Granite, colour of, 183, 197, 208
    crushed, 183, 186, 191
    imports of, 183, 187, 196, 198, 201–7
    industry, 7–8, 181–208
    manufacture, 192, 194–5
    manufacturers in Aberdeen, 193
    polished, 187, 188
    products, 185, 186, 189, 191
    transport of, 185
    sources, 188–90, 201–5
    utilization, 181–5, 199–200
Great Grimsby Coal, Salt and Tanning Company Ltd., 143
Grimsby, 9, 14, 45, 101, 103–4, 106–7, 110, 112, 128–45, 147, 150–1, 157, 166–7

Grimsby Ice Co. Ltd., 144
Grimsby Trawler Owners' Exchange, 139

Haddock, 102, 135, 148, 149, 157, 164, 166
Hake, 102, 135, 157–9, 166
Halibut, 102, 135, 148
Heriot-Watt College, 212, 218
Herring, 101, 116, 122, 133, 135, 149, 151, 164,
History of Aberdeen, 108–12
  of Brewing Industry, 209
  of Fleetwood, 157
  of Granite Industry, 181–3
  of Grimsby, 129–32
  of Hull, 145–52
Home-grown wheat, 32–6, 65, 67, 71–2, 94, 96, 98–9
Hops, 210
'Households', 31
Hovis Ltd., 46, 82
Hull, 8, 9, 14, 38, 45–7, 80, 83, 89, 91, 101–7, 110–13, 128–9, 131–4, 135–57, 159, 162, 167
Hull Steam Fishing and Ice Co. Ltd., 148

Ice, 121, 134, 144, 150, 158, 165
Iceland, 116–17, 127, 135, 142, 147–8, 157, 167
Import Duties Act, 85, 205
Import Duties Advisory Committee, 85
Imported flour, 83, 84, 87, 89, 90
  granite, 183, 187, 197, 198, 201–7
  granites, Quantities of, Table, 206
  wheat, 22, 65, 67, 72–3, 89, 94
Imports of foreign fish, 110, 127, 150–1
  of Granite—Monumental and Architectural, 204
'Improvers', 26, 75, 77–8, 96
India, 65, 74, 203
Inland mills, 35–40, 92
Institute of Brewing, 218
Interlocking, 110, 114, 117–21
Isaac Spencer & Sons Ltd., 164

Joint Industrial Council, 64

Kelsall Brothers & Beechings Ltd., 148
Kemnay Quarry, 181–3, 190, 192, 197

Labour problems, 4, 106–8, 128, 145, 149, 187–8, 196–7, 208
Landings of fish, weight of, 8, 101–2, 109, 111, 130, 132, 151–2, 157–8, 166, 179–81
  of White Fish, Table, 179
Leeds, 45, 141

Leicester, 141, 188, 190
Leith, 46, 83, 89, 91
Lessons from the four studies, 16–18
Ling, 110, 135, 145
Liver oil, 13, 150, 152, 164–5
Liverpool, 38, 45, 47, 80, 83, 89, 91, 124, 166
Location of flour mills, 22, 33–9, 45, 46
  of the granite industry, 183–8
London, 38, 45–7, 80, 83, 89, 91, 148, 166
London Wheat Agreement (1933), 68

McDougalls, 46
MacFisheries, 113, 118, 136, 162
Malt, 211, 215, 219
Manchester, 38, 45, 46, 124, 166
Manitoba, 30, 31, 65, 87, 95
Marketing of wheat, 41, 67–9, 98
Markets for beer, 222–3
  for fish, 104, 110, 121–5, 128, 141, 148, 154, 156, 163, 166
  for flour, 80, 88–9, 97
  for granite, 187, 198–201, 208
Merchant Shipping Act, 1894, 103
Millers' Mutual Association, 4, 46, 49–58, 82
Ministry of Food, 91, 95, 113

National Association of British and Irish Millers, 46–9
National Association of Flour Importers, 85
National Association of Master Bakers, Confectioners and Caterers, 93
National Joint Industrial Council, 48–9, 63
National wheat meal flour, 95
Newcastle, 38, 45
New Zealand, 187, 201
North Sea, 116, 131, 134, 147
Norway, 203
Number of Granite Manufacturers in Aberdeen, Table, 193
  of Port Wholesalers, etc., Table, 178
Nutritive content of flour, 24–7, 32, 77–8, 99

Obsolescence of fishing vessels, 115, 161
Offals—fish, 141, 150, 160
  —wheat, 24, 27–8, 67, 89–90, 97, 99
Operatives, 41–2, 61–5, 106–8, 126, 130, 144, 152, 163, 165, 192, 212–14
Ottawa Agreement (1932), 73, 84
Output of beer, 209
  of flour and meal, 28, 39, 42, 48
  of flour mills in the United Kingdom, Table, 42
  of port and inland flour mills, Table, 40

Over-fishing, 131, 147, 157, 166, 168
Ownership of Trawlers, Table, 113–17, 174

'Patents', 31
Penryn, 184, 186, 192
Peterhead, 149, 183
Plaice, 102, 135, 147, 148
Port Mills, 22, 33–8, 40, 43, 66–7, 80, 86, 92, 98
Preston and Wyre Harbour and Dock Company, 158
Prices, 10–11, 47–50, 52, 55–9, 82, 85, 94–5, 100, 112–13, 142, 210
 of fish, 105, 111, 123–5, 140, 142, 156, 169
 of wheat and flour, 28–9, 51, 72, 86, 87
Problems of the fishing industry, 167–71
 of the flour-milling industry, 96–100
Processing of fish, 117, 141, 142, 163–4
Proportions of Total Available Flour Used in Various Trades, Table, 78

Quantities of Flour Delivered by U.K. Millers, Table, 28
Quantity of Fish landed by British Steam Trawlers, Table, 181
Quarrying, 184, 190, 191, 195

Rank, J., Ltd., 45–6, 53, 81, 88
Rate of extraction, 27–8, 31–2, 39, 95–6, 99
Rationalization, 4–6, 22, 36, 48, 54, 57, 62, 80, 81, 92, 121, 161
Raw materials of beer, 209–11, 219
 materials of the granite industry, 197–8
Reconstruction, 121–2, 127–8
Retained Imports of Flour, Table, 83
Royal Commission on Food Prices, 1924, 97
Rubislaw Quarry, 181–3, 190–2, 197

Sale Note Clauses, 59
Sales of Manufactured Granite, Table, 186
Sea-Fish Commission, 103–5, 132
Sea-Fish Industry Act, 1938, 11, 105, 108, 171
Sea-Fishing Industry Act, 1933, 102, 151, 168
Self-raising flour, 32–3, 35, 82
Share of Supplying Countries in Total Flour Imports, Table, 84
Shetlands, 116, 117
Silos, 23, 33, 94, 98
Skate, 135
Southampton, 38, 45

Sowerby Bridge, 37, 46
Spillers Ltd., 45–6, 68
Straight-run flour, 31
'Strong' wheats, 30, 65
Subsidiary industries, 114, 117–22, 127, 130, 134, 137, 143–4, 160, 162
Sunderland, 45
'Super', 31
Swansea, 38, 45
Sweden, 187, 197

Torry Research Station, 117
Transport and General Workers' Union, 107, 213
Transport costs, 33, 35, 38, 121–2, 128–9, 149
 facilities, 109, 125, 129, 133, 137, 166
Trawler Owners, 103, 106–7, 112–14, 117–18, 122, 126, 136–7, 149, 151, 159, 160, 174
Trawlers, 115, 116, 134, 136, 148, 151, 155
 age of, 103, 114–15, 155, 161, 173
 numbers of, 109, 110–11, 148, 152, 159
Trawlers Grimsby Ltd, 137
Treatment of Four with Chemical Substances, Departmental Committee on the, 27
Tyne ports, 38, 45, 46, 83

United Alkali Co., 158
United Kingdom Average Annual Production of Wheat, 69
United Kingdom Output of Flour and Meal, 28
U.S.A., 65, 73, 74, 84, 86, 87, 95, 187, 201
U.S.S.R., 65, 72, 74, 88

Vessels trawling in distant waters, expenses and profits of, 176, 177
 trawling in near waters, expenses and profits of, 175, 177
Vitamin B_1, 25–6, 95–6, 99

Wages, 43, 63, 64, 107, 120, 203, 212
Walker Steam Trawl Fishing Company, 118
War, effects of (1914–18), 22, 90, 110–11, 131, 147, 156, 159; (1939), 90–4, 96, 112–13, 138–9, 140, 155–6, 167, 207–8, 212, 219
'Weak' wheats, 30
Wheatings, 27, 89
Wheat Act (1932), 36, 69–70, 72, 86, 94
Wheat, cut and kibbled, 27, 28
Wheatfeed, 24, 27, 67, 89, 90, 97, 99
Wheat germ, 25–8, 32, 77–8, 99
 grain, 23–5

Wheat, home-grown, 32–4, 36, 65, 67, 70–2, 94, 98–9
  imports, 22, 65–9, 72–5, 83–4, 87, 89, 94
  prices, 28–9, 51
  production, 69–70
  rolled and flaked, 27–8
  stocks of, 94–5
  supplies, 65–75, 93–4
  types of, 30, 65
White fish, 101, 102, 135
White Fish Commission, 106
White fish industry, 8–12, 101–80

White Fish Industry Joint Council, 106
White flour, 25
White Sea, 135, 147, 148
Whiting, 102, 135
Wholemeal flour, 25–31
Wholesalers, port and inland, 104, 123–4, 178
Winchester, 45
Working Party Reports, 16–18, 20

Yarmouth, 149

Zoning, 106, 113, 140

Printed by Jarrold & Sons Ltd., The Empire Press, Norwich

For Product Safety Concerns and Information please contact our EU
representative GPSR@taylorandfrancis.com Taylor & Francis Verlag GmbH,
Kaufingerstraße 24, 80331 München, Germany

Printed and bound by CPI Group (UK) Ltd, Croydon, CR0 4YY

01/05/2025

01858351-0008